ABT

DO-OVER!

DO-OVER!

In which a forty-eight-year-old
father of three returns to kindergarten,
summer camp, the prom, and other
embarrassments

Robin Hemley

Little, Brown and Company
New York   Boston   London

Little, Brown and Company
Hachette Book Group
237 Park Avenue, New York, NY 10017
Visit our Web site at www.HachetteBookGroup.com

First Edition: May 2009

Little, Brown and Company is a division of Hachette Book Group, Inc.
The Little, Brown name and logo are trademarks of Hachette Book Group, Inc.

Author's Note: Most of the names of those under eighteen in this book have been changed. Many of the names of the adults have been changed too, though not all, for the sake of privacy. I suspect that some of those whose names have been changed would have been happy *not* to have their names changed, but I decided to err on the side of caution.

Photographs by Alex Sheshunoff (pages 3, 15, and 85), Wendell Brock (page 30), Jeff Mermelstein (pages 60 and 74), Margie Hemley (pages 112 and 220), Robin Hemley (pages 139, 211 [top], and 316), Kate Hrdina (page 140), Diane Strotbeck (page 151), Bob Hoagland (page 172), Elaine Hemley (pages ix, 211 [bottom], and 237), and Lisa Rodriguez Ortiz (page 238)

Parts of chapter three, "Camp Echo," first appeared in a different form in the *New York* magazine article "Big Man on Camp."

Library of Congress Cataloging-in-Publication Data
Hemley, Robin.
    Do-over! : in which a forty-eight-year-old father of three returns to kindergarten, summer camp, the prom, and other embarrassments / by Robin Hemley. — 1st ed.
        p. cm.
    ISBN: 978-0-316-02060-2
    1. Hemley, Robin.   2. Authors, American — 20th century — Biography.   I. Title.
PS3558.E47915Z463 2009
813'.54 — dc22   2008022588

10 9 8 7 6 5 4 3 2 1

RRD-IN

Text design by Meryl Sussman Levavi

Printed in the United States of America

For Margie, who, in marrying a writer,
didn't quite know what she was in for

Contents

Every man's life is a fairy tale written by God's fingers.

—HANS CHRISTIAN ANDERSEN

The fairy in whose presence we are granted a wish is there for each of us. But few of us know how to remember the wish we have made; and so, few of us recognize its fulfillment later in our lives.

—WALTER BENJAMIN

MY DO-OVER LIST

When a child shouts "Do-over!" he wants a second chance. He wasn't ready the first time. It was just practice! The pitch came while he was daydreaming about a movie he wanted to see. Or she meant to make her fingers into scissors, but her hand had a mind of its own and formed a rock instead. As a kid, I never took full advantage of do-overs. Either I wasn't forceful enough in asserting my natural-born right to do-overs, or I was a young fatalist, accepting all outcomes, no matter how unfair they seemed or how unprepared I felt. I'd like to think I was just saving up my do-overs, banking them, because one day deep into adulthood, I suddenly remembered this simple perk of childhood and thought, *If kids can do it, why can't I?*

I've never quite bought Thomas Wolfe's famous dictum, "You can't go home again." I know you can't change the past, but you *can* change the way you think about the past. Sometimes you need to reevaluate what you think you've left behind forever as a way to find out who you are now, to put into perspective those rites of passage we all must survive and which more often than not linger in our minds as disasters. There's nothing that says you can't go back and run toward those hurdles again, doing over those moments from kindergarten to college you filed away as failures or mistakes.

There are some things that I did or that were done to me that I'd like to erase. Why not simply go back and get them right this time? In many ways our regrets form who we think we are, and I'd arrived at midlife, forty-eight years old, a divorced and remarried father of three girls, with a passel of regrets, a Santa Claus bagful. *Enough is enough*, I thought. Perhaps if I could revisit some of the early episodes of my life that I hated or had trouble with the first time, I could start unburdening myself, and the way I thought about my life as a whole would improve. Not that I thought of myself as a failure. In fact, by outward measures, I probably seemed successful (a college professor, great family, nice house, ballooning debt). But inside, I was still the kid who flubbed the line in the school play in second grade, the last one picked in sports at camp, the awkward teenager who couldn't get a date for the prom. All of these failures were holding me back, I sensed. I didn't want to be that awkward teen anymore or that skinny kid who tripped over his feet. I would never want to banish these versions of me completely. I held them as close as family. But I didn't want them to control me, to tell me what to do and how to act. After all, I had my own kids to raise, and I wanted them to be healthier specimens than I was. I had to set a good example.

I've never been good with to-do lists, but do-overs come easy. The problem with to-do lists for me is that I always forget them somewhere or I simply ignore them. They get buried or lost. I couldn't do that with a do-over list. The list took all of five minutes to create, and these things wouldn't be ignored. They hung like chattering monkeys rattling a cage close to the surface of my consciousness.

1. Kindergarten: Psychologists claim your personality is pretty well formed by the age of five. My kindergarten teacher, Mrs. Collins, certainly seemed to think so. She predicted I'd grow up to be "a thug" someday. Did I?

2. The school play, *The Littlest Angel:* Putnam Elementary School, Athens, Ohio. In the role of the Heavenly Messenger, I had one simple line that I blew completely and ruined the play. I wanted to get it right this time.

3. Summer camp: I was a terrible if frequent camper, a failed specimen of boyhood, always picked last for everything. I went to three summer camps, one in Long Island, one in North Carolina, and one in New Hampshire. I wanted to return to one of these camps and beat everyone at the sports I had been so bad at. I had some scores to settle.

4. Sixth grade: I went to two different sixth grades, one in Slippery Rock, Pennsylvania, and the other in Hollywood, Florida. In both I was bullied mercilessly. I wanted to go back and overcome the bully.

5. Joining a fraternity: My family moved to Columbia, Missouri, when I was in seventh grade, and when I was thirteen, the local chapter of the Sigma Alpha Mu fraternity made me an honorary member after I helped them with a humanitarian project. In college I lost my honorary membership, and now I wanted it back.

6. Eighth grade: By eighth grade I was a miserable outsider. Who likes eighth grade? Not many people. Even so, I was never a cool kid. I was least cool in eighth grade. I wanted to remedy this.

7. The prom: St. Andrew's School, Sewanee, Tennessee. When I was sixteen, I didn't want to attend the public high school in South Bend, Indiana. With my grandmother's financial assistance and the recommendation of a friend, I spent my junior year in Sewanee, Tennessee, at an Episcopalian high school. The school had only 186 students, most of them boys. Although I had a crush on Lizzie Clark, my costar in the high school play, I didn't have the guts to ask her to the prom. So I stayed outside the cafeteria that night and looked in the window at the couples dancing. I wanted to go back to St. Andrew's and do over the prom.

8. Standardized tests: I was terrible at these. I took my PSAT but never my SAT, for a number of complicated reasons. As

a kid, I was always being administered tests that in some way pretended they could foretell my future: IQ tests, aptitude tests, and one odious test in high school that claimed that the best professions for me were (a) gas station attendant, (b) fingerprint technologist, and (c) bookstore owner. I now wanted to beat one of these tests. I wanted to take an SAT or ACT and either do well or, better yet, not care about doing well.

9. A childhood home: My family and I lived in a series of homes throughout my childhood, rarely staying in one for more than a few years. As a result, I'd always felt like a bit of a displaced person. I wanted to revisit one of these childhood sites, camp out for a few days, and come to some peace with my notions of Home and Family.

10. Being an exchange student in Osaka, Japan: From St. Andrew's, I went to our sister school in Japan: Momoyama Gakuin. After six months of fighting with the head of the exchange program and skipping school, I'd had enough. I was homesick and culture shocked to the extreme. I quit my exchange program early and went home to South Bend.

Other possibilities presented themselves — a bar mitzvah, being in Boy Scouts, my first kiss — but for one reason or another, these do-overs never completely gelled. The problem with the bar mitzvah was that I'd never had one in the first place, so it didn't really qualify as a do-over. As for the Boy Scouts, I'd only been a scout for a couple of weeks after we moved from Athens, Ohio, to Slippery Rock; my mother thought I might like to get involved with scouts as a way to meet other boys my age. Actually, I wanted to flee from boys my own age. Ultimately, I felt indifferent about doing over the Boy Scouts. Nothing more eventful had happened to me in the Boy Scouts than learning how to tie a slipknot. And a first kiss? Some things, like first kisses and circumcisions, are un-do-over-able.

There were plenty of things I didn't want to do over too — my first marriage, for instance, something that more than a few people jokingly suggested. But in some inescapable ways, this project *would* be a do-over of if not my first marriage, then fatherhood. When my ex-wife and I divorced, she picked up and moved with my two daughters, Olivia and Isabel, across the country. With no way to follow them, and no job prospects in the middle of the country where they had moved, I felt I would see my daughters at major holidays at best and that we'd recede gradually from one another's lives. It took three years, but eventually I found a good job in Iowa City, within driving distance at least of my daughters in Wisconsin.

Life is complicated and a bit messy, but we've found a way to make it work, more or less. I remarried, and my wife, Margie, and I had another daughter, Shoshanna, whom we call Shoshie. My older daughters spend all the major holidays, spring break, and half the summer with us, as well as the weekends we can all manage to coordinate our schedules. As the girls get older and become more involved with extracurricular activities, mainly involving drama and music, just seeing them once a month seems hard to negotiate. Even so, Margie and Shoshie and my older daughters get along well. Olivia and Isabel adore their younger sister, and Isabel especially is close to Margie. Olivia and Margie get along, but Olivia, who in the best of circumstances is a bit shy, sometimes seems to hold back with Margie and even me. Isabel, by contrast, throws her arms around me and throws her arms around Margie, occasionally before greeting me, whenever she sees us. Olivia seemed initially worried that her affection for me was at the cost of loyalty to her mother. But as the years pass, she seems less concerned about this, to the point that she and Margie have become friends and shopping buddies.

I don't think of this as a midlife crisis as such, though perhaps there's some of that involved. I've been having midlife crises since I was twenty-five, feeling acutely my senses of age and failure, on the average of one a year, so that's nothing new. My do-overs really have as much to do with what kind of parent I am and want to be as with how the past shaped me. My daughters are heading toward all of those hurdles I've jumped (or not). How can I understand what they're going through if I can't understand what I went through?

Coming to Iowa City in itself has been a kind of do-over. I received my graduate degree from the University of Iowa in 1982, and then I returned to teach at the university after an absence of twenty-two years. The house Margie and I bought is a block and a half from the house I lived in as a student, and all that first year, I kept having flashbacks of myself arriving as a gawky twenty-two-year-old. I even teach in the same building, on the same floor, in the same classrooms in which I was taught. My office is *literally* on the other side of a wall from the office I shared with other teaching assistants a quarter of a century ago. Sometimes it feels as though if I could break down that wall, I could meet the twenty-two-year-old me on the other side, and we could be friends. Whenever I walk by this office, I peek inside as though I might see him. I think I'd like him, but I'd be wary because I know his tricks.

⌒

If I only knew then what I know now. How many times have I thought that in my life? The more I considered this project, the more I wondered if knowing what I know now *would* make any difference when I revisited my young life. That's not to say that my do-overs involved moral or ethical tests I hadn't passed the first time. For me, a do-over wasn't a correcting of karmic imbalance, though there was some of that. It wasn't always a matter of *my* choices, *my* wrong-doings, either. It was a matter of roadblocks. What were the roadblocks in my life that I had never completely negotiated?

After I created my list, I resolved, when possible, to do over the original event in its original place, though this wouldn't always be feasible. I wanted to spend a week or so doing over each of the events on my list, but I *did* have a career and other responsibilities to consider, so I couldn't always return to the original scene of the crime or else I'd have to do over finding a job too. I originally attended kindergarten at East Side Elementary School in Athens, Ohio, before transferring to Putnam, but for my do-over I decided to go to Horace Mann Elementary School, a few blocks from my present home. I justified this choice because my daughter Shoshie, who was three when my project started, would most likely attend this same kindergarten in a couple of years. I would be her advance scout. In fact, every time we pass by Horace Mann now, she points it out as "Daddy and my kindergarten." For similar reasons, I figured that since I'd gone to two separate schools the year of sixth grade, I didn't need to revisit a particular school in Slippery Rock, Pennsylvania, or Hollywood, Florida. Instead, I chose Longfellow Elementary, which, like Horace Mann, was within walking distance of my house and another possible candidate school for Shoshie when she gets older.

In the case of summer camp, the three camps I attended when I was a kid are all defunct now, so I chose Camp Echo, in upstate New York, where I had briefly been a counselor when I was eighteen. In this case, I bunked with a group of ten-year-olds in the same bunkhouse where I had been a counselor of a particularly bratty group of ten-year-olds thirty years earlier. But I wasn't a counselor this time. I was a camper again, beholden to no one but my counselor overlords.

My do-overs are presented in the order of the original experiences, though, logistically, I couldn't always do over the events in the same sequence as the originals. My first do-over was summer camp, and my second was kindergarten, but for the sake of continuity in reading, I've swapped them, as I've swapped several other experiences, so that eighth grade, for instance, doesn't follow twelfth grade, a demotion that in real life would emotionally wreck even the hardiest among us. Throughout this journey, I had to rely on the schedules of school districts and administrators, not my own, and so the timing of my do-overs was rarely up to me. Even so, I was often flabbergasted and always grateful that I was allowed, time and again, to storm the halls of childhood and be, for a week at least, an insider again.

As I started performing my do-overs, people felt compelled to confess to me the things in their lives they'd like a chance to do over. Some commended me for my bravery. Some claimed they would never want to revisit the scenes of their childhood defeats. But the majority of people I encountered seemed ready to do the same in *their* lives. At one point I feared I might spark some awful social movement: hordes of grown-ups invading summer camps and elementary schools, determined to retake the math exams they'd failed in third grade or to pass their swimming tests. What a crazy trend this would be. Society would soon disintegrate, and the children would need to grow up even faster than we already expect them to in order that they might wrest society back from the brink, after their parents had regressed and fled their jobs for recess and quiet time on their blankets. This seems an immensely bad idea. In the end, childhood should still be left to the children, though there's nothing wrong with a little vicarious pleasure in watching them play and fall and get up again.

DO-OVER!

CHAPTER ONE

ALPHA FRIEND OF THE DIAMOND CLASS
Kindergarten Do-Over

ORIGINAL AGE: 5
DO-OVER AGE: 48
ORIGINAL LOCATION: EAST SIDE ELEMENTARY, ATHENS, OHIO
DO-OVER LOCATION: HORACE MANN ELEMENTARY, IOWA CITY, IOWA

Most likely, you don't remember your nemesis in kindergarten, but I remember mine, probably because I had two. Virginia Adams was the teacher's pet, and our teacher, Mrs. Collins, hated me. She told my mother I was going to grow up to be "a thug." Those were her exact words. But she loved Virginia, and Virginia took every opportunity to flaunt her superiority. Often Virginia would sing to me: "I'm named after a state, and you're only named after a bird."

Mrs. Collins hated me because of an unfortunate encounter with a small rubber lobster. When we received our first report cards — full of Es and Ps and other letters hardly ever used beyond kindergarten — Mrs. Collins told us to bring them home to our parents, who had to sign them. In 1963, *parents* meant "Mom," and maybe that's even how Mrs. Collins phrased it: "Bring this report card home, and make sure your mother signs it before you come to class tomorrow." Most fathers, mine included, left the signatures and just about everything else to moms.

After my mother signed, I took a bath, and she allowed me to look at the card while in the water. I loved the pink report card and all those letters and words I couldn't read, and I loved my mom's signature, which was bigger than any other words inside the card.

Enter the lobster. Somehow, one of my little bathtub playthings, a thin rubber lobster about three inches long, found its way into my report card. Wet when it entered the report card, it dried and stuck between the thick pages. My older brother Jonathan probably did it, perhaps in payment for my flushing of his goldfish down the toilet the week before. I just liked magic. Now the fish is swimming in the toilet bowl. Flush. Now it's not.

When Mrs. Collins opened the report card the next day and brought it to her eyes to look at my mother's bold and beautiful signature, we both had a nasty surprise. The lobster popped up from the fold of the report card as though attacking her lips. She dropped the card and screamed, and after that I don't remember anything except that Mrs. Collins called my mother to school for an emergency conference and ranted for half an hour about me growing up to be "a thug."

At home, this type of incident would have provided great amusement for my family. But in my school life, this was serious. After the lobster, Mrs. Collins started a campaign against me. At sing-along, she accused me of mouthing the words (I most certainly did not! I shouted them!). When we finger painted, she accused me of finger painting "wrong" (is that even *possible?!*). For each offense, she sent me to sit facing the corner. At nap time, she'd hover over me and then press her foot into my back. She stepped on me almost every day.

Our classroom had its own bathroom, and we had to line up for it when we wanted to use it. Whenever I reached the front of the line, Mrs. Collins would grab my hand roughly and lead me to the back of the line. Of course, I'd do things in my pants as a result and then I'd get punished for that.

If I could have flunked kindergarten, I would have.

But I didn't hate Mrs. Collins. I was just baffled and wanted more than anything else to figure her out. The only clue I had that Mrs. Collins's Laws were not universally observed was when I tested her graham-crackers-and-milk rule at home. Mrs. Collins absolutely forbade us to dip our graham crackers in milk at snack time. Nothing upset her more, except maybe rubber lobsters. She explained to us that soggy graham crumbs, breaking off the Mother Graham Cracker, bobbed like little drowned bugs on the surface of a swimming pool or sank to the bottom like dead babies. And. This. Was. Disgusting! And she wouldn't tolerate it! Did we understand?!

So, of course, whenever she turned her back, we dipped our graham crackers in our milk, like some precision dipping team, and then stuck them in our mouths, gumming the soggy and delicious crackers. Nothing tastes better than disobedience. And one day when I went home, my mother asked me what I wanted for a snack, and I said, "Graham crackers and milk!" When she set them down in front of me at the kitchen table, I started defiantly dipping my graham crackers in my glass of milk and eating them. My mother seemed not to care. In fact, she turned her back on me!

"Look, Mom," I said. "Look what I'm doing!"

She turned around. "What?"

I dipped my graham cracker in my milk and stuck it in my mouth and bit down. Hard. There were crumbs in my glass, floating and sinking.

She thought this was a joke. She laughed. I was cute.

This should have been my first clue that all was not right in the grown-up world, but I thought the fault lay with my mother, that she had not been properly educated. I started to cry, ashamed that my mother was so uncouth.

On the last day of school, Mrs. Collins took me from the front of the bathroom line and put me in the back. Once again, I pooped in my pants, and I was mortified that Mrs. Collins would find out. While not quite as awful as dipping graham crackers in milk, pooping in your pants was right up there.

Every day, we had cubbyhole inspection. It's where we kept our blankets neatly folded and extra supplies. Before she'd dismiss us for the summer, on that fateful day, Mrs. Collins made us stand at attention beside our closed cubbies and await her verdict. She told us that we would not have summer if our cubbies were dirty, that we would stay in kindergarten forever and never go home. Ever. We all stood cowering, terrified by this possibility. Not having summer was one thing, but having to stay with Mrs. Collins forever seemed too much to bear. I was sure she was going to smell what I'd done when she approached my cubby, so I reached into my pants and pulled out what I'd done, which was luckily very hard and dry, and I secretly opened Virginia's cubby next to mine, expertly palming the turd, and snuck it inside. Then I closed the door.

When Mrs. Collins approached my cubby, I stood at the straightest attention I could muster, my eyes locked ahead of me.

"Step aside," she said and slid open the cubby and sniffed tentatively. She closed the door, said nothing, and moved on to Virginia's cubby.

"Why hello, Virginia," she said. "Do you have any pleasant plans for the summer?"

"My parents —" Virginia started and then stopped as soon as Mrs. Collins slid the door open and peeked inside. Mrs. Collins jumped back as though my dry turd would leap toward her mouth the way my rubber lobster had.

"Virginia!" she screamed, high-pitched, sounding like a bird in a state.

And then the scene blanks, and all I remember is looking in the window of the kindergarten after she had dismissed all of us but Virginia, who stood with her face in her hands, crying, while Mrs. Collins stood above her.

As much as I didn't like Virginia, I did not want her to lose summer and have to spend the rest of her life with Mrs. Collins. But I wasn't going to stick around to spend it with her either!

That turned out to be the last year Mrs. Collins ever taught. She was carted away shortly after to the Athens Lunatic Asylum, also known as the Ridges, an imposing Victorian brick institution that sternly overlooked Athens and warehoused its misaligned and misanthropic. I can't say that I tipped her over the edge or that the cubby incident did, but I'm sure I was a contributing factor. She died there and undoubtedly still haunts the place, which was featured a while back on a TV show titled *The Scariest Places on Earth.* And I have no doubt that the place is just like kindergarten was for me, with Mrs. Collins keeping all the other ghosts in line.

↶

I often wondered in the intervening years what had happened to Virginia and how she remembered me. Since kindergarten I'd seen her only once, when we were both eighteen and I'd returned to Athens to visit my brother Jonathan who was attending Ohio University. My childhood friend John Kortlander pointed her out to me at a party — she had blond curly hair and radiated poise and confidence, which completely undid me. I had neither. At eighteen, I looked like a stalk of broccoli: emaciated, wearing seventies polyester, sporting a Jewfro. So I didn't approach her to tell her what I'd done to her when I was five. I thought she'd think I was crazy or trying some weird line to pick her up. So, I went back to my life and she to hers.

But I had a chance to meet her again years later when John Kortlander and some other childhood friends from Athens decided to piggyback an elementary school reunion and the thirtieth reunion of the Athens High Class of 1976. I've never been big on reunions, but an elementary school reunion was too enticing for me to pass up. I hadn't seen most of my old classmates since fifth grade, when my family moved to Slippery Rock. And I wasn't the only one lured to Athens by the prospect of this reunion. About 80 percent of my old classmates showed up. Virginia and I hadn't been classmates since kindergarten, but she graduated from Athens High, and my friend John dragged me to several Athens High events that weekend, including a party at a local watering hole where many of my old schoolmates gathered, including Virginia. My friend John, who knew the whole story of Virginia and me, made a point of reintroducing us as soon as he spotted her among the crush of middle-aged men and women in the bar. John had suggested in an e-mail that I might want to bring some poop with me for old times' sake. I let that one pass. Virginia looked almost as I remembered her from when I was eighteen, and I suddenly had the urge to run. But I reasoned that the statute of limitations should apply to things you did when you were five. Maybe she'd think the incident of the Poop in the Cubby was funny.

Happily, she *did* think it was funny, but she had no memory of the incident. Still, I think the episode must have had an impact on her. She'd grown up to be a therapist. Not a Freudian therapist, but even so, the surprise of poop in your cubby has implications you might like (or need) to spend a lifetime exploring . . .

"I'm glad you told me all this," she said. "I always wondered if I had imagined the things that Mrs. Collins did. I remember her sitting on some of the kids — even then, that troubled me."

This was news to me. "She *sat* on some of the kids?" I asked. "I remember her stepping on my back, but not sitting on me."

"I remember her sitting," she said.

Mrs. Collins was a small woman, but I was an even smaller boy. What Virginia was telling me gave me the oddest feeling. If Mrs. Collins sat on kids, then I was the most eminently sittable kid in that class. I would have been the equivalent of a plush Victorian loveseat to her. If she sat on anyone, she had certainly sat on me. Either I had translated this into stepping on my back (still despicable but slightly less so in my mind), or Virginia was misremembering. Regardless. Though stepping on kindergartners is creepy, sitting on them redefines *creepy*. It takes a connoisseur of malevolence to sit on five-year-olds. Did this qualify as abuse? I had never thought of myself as abused, and the word seems too loaded, potentially fraught with societal baggage and the Look-at-Me brand of sensationalism and self-pity. I wasn't having a Talk Show Moment, but I was having *some* kind of moment, a reassessment, one of those cartoon word bubbles filled with exclamation points and symbols that are nonverbal but absolutely expressive of inner turmoil and alarm. Something that can only be approached in a curse.

Shortly after that reunion and meeting Virginia again, I began my do-overs. There definitely were things from my childhood I needed to investigate, to redefine, to get over, and kindergarten was chief among them. I wasn't going to let Mrs. Collins haunt me forever.

But wanting a do-over and setting one up are two different things, I quickly learned. For reasons that should be obvious, most school districts do not simply welcome forty-eight-year-old men into kindergarten as students. There are a lot of logistics involved: writing letters, cold-calling people, getting background checks. Fortunately, a colleague in the education department at the University of Iowa vouched for me and helped me get my foot in the door at Horace Mann Elementary. Before long, I met with my proposed teacher, Janis Statler, and the principal of Horace Mann, Jodi Rickels. Not only did I have to undergo a background check, but I also had to write a letter to the parents of Janis's kindergarten class to tell them about my project. If any of them objected, that would be the end of it, at least at this school. Thankfully, no one objected. Still, the parents were given a chance to meet with me one evening — a couple of parents and their kids showed up. The parents all seemed amused but supportive. Not only did they think my project was a good idea, but they wished they had the chance to do over a few episodes from their own lives too.

One of my new classmates, Haley, and her mom told me about the routine. I learned that hands are for helping, not hurting. This seemed like a good rule, something that Mrs. Collins hadn't subscribed to. Haley also mentioned something about "Alpha Friends," and I tensed. Was she talking about dominance? Shades of Virginia Adams? I vowed to be the Alpha Friend of *this* kindergarten class. But Janis explained that *Alpha Friends* refers to the alphabet; they're personifications of the letters. Alice Aardvark. Bradley Beagle. *Not* Alpha Wolf. I wasn't quite in the kindergarten groove yet.

Janis and Jodi figured that the kids would accept me the way they accept any adult in their room, that they'd see me the way they see student teachers who regularly come over from the education department. That worried me a bit. The important thing, I thought, was not to try too hard. Over twenty years ago, I reviewed a book by educator Vivian Gussin Paley, *Mollie Is Three*. Paley, a recipient of a "genius grant" from the MacArthur Foundation, spent a year observing a class of three-year-olds at the University of Chicago's preschool, and one of her main points was that children spend a lot of their time telling each other stories and role playing as a way of learning about the world. Simple enough. But what struck me was that when an adult tried to join their play, it freaked them out a bit. Once, when they were pretending to fly to the moon, the dad of one of the kids tried to fly to the moon with them. "It's just pretend," one child said, alarmed. The dad said he knew this but wanted to play. No, grown-ups aren't supposed to pretend.

So that was a depressing possibility. The kindergartners might well freeze me out and refuse to let me fly to the moon with them. Another depressing thought: the Mollie of Paley's book is about twenty-seven now.

↶

On my first day of kindergarten, I'm awakened from a troubled sleep at 6:58 a.m. by the sounds of traffic on rain-slicked streets.

My wife, Margie, stretches and we say good morning.

"I couldn't sleep," I tell her.

"Why not?"

"First day of school."

"Excited?"

"Nervous."

I'm worried of course about how my new classmates will accept me. I'm a new kid and a grown-up besides, and they've been in class for about six weeks already. It's not that I think I'll have any trouble catching up. After all, last night I read a book to my three-year-old daughter, Shoshie, *Small Pig* by Arnold Lobel, an "I Can Read Book." Not many kindergartners know how to read. Fewer have children.

But it's not easy being forty-eight and going back to kindergarten. There's the embarrassment factor, and I figure I'm going to get a few stares, maybe be ridiculed by the older kids, maybe even the teachers. The whole week might be awkward and uncomfortable.

Margie drives me to school before dropping Shoshie at her preschool, and both of them wish me luck as I grab my book bag and my towel for quiet time and hurry to join some kids crossing the street under the benevolent protection of the crossing guard. I'm welcomed to kindergarten by my classmate, Martine, throwing up. I don't take it personally because kindergartners do a fair amount of that — I remember throwing up on a kid in lunch line in kindergarten, an accident of course, though Mrs. Collins accused me of doing it on purpose. "Why didn't you tell me you were going to throw up?" she yelled at me.

I just looked at her like she was crazy because, well, she was.

From the outset, I can see that Mrs. Statler is a much kinder kindergarten teacher than Mrs. Collins, though, of course, that's not saying much. Mrs. Collins looked and acted much like the original Wicked Witch of the West, and Mrs. Statler seems much more like Glinda the Good Witch, though only superficially. Like Glinda, she's blond, but she's not sickly sweet, and she doesn't float around on a bubble. She's friendly but firm, which I learn almost immediately when I sit on the floor near her chair with the other kindergartners. It's reading time, which precedes the official start of the day, and I've grabbed a book and plunked down with it.

A crowd of children has gathered around me, amazed by my advanced reading skills.

"Can you teach Robin that we don't sit near the books so other kids can get to them?" Mrs. Statler tells the group.

I flush a bit. Oh, so that's why they were crowding around me — because they couldn't get to the books.

But they're definitely curious. One girl with dark hair, Jasmine, book in hand, asks me, "Why did you have a bad time in school, Robin?"

I'm about to tell her about my teacher sitting on me when Stefan asks me a follow-up. "Are you coming back to school to have a great time because when you were a kid you didn't have a great time?"

"Yes, that's it, exactly," I say.

Jasmine nods and shows me her Barbie watch.

At the start of the day, we need to choose what we're having for lunch, and we have to do attendance. Like all the other kindergartners, I have a popsicle stick with my name neatly written on it, and I place that by my choice for lunch today (chicken tenders), and I also have an attendance cube that I stack with the other attendance cubes.

"All right, my little chickadees," Mrs. Statler says, sitting in her chair, starting the day's activities. We all gather in a semicircle around her, respectful of the paper-toweled vomit spot of our fallen comrade, Martine, who, Mrs. Statler explains, isn't feeling well.

Almost every activity in kindergarten has at least one song attached to it, with the possible exception of vomiting. When I was a kid, we did have a vomit song. Left to our own devices, we sang it for years and years, never growing tired of it. The song was sung to the tune of the theme of *The Bridge on the River Kwai:*

Comet, it makes your mouth turn green.
Comet, it tastes like Listerine.
Comet, it makes you vomit.
So buy some Comet and vomit today.

The Good Morning Song is less memorable and not as much fun to sing, but I don't make the rules here. Maybe the next time someone vomits, I could suggest to Mrs. Statler that she add it to the kindergarten repertoire.

One of the first things that I notice about this kindergarten class as distinct from my kindergarten class is how ethnically diverse this group is. In my day, Erica Marks and I represented multiculturalism, the two Jewish kids in our class. One aspect about Horace Mann that recommends it is that a number of the children are the sons and daughters of international students and other immigrants: Hispanic, Asian American, African American, and Arab American. Shoshie, as a Filipino American, will fit in well in this group. The only sign that all is not hunky-dory — the parents of one Mexican American boy, Jesus, wouldn't sign a photo release for me, Mrs. Statler suspects, because they're illegal immigrants and they're concerned about deportation.

Other than that, the Diamond Class, as they've named themselves, seems as harmonious a place of racial and ethnic harmony as one could find, with Mrs. Statler their benevolent Queen, sitting in her rocking chair dispensing kindergarten justice and compassion.

The rules are posted on the wall near her chair, though I suspect I'm one of the few kindergartners who can read them:

I-Care Rules
1. We listen to each other.
2. Hands are for helping, not hurting.
3. We use I-care language.
4. We care about each other's feelings.
5. We are responsible for what we say and do.
6. Different is great.

and

1. Ignore.
2. Tell to stop.
3. Walk away.
4. Get help.

My three best buddies from the get-go are Louis, a kid with blond hair; Stefan, an African American kid; and Abdul, an Arab American boy. Stefan takes it upon himself to show me the kindergarten ropes. My classmates, though they don't know my checkered kindergarten past, are leaving nothing to chance. Stefan gives me the lay of the bathroom land. He shows me the "bathroom clip" that you take when you need to go — and what an innovation — you don't need to tell anyone you're going. If you've got to go, you've got to go. He shows me the bathroom, shows me the water fountain, and starts to tell me how to stay out of trouble. But Mrs. Statler's attention lands on him. "Signals on, Stefan and Robin," she says. "It's time for learning, not talking," and I fold my hands in my lap as does Stefan. When she says this, Mrs. Statler uses hand signals, pointing to her eyes or her ears, as though she's interpreting for the deaf. No one in class is deaf, but we're attention impaired. Nothing as serious as ADD as far as I can tell, but it's not easy to pay attention when you're five — we're a visual culture. Point to your eyes when you're telling me to watch you. Point to your ears when you're telling me to listen.

We're going to learn about our new Alpha Friend for the week, the moment we've all been waiting for.

"The Alpha Friend," Mrs. Statler starts in her soothing voice, "is red on the outside and white on the inside . . . and he's an acrobat. Can anyone tell me what an acrobat is?"

"Signals on," she says. "Thanks for raising your hand, Abdul."

"It's a stick you throw in the air and then you catch it," he says.

Not exactly, Mrs. Statler says, but finds the closest correlation to Abdul's interpretation. She asks if anyone knows what a trapeze is. No one has the foggiest, so she draws a person on a trapeze and then introduces our Alpha Friend, Andy Apple, a smiling apple on a card. "Andy Apple is an acrobat," she says in a lilting voice that I know will now get stuck in my head and make me hate Andy Apple and want to crush him underfoot if he ever gets off his trapeze. Hands are for helping, I know, but no one said anything about feet. We repeat Andy Apple's occupation back to her, though I have a very kindergarten urge to tell Mrs. Statler and the rest of the class that I've been on a trapeze before. Signals on, Robin!

And so it goes in orderly fashion through much of the morning. It looks like it might rain outside and who knows what the family lives of these kids are like, though I suspect most come from pretty stable homes, but, boy, does it feel safe in here, even with the ever-present threat of a time-out hovering in the wings. Despite my initial antipathy toward Andy Apple, I make my peace with him and alliterate my way along with my twenty-two classmates, minus Martine the Nauseated and one or two other absentees. After we have exhausted all possible avenues of discussion about Andy Apple and his day, we get up and, just like that, run, hop, skip, tiptoe, and skate to music as if this were the most natural thing in the world.

Besides the I-Care Rules, I learn two important things on day one of kindergarten. First, I learn that kindergarten is hard work. It may look easy, but it's not. By 10:45, we've already done eight activities, and I'm exhausted. The second thing I learn is that I've missed recess terribly all these long adult years. Out on the playground, Stefan wants to play tetherball with me, so he smacks the ball my way, and I smack it back and it busts him in the jaw. Although he seems fine, he takes the opportunity to lecture me on proper playground etiquette.

"You can't hurt anyone on the playground," he tells me. "And you really can't hit or else you get a time-out for a long, *long* time, a

time-out until school is over. And you can't run. And if you get a time-out for a long, *long* time, that wouldn't be much fun because people like to play."

Stefan gets stuck on his "If you do really bad things" speech, I suppose, in part, because I'm listening so intently, even taking notes. He's struck a bit of a self-important pose, like some politico outlining his platform. "If you do a really *really* bad thing," he says, "you'll be taken to the office."

I was only taken to the office once as a child, in fourth grade, when I yelled at my teacher, Mrs. Hill, not because I was angry but because I felt like yelling at her. It was an experiment. I told her so, and she told me she felt like taking me to the office, the direct result of my experiment. Most of the stuff I did in grade school couldn't be considered bad so much as misguided. That same year, I wore my pajamas to school one day after telling my mother that I thought they looked like street clothes. She said they didn't, that they looked like pajamas, and I said no, they looked exactly like regular clothes. They had a collar and were made of corduroy, and that somehow struck me as unpajama-like, despite the elastic waistband and the fact that they were obviously, in all important respects, pajamas. "Okay, wear them then," she said. In this way, she really was an enlightened parent, knowing that experience is indeed the best teacher. So I wore my pajamas to class and, amazingly, the only one who noticed was Mrs. Hill. During a math quiz, she called me over to her desk, where she and her student teacher were trying to stifle their laughter.

"Robin," she said. "Are you wearing your pajamas?"

"No, Mrs. Hill," I said.

That was my real problem, lying. I was an inveterate liar. I suppose the flip side is that I had an imagination and saw all things as possible.

When, in first grade, a classmate brought in some rabbits, our teacher told us we could have one if we brought back a note from a parent the next day. I knew my mother wouldn't allow me to have a rabbit, so I went home and that night forged a note from my mother in my best first-grade block lettering.

Robin can hav rabbi

Sined Mom

That's the kind of thing I got in trouble for, not hitting people.

↶

One of the nice things about kindergarten is that you can't get too much of a good thing. After we sing with Mrs. Statler and her associate, Laurie, we go to music class. Before lunch there's snack time, and there's recess before lunch *and* after. Music begets music. Food begets food. Play begets more play. It's all very civilized and is probably much the way life was in the Garden of Eden.

At snack time, we have bagels and cream cheese, and in unison we all thank Annie, our classmate who brought the snack today.

Then we have a serious discussion about potential Alpha Friends, at my table at least. Mrs. Statler, meanwhile, patrols the room, gently reminding us of social norms.

"It would be funny if we had a bagel Alpha Friend," says Stefan.

"It would be funny if we had a human Alpha Friend," says Abdul, snorting his juice.

"Maybe we could have a sandwich Alpha Friend," says Haley.

"Make sure you're chewing with your mouth closed," says Mrs. Statler. "Because it's gross if we see your chewed-up food."

"I wish we had an Alpha Friend that was a stop sign," says Haley, showing me a mouthful of gross, chewed-up food. I stifle the urge to show her my chewed-up food too. The teacher is near.

"Make sure you're doing as much eating as talking, Haley," Mrs. Statler says in a grown-up voice I know well, one that I have used on my three daughters that means you are about to pass a boundary from which there is no return. You are about to lose something. You are about to have a (gasp!) consequence. I would like to join in the Alpha Friend Roundup, but they're doling out Alpha Friends faster than I can think, and, anyway, I'm mindful of Vivian Paley's assertion that if I join in, I'll ruin my cover, and they'll just think I'm some odd grown-up who doesn't know Alpha Friends from a hole in the ground.

"I wish we had an octopus Alpha Friend," says Abdul, giggling.

"I was just going to say that," says Haley, opening her mouth as though it's a three-car garage.

Oh, Haley, I think, mentally slapping my forehead with the palm of my hand. But, kindergarten rebel that I am, I wonder why showing your food while you eat isn't simply a sign that you're enjoying your food tremendously. Look what happens when my teeth meet my food! It's delicious, and it's going in *my* stomach! When I was an exchange student in high school, in Osaka, Japan, my host family, the Oshiros, used to constantly prod me to slurp while I ate noodles. My host mother wasn't sure I was enjoying my food.

"Make more noise, Robin," my host brother, Hiroshi, used to tell me, as they all slurped soup or sukiyaki while I sat there primly taking quiet nibbles. It used to really bother them, but, try as I might, I couldn't cast aside my upbringing and make the requisite noises that sounded to my ear only slightly less grating than a pig at a trough.

Of course, kindergarten exists in part to teach us the social norms of America, or at least of Iowa. Andy Apple is Assimilated, and Mrs. Statler asks Haley to leave the table and takes her aside to show her proper table manners. There are no raised voices, no punishments, and no tears. I just see Haley nodding and Mrs. Statler talking softly to her, out of earshot of the rest of us.

Lunch for me is chicken tenders, animal crackers, iceberg lettuce, and applesauce. I squeeze in among my classmates and chow down while the kids instruct me on lunchroom etiquette.

"If you take it, you got to eat it," Jasmine tells me.

"When you're done with lunch, you throw things away and then you come back and sit down," Louis says.

"Robin, you're the only one in our class who took salad," Stefan notices.

What of it? I'm thinking. Obviously, this marks me as different, but then I remember the I-Care Rules. "Different is great," I tell my classmates, and they nod. The I-Care Rules are widely respected in these parts.

At quiet time, I consider asking Mrs. Statler to step on my back for old times' sake. But it wouldn't go with the ambient music she's playing. It's kind of Andean with birds chirping in the background. I can hear pages being turned, small voices reading aloud, "Boys can be friends. Girls can be friends."

"You're having a great day," I hear Mrs. Statler telling Abdul. "You're making a lot of good choices. Way to go, kiddo."

"Babies can be friends. Grown-ups can be friends."

My sentiments exactly, but I'm trying to concentrate. Not only do I have kindergarten every day from 8:25 to 2:55, but I also have a class to teach at the university at night. It's a class about "truth" in contemporary memoirs, and this week we're reading James Frey's *A Million Little Pieces*. To keep up, I have to reread the book at nap time, on my blanket. I actually need to have it finished tonight, and it's hard to stress out properly amid all these peaceful sounds.

After quiet time comes choice time, and Stefan asks me if I want to play in the Let's Pretend Center. My first kindergarten wasn't zoned, but this one is. There are different "centers," and a number of children are allowed to play in each at any given time. The Let's Pretend Center has a capacity of four. The Writing Center can handle seven, the Art Center six, and the Building Center four. It's strictly first come, first served. After I stow my blanket back in my cubby, I'm approached by Louis and Abdul, who both ask if I can play a board game with them, but I say sorry, Stefan has first dibs. In my old kindergarten I would have ditched Stefan without remorse, much preferring board games to the Let's Pretend Center, but I want to do things right this time so my teacher and the others will like me.

The first thing Stefan does is to confiscate my copy of *A Million Little Pieces*.

"Hey, this can be a pretend recipe book," he says.

I agree. I suggest calling it *A Million Little Pizzas*.

"Okay," he says. "What do you want on your pizza?" he says, going to the oven, the centerpiece of the Let's Pretend Center. He pulls out a plastic pizza from the oven and says, "You want sauswidge?" Then he offers me an array of drinks, including Dr Pepper, Coke, and "things that kids can't have," which, he elaborates, means alcohol. A kindergartner serving up pretend alcohol, out of a pretend recipe book, made from a pretend memoir about alcohol addiction, to a pretend kindergartner. Sounds like a dangerous mix, so I opt for water instead.

⌒

By the end of my first day, we're all a bit confused. If I wasn't having a midlife crisis before, I am now. And my classmates are having a bit of a beginning-life crisis — not quite sure what to make of the new kid.

As we're waiting at the end of the day to be dismissed, we sit on the floor with our coats and backpacks, legs "crisscross applesauce," which is a little difficult for me.

"Are you going to Extended Day?" Stefan asks me.

"No," I say. "I'm going home."

"Do you ride the bus?" Louis asks.

"No."

"Oh. Well, who's picking you up?" Haley asks

"My wife," I say.

There's a long moment of silence as they take that in and blink at me like cats.

"Oh," says Stefan finally. "I thought you were going to say your dad."

I spoke too soon. I wait in front of the building for a while for Margie to pick me up, but she doesn't show. The principal comes by and tells me that I can wait by the second-floor window with the other kids waiting for errant grown-ups to show. After fifteen minutes, I grow impatient, and I look for a phone, admittedly not a very kindergarten thing to do, taking charge in this manner. But after 2:55, I'm off the kindergarten clock. Mrs. Statler tells me I can use the phone in her classroom.

Maybe Margie is running behind, I think. *Maybe she lost track of the time.* But no, it turns out she's only lost track of *me.* This, of course, is one of the negative side effects of going back to kindergarten for a week. Your spouse, in an act of subconscious self-preservation, will completely forget about picking you up after school, claiming that she thought you said 3:55 when you clearly remember telling her 2:55. It's hard to blame her. After all, we're treading on dangerously thin psychic ice here, with the potential of turning her into my mother for a week.

For similar reasons, I'm not going to invite Mrs. Statler over for dinner, though I'd like to thank her for treating me like a real kindergartner. I'm too exhausted after a school day to cook for her, and I wouldn't ask Margie to cook for my teacher and risk turning her irrevocably into my mom. Still, if I were a kid, I'm sure I would have a crush on Mrs. Statler. She radiates a kind of serene and confident poise that would have made me want to marry her when I was five or six. *Marry,* of course, was a murky word when I was five — it was something like being it in freeze tag. At five, I planned to marry a four-year-old named Christy, who suffused me with a sense of inner joy as we played in the sandbox. Shoshie too sees marriage as both flexible and easy. Sometimes she wants to marry me, and sometimes she wants to marry Margie, and she often wants to marry Peter, her classmate in preschool, or Oliver, our three-year-old neighbor. Sometimes she wants to marry the lot of us.

Although I never would have wanted to marry Mrs. Collins, I thought differently about my first-grade teacher, Mrs. Drake, whom, after having Mrs. Collins, I would have followed into the fiery pits of hell. Just the fact that she was nice to me made me love her. I figured we should marry, but I knew that she had to meet my parents first. She was probably in her early twenties, and this was her first year teaching. I invited her to dinner one day, and she asked if I had cleared this with my parents.

"Yes," I said, not quite understanding what "clearing with parents" meant exactly.

She asked me what time she should show up, and I told her nine, which was actually my bedtime.

I went home and completely forgot about the invitation. That night, my mother and I were in the kitchen at the sink doing dishes from our dinner when the doorbell rang.

"Who can that be at this hour?" my mother wondered, drying her hands on the dish towel. "Robin, go see who it is."

I went downstairs, peeked through the window, and saw Mrs. Drake all dressed up with a fur collar and her hair in a bouffant. She was the most beautiful creature I'd ever seen, but I knew she spelled Trouble with a cursive *T*. She waved at me, and I waved back, and then I closed the curtain and went upstairs.

"Who was it?" my mother asked.

"No one," I said.

The doorbell rang again, and my mother looked at me and headed downstairs, with me trailing after her, shouting, "No, don't let her in. She wants to eat!"

After my mother let in my teacher, all of us sat around, embarrassed. We didn't have any food left for poor Mrs. Drake, so my mom fixed her a drink, and they tried to relax and chat about me as if I wasn't a holy terror. Even though Mrs. Drake was calm and polite, I knew one thing for sure, that she and I would never marry now.

✍

In most ways, it turns out, I'm the same as a forty-eight-year-old kindergartner as I was as a five-year-old kindergartner. Little has changed internally, I'm afraid. I still love recess as much as I did when I was five, and I still have some of the same problems. When I was five, Erica Marks used to chase after me and tackle me and then plant me with kisses. Now the kids still chase after me, but only because I'm it. I'm always it in freeze tag. From day one, as soon as we're let out on the playground, the kids shout at me, "You're it," and they swarm around me, not only from my class, but from the other kindergarten class as well. Half of them want to be tagged by me, and the others don't. I chase after those who don't, and I succeed in tagging a boy from the other kindergarten class, who turns around immediately and starts pursuing me. The kids decide en masse that they're all suddenly it and I'm the one who needs to be tagged. Ah yes, the make-up-the-rules-as-you-go version of every game I ever played as a kid. I remember it well. I run close to the building, then dart to the swing sets and around the jungle gym, and I can't shake them, so I head for the big field behind the school, where some older kids are playing. The swarm stops and I stop too, catching my breath, my hands on my knees.

"You're not allowed to go there," Stefan yells at me. "We're not allowed to go there."

Okay, so I head back to the playground and run to home base. Safe. I don't want to play anymore. I'm tired. Happily, a little girl named Sophie who's missing four front teeth comes over to rescue me. She wears a crooked smile and looks up at me mischievously. On the first day of school, I'm told, she came up to her teacher and announced, "I'm in kindergarten!" as though all her ambitions in life had been realized.

"Let's play a new game," she says now. "Princesses!"

"Don't say *Princesses*," Stefan groans. "I hate that game."

Stefan and the others run off to continue playing freeze tag. "I'm Cinderella," she tells me. "And you can be Belle."

Of course, I'm intrigued. I've never played Belle before, but apparently playing Princesses largely entails standing around sipping imaginary tea and admiring each other's ball gowns.

I think I've got this kindergarten thing down. The kids don't seem to have *any* problem accepting me as a fellow kindergartner or accepting me into their play. I would even go so far as to say I'm popular. I think the real reason that the dad of Paley's book wasn't accepted by Mollie and her friends when they went to the moon was because he was so obviously faking it. "Can I come to the moon with you?" he probably said, in that saccharine grown-up voice that some grown-ups think passes for Kidspeak. Get this: It doesn't. They know you're faking it. (I'm not, though; of course, I *know* I'm an adult.) And they think they talk like us!

But this isn't a Peter Pan complex or some *Whatever Happened to Baby Jane?* psycho thriller. And though I clearly have one, I loathe the term *inner child.* When I was a kid, I used to plunk myself down on strangers' beach blankets in Long Beach, Long Island, where my grandmother had a little beach house, and I'd introduce myself to them. I'd do that still if I wouldn't get arrested.

I actually *was* arrested for this when I was five, though not booked. One time I was begging my mother for a banana popsicle as we walked toward the Borden's Dairy store. I was whining, and my mother was just sick of me and told me I couldn't have a popsicle.

"Fine," I said. "I'll run away."

"Fine. Run away," my mom said and started walking away. I headed in the other direction, and I soon found an alley that I turned down. I hadn't gone more than a hundred yards or so when I spotted a boy about my age playing in his front yard. I went over and introduced myself and told him I had run away and asked if I could play with him.

We played for two or three hours before his mother came to the door and told him it was time for dinner.

"Mom," he said. "This is Robin. Can he live with us?" The request seemed reasonable to us both, but his mother looked puzzled.

A police car then stopped in front of the gate, and a policeman rolled down the window and asked me if my name was Robin Hemley.

That was a nifty trick, I thought. Of all the lucky guesses, that the policeman would know my name. For a moment, I thought of telling him no, it wasn't my name, but I wanted to see where this was going, so I told him yes.

He opened the door. "Get in," he said. "Your mother is worried about you."

My mother. Oh, I'd completely forgotten about her. Yes, she was beyond worry. She was frantic. As she later explained it to me a number of times over the years, she'd walked only fifty feet or so when she turned around to find I'd completely vanished. She didn't see the alley I'd walked down. Maybe it was obscured by bushes. Only now can I truly comprehend how she must have felt. Once in the Cincinnati airport, Margie and I and Shoshie, who was two, walked into a store together. Both Margie and I thought Shoshie was with the other, and by the time we realized she was with neither of us, she was no longer in the store. We rushed outside, frantically scanning the concourse until finally, a minute or so later, we saw Shoshie holding hands with a woman who, when she saw us, gave us a look of both perplexity and utter condemnation. How could you lose your child? her look said. Actually, it's easy. They're slippery things.

"Are you arresting me?" I asked the policeman as we drove away from my would-be adopted brother and his quizzical mother.

"We'll see," he said. "If you promise not to do that again, I might let you go this time."

"I promise," I said. As we drove by my school, I saw the kids from the afternoon kindergarten class, a number of whom were my friends, playing on the playground. One even pointed at me, and I ducked down. What if this got back to Mrs. Collins? I felt like the thug she thought I was.

The next day, my classroom was abuzz with news that I'd been spotted in a police car. "Were you arrested?" one of my friends asked me.

"No," I said. "That wasn't me. That was just someone who looked like me."

This episode spawned in me a lifelong fear of police. I share this phobia with Alfred Hitchcock, whose father once had him locked up in a jail cell as a very young boy. In his films, the police are always menacing. Margie loves to tease me about this — whenever we pass a police cruiser, she waves, and I cringe. "Don't do that!" I tell her invariably, as though waving to a cop is a crime.

↶

Kindergarten has always implied threat and alienation to me, but in the Diamond Class, no one needs to fear being arrested (with the possible exception of Jesus, the boy whose parents might be illegal immigrants), and everyone is made to feel special in their turn.

"Different is great" is drummed into us day after day. I'm glad of this. I'm glad, for instance, that Jesus doesn't taunt me: "I'm named after the Messiah, and you're only named after a bird!" But sometimes I feel as though I'm in an indoctrination camp. One day Mrs. Statler reads us a book about ants and explains that ants smell with their antennae, while we smell with our noses.

"But that's okay," she says, "because different is great!" And she makes a raise-the-roof sign.

"Different is *great!*" the kids repeat in unison.

We're talking about ants here.

Sure, different is great, except when it isn't. Different isn't great if you're chewing with your mouth open. Different isn't great if you can't communicate. One day on the playground, Mrs. Statler sees Jesus, who barely understands any English, having trouble comprehending tag. She shows him how to tag a girl. "Say, 'Tag, you're it!'" she says. The boy looks unsure, almost scared, looking at his hands as if Mrs. Statler's asking him to take a swing at the girl. So she gives him a ball and mimics shooting a basket, but he shakes his head. Both Mrs. Statler and the boy earn my sympathy. Sometimes different is different, and it's hard to mitigate the pain of that, though Mrs. Statler tries.

I wonder if part of the reason my classmates have accepted me so readily into their group as a fellow kindergartner is because "different is great." Laurie, Mrs. Statler's classroom associate, tells me one morning that Jeffrey, one of the Asian American kids, told his parents about me. "There's a new kid in class," he told them. "He's very big. I don't know what to think about that."

Maybe I'm the "different is great" slogan taken to its preposterous extreme.

⟨⟩

At lunch on Wednesday, I pay for all my hubris about being so easily accepted into this cult of five-year-olds. A boy from another class speaks to me in the lunch line.

"Why are you always here?"

"I'm not always here. Only this week."

"Are you someone's dad?"

"I am, but not here."

"Is this your work?"

"No, it's my experience. I'm going back to kindergarten for the week."

"Cool."

No sooner have I put out this psychic fire than I have an odd encounter with one of my buddies, Abdul. It's my fault. Inadvertently, I slip into my parent role when I see that Abdul isn't eating much of his hamburger.

"Are you not hungry anymore?" I ask him.

He gets a dark look, and suddenly I feel like a spy caught in some World War II flick. Darn. What self-respecting kindergartner would chide another kindergartner for not eating all his food?

"Are you a teacher?" he asks.

"Me? No, I'm one of you," I tell him, perhaps a little too desperately, and he gives me a doubtful look.

Jodi, the principal, comes up to us then. She wasn't eavesdropping — that's impossible in the bedlam that's an elementary school lunchroom. It's just a coincidence that she asks him, "What do you think of Robin?"

He's silent.

"It's kind of silly, isn't it?"

Hey, Principal Lady, I'm thinking. *This isn't helping.*

Abdul nods. "He's coming back because he had a worst day?" he asks.

"That's right," she says. "And now he's trying to make a new memory."

What a masterful move on her part. Unlike me, by acknowledging his doubts, she gives him a path to understand, in his own way, what I'm doing here. I had a worst day, and now I'm going to replace it with a better day. Simple math. Or, in the lingo of the Diamond Class, "Mustang Math!"

Abdul is having a worst day too, as I find out after lunch at recess when I notice him standing alone, looking glum.

"What's wrong, Abdul?" I say.

"I'm sad."

"Why?"

"No one wants to play with me."

"I'll play with you," I say, and just like that, in that kindergarten way, we're friends again.

⟲

The Octopus Song, the Dracula Song, the Pumpkin Stew Song, the Good Morning Song, the Mustang Math Song. We sing and play our way through the week. Never mind that we shout the lyrics. Never mind that the percussion in music class is so off tempo and so jarring that you envision a Monty Python skit — an ox cart full of plague-ravaged bodies, and the call "Bring out your dead! Bring out your dead!" instead of twenty-two five-year-olds singing about pumpkins. We are the Diamond Class! We know who are our Alpha Friends and who aren't. We are learning to share, and we are learning to make good choices, and we know our I-Care Rules. We know who the line leader is today, and we know what the weather is outside, and we know the days of the week and how many days we've been in school. We are all different, and we are all special, but some are more special than others.

The most special among us are those who are line leaders and those who get to do Surprise Box. The Surprise Box always stays the same, but what goes in it changes from day to day and so does the person who gets to put the surprise in the box. Whoever guesses the surprise correctly gets to take the box home that night and put a surprise in it and write three clues or have Mom or Dad write the clues. You only get to do Surprise Box once until everyone in class has had a turn. So when one of my classmates, Lottie, the daughter of an English department colleague of mine, guesses the surprise correctly one day, she generously turns over the box to me, because she's already had a turn.

That night, I can't sleep. I awake at two in the morning and go to my study where I read work by my students. The strain of the week has shown on both Margie and me. We're both crabby and a little overwhelmed. I was too tired to read to Shoshie tonight, too tired to give her a bath. I just collapsed, which, understandably, didn't make Margie too happy. Or Shoshie. She wants to come to kindergarten with me, but I told her she'd have to wait a couple of years, an incomprehensible amount of time to her, all too comprehensible to me. I check on her now and give her a kiss, then I roam around the house trying to find something for Surprise Box. In a way, I'm an old hand at Surprise Box, but forty-three years ago, it was a rubber lobster in a report card, and it was as much a surprise for me as for my teacher. After all that time, a rubber lobster just won't do. I find a dragon incense burner I picked up once in a market in Hong Kong.

I write down my clues.

I'm an animal that doesn't exist. A pretend animal.
There are stories of knights in shining armor battling me.
I breathe fire.

Yes, that's right. A dragon. Something transformative and mythic.

The next day, before Surprise Box, we have Writers' Workshop. Although it's called Writers' Workshop, it mostly involves drawing in journals, though my classmates practice their letters and numbers too. Our assignment is to write and draw about what makes us happy. Lottie draws a lamp. Haley draws a hill with an olive on a toothpick on top of it. No, it's a tulip, she says. Jasmine is drawing some kind of green blob. Jeffrey is writing a calendar. Lottie is drawing another lamp. No, it's someone under an umbrella, and it's raining, she tells me. Mrs. Statler is giving Stefan some help with his lowercase *a*'s. I scribble my drawing, and they all tell me not to go so fast. Then they try to decipher what *I've* drawn. "Go show it to the teacher," Jeffrey tells me, and I obey.

I've drawn a hillside with blueberry bushes on it, and people with buckets picking the berries.

I stand in line with the other kindergartners, and when it's my turn, Mrs. Statler asks me if it's a happy memory. Yes, I tell her. It's a picture of blueberry bushes on Mount Baker in Washington State.

"Did you go berry picking?" she asks, and suddenly I find it difficult to speak. I try to tell her about blueberry picking on Mount Baker with my daughters Olivia and Isabel. I try to tell her about making blueberry pies with them and making jam, and how we labeled the jam "Izzy's Jam" and how proud it made her feel to have these delicious wild blueberries named in her honor. But I don't really tell her all that. I only tell her the bare facts. I don't tell her that I haven't made jam or picked wild blueberries since my divorce. I don't tell her how infrequently I get to see my children, even now that we live in adjoining states. I don't tell her that my ex-wife and I divorced when Isabel was in kindergarten. I wasn't expecting this. I wasn't expecting these feelings at all. I thought this would be a lark. It's kind of crazy, I know, but I'm sure something is visible on my face, and besides I can't speak. This is embarrassing, and I'm grateful to Mrs. Statler that her face doesn't betray anything that would shame me further. I guess this is why I needed to return. This picture. This happy memory. This teacher telling me that there's nothing wrong with me drawing the picture the way I want to draw it. "It's very nice," she says, and I rejoin my comrades without glancing at my journal again. Haley looks up from her drawing and politely asks me for my green pencil, if I'm not using it anymore, so that she can put the final touches on her small and indecipherable creation.

CHAPTER TWO

HONORARY ANGEL
School Play Do-Over

ORIGINAL AGE: 7
DO-OVER AGE: 48
ORIGINAL LOCATION: ATHENS, OHIO
DO-OVER LOCATION: MARIETTA, GEORGIA

For Thanksgiving, we were going as a family to London for the week. I suppose, in part, we were going to London because of the kind of parent I am, a self-avowed Disneyland Dad. It's undeniable. This is the kind of dad who, as the name implies, tries to make up for the fact that he can't see his children all the time by taking them to Disneyland and other resortish places. But there's a difference between me and your average Disneyland Dad, I think. I want to go to these places myself. I love to travel, but from the time I was nineteen to forty, I couldn't afford it and left the country only once, for a short business jaunt to Germany. Having rediscovered the joy of travel midlife, I've come to the conclusion that there's hardly anything better I can do for my children than to open up the world to them. Whenever I have a chance to bring my family somewhere, I do it by hook or by crook, cashing in frequent flyer miles, taking on extra teaching gigs, and too often racking up an impressive credit card bill. But I've seen results. In San Sebastián, Spain, Olivia and Isabel ate and loved squid cooked in its own ink. In Japan, they shed some of their midwestern shyness and their clothes to take a communal bath at a traditional Japanese inn. In Slovenia, we toured a museum that had once held captured partisans in World War II. In France, we stood where Joan of Arc presented herself to the Dauphin to lead her countrymen against the English.

Of course, it's impossible to be a Disneyland Dad and not concede that there's guilt mixed up in there, and yes, probably on some level I'm trying to buy my daughters' affection. But if we presented my motivations in a pie chart, I think these reasons would get only slivers of the pie.

For our Thanksgiving London getaway, I bought the tickets on the Internet from British Airways during a promotion well in advance of our trip. The tickets were relatively cheap, but the catch was that once you purchased them, you couldn't exchange them, change the date or time, or receive credit on a future flight if you missed yours. I called Isabel and Olivia to make sure the dates were okay, that they didn't conflict with any of the dozen activities they're involved in: solo and ensemble music competitions, chamber singers, concert choir, women's vocal jazz, forensics, and their plays. Olivia was going to be Auntie Em in her high school's production of *The Wizard of Oz*. Like so many kids in America, mine seemed overscheduled and stressed out. In some ways, childhood may have changed for the better over the years, but this was not one of them. Of course, Olivia and Isabel shrugged off my concerns. They could handle it, they said. And the dates were fine, they told me, so I bought the tickets.

You can see where this is going, I'm sure.

The next time I spoke with Olivia, she said, "Dad, I can't go to London with you."

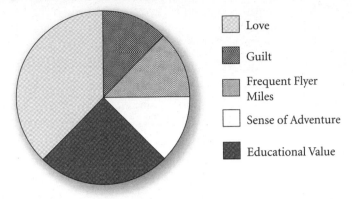

Love

Guilt

Frequent Flyer
Miles

Sense of Adventure

Educational Value

She seemed to be speaking a foreign tongue. I couldn't quite understand this language. "What do you mean?" I said. "Can't go to London? I bought the tickets already."

"I know," she said. "But I didn't know exactly when the play was scheduled when you were buying the tickets, and one of the performances is scheduled during the trip."

"But I bought the tickets," I said. "And they can't be changed."

"I'll pay you back, Dad," she said.

"You can't pay me back," I said. "That's too much money, and, anyway, it's not about the money."

But I had lost this battle before it began. This is the battle I have long had with Olivia, in one form or another. It's hard to tell how much is simply the inevitable result of growing up, and how much can be traced back to the divorce. The two seem tangled together too often. Isabel was too young to understand the divorce when it happened, but I remember a single tear tracing its way down Olivia's cheek when her mother and I told her we wouldn't be living together anymore. That tear has haunted me ever since, and sometimes I've felt that what it washed away is irretrievable.

Okay, I suppose I need to revise that pie chart and add a little more guilt.

"You have to face facts," my wife, Margie, has told me a number of times through the years. I remember my ex-wife saying to me in the bitter days of the divorce, "You'll never have this again," curse and prediction rolled into one. And my life since then, in part, has

Why I *really* travel with my kids

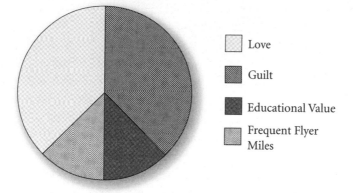

- Love
- Guilt
- Educational Value
- Frequent Flyer Miles

been about trying to prove her wrong, but at the same time knowing that I'll never have Olivia and Isabel again. Not completely the way I might have. I guess I've never been good at facing facts.

In my smaller moments in advance of our trip, I reasoned that I might have been more supportive of Olivia's decision to stay home if she'd won a bigger role. But Auntie Em? Missing a chance to visit London so she could play a dowdy matron from Kansas?

But the part doesn't matter. In some ways, they're all big parts, especially when it comes to not making mistakes and keeping a play flowing smoothly. Olivia is already a pro, but I didn't know what I was getting into the first time I appeared in a play. At age seven, I took part in a disastrous production of *The Littlest Angel*, in the role of the Heavenly Messenger. Never mind that I'm Jewish and the play is about the birth of Jesus — this was 1960s Ohio, and although I attended a so-called laboratory school, supposedly progressive, no one questioned the propriety of staging this play. My family was about as secular and assimilated as you can get without actually becoming Christian — we attended services at the Unitarian Church. We had a Christmas tree and presents underneath, and I ran through the fields near the church in search of Easter eggs, just like all the other children. I trick-or-treated for UNICEF, collecting more money than any other kid at church two years in a row. In many ways, I was the model Christian kid — Christian Lite. I was still going to hell perhaps — I did, after all, skim a little off the top of my UNICEF collection box for necessary candy bars — but at least I wasn't taking any of my Christian friends with me. Being cast in *The Littlest Angel* as the Heavenly Messenger posed no problems for me or my parents.

I envied David Ransom, the boy who was given the leading role, typecast because he was the shortest kid in class. When I saw David at my elementary school reunion, he told me that far from an honor, the role had been a curse and had dogged him all the way into high school. I hadn't considered that this leading role would have been more curse than honor. Boys *were* supposed to be tough and big. Not angels. Not littlest. That *would* have been a heavy cross to bear.

At the reunion, David also revealed something that surprised me even more. He told me that he had never been to church before my family brought him with us one Sunday morning after he spent the night at our house. That floored me. *I* brought the Littlest Angel to church for the first time? Only in 1960s America. Keep your head low. Wear camouflage and become more Christian than the Christians. Different wasn't so great back then.

The Littlest Angel centers on the goings-on in heaven right before the birth of Jesus in Bethlehem, its main character a mischievous little boy, from that same town, who has recently died and is now wreaking havoc in heaven, playing all sorts of pranks on his fellow angels. All the angels, even the littlest, prepare gifts for the holy infant and his is the humblest of all. This is where I came in. The Heavenly Messenger is sent down to Jerusalem by the Littlest Angel's guide and mentor, the Gatekeeper, to fetch the Littlest Angel's box of worldly goods to give to the Christ child. The box contains things like feathers, rocks, and dead butterflies, not the usual gifts for a baby shower. But God is impressed and honors the Littlest Angel's gift above all others, raising it high in the heavens until it shines for all eternity as the star of Bethlehem. Sorry if I spoiled the ending for anyone, but it's not a nail-biter.

Bill Greer's dad, a radio announcer, played the Voice of God, and this was the part of the play that impressed me the most. When God spoke, we were all to bow down to the ground and not look up as the box ascended on a piece of fishing line up, up, up into heaven. Of course, I sneaked a peek, though our teachers hovered around us in rehearsals as we knelt in a semicircle, yelling at us to keep our heads down. I remember the rehearsals as being more like dog obedience classes than actual rehearsals. *Now . . . kneel! Heads down! Heads down!* But I was in awe of that last scene when the Voice of God spoke. It almost seemed as though God truly *was* speaking, not just a radio announcer, and that's why I wanted so much to misbehave and look him in the eye. When I did glance up, all I saw were rafters.

The night of the performance, I stepped out on stage and froze. I saw my parents in the front row. I knew they would be there, but I hadn't quite understood that others would be there too. At seven, I had no concept of an audience. Or performance. I still thought the people on TV were little people who lived in the TV.

I was supposed to go out onstage and make a brief speech about the box I had retrieved from earth, how it didn't contain much, and how I thought it wasn't a good gift to give the Christ child. That was about it. Easy enough. But as I stood onstage, my meager lines flew out of my head, and I waited there dumbly facing David Ransom, who watched me expectantly, ready to receive his treasures. I looked at the audience and figured maybe they'd think it was funny that I was just standing there. But my mother was reaching her hands out as though she had a box to give the Littlest Angel too, and my father had his eyes averted. I smiled, but no one else smiled. This flustered me more than anything. I had never before smiled at grown-ups without them smiling back. I was a cute kid. People told me this all the time. They loved my smile. But this was a whole roomful of grown-ups, looking grim and nervous, and my smile seemed to have no effect on them at all.

I hurled the box at the Littlest Angel, who shielded his face in surprise as its contents scudded across the stage.

"Here's your stupid box!" I yelled at him, and ran offstage.

After that experience, I never flubbed a line again in a play, but the memory of that first play still makes me cringe. There's something about failing in public in front of your parents at an early age that doesn't wash out easily. My father died later that year of a heart attack, so he never had a chance to see me in another play. Perhaps that's why, in part, the Littlest Angel still looms so large.

Do elementary schools even put on plays in twenty-first century America? Not many do in Iowa City, as I found out when I asked around. Some of the individual classes put on little skits now and then, but no one puts on a Christmas play anymore. At least not in public school.

So I call around to the private schools in the area, ranging as far from Iowa City as Des Moines, over a hundred miles away. There's a Christmas pageant or two, but that's not quite the same thing. The search takes me a couple weeks in September, and I start to worry that I'm not going to find *any* school play to do over. One of my friends tells me that *The Littlest Angel* was performed last Christmas season by a local church. After all, the original story, on which the play was based, was written by a native Iowan, Charles Tazewell, so it makes sense that someone in Iowa is putting it on. I call every church I can, but it's still too early for those that are putting on Christmas plays to have settled on anything. And it's not easy explaining my project to music directors and ministers. One minister says he'd feel uncomfortable with an adult in a production with children. I want to tell him that, actually, there's more reason historically for parents to be worried about clergy around their kids than writers. But that wouldn't be nice. So I thank him for his time and hang up.

Finally, the Internet yields some promising results. Apparently, there are two semiprofessional theater companies putting on *The Littlest Angel* this season, one in Brevard, North Carolina, and the other in Marietta, Georgia. As luck would have it, my timing seems pretty good, as the audition schedules are posted for each playhouse. The playhouse in Marietta has just gone through auditions, and the one in Brevard is about to have them.

First, I call up the playhouse in Brevard, which is in western North Carolina, and I leave a rambling message on their voice mail. According to Margie, I practically give people my résumé, even when I'm asking for something simple.

"Hi, my name is Robin Hemley, and I have three daughters, and I'm divorced and remarried, and I teach at the University of Iowa and live in a white brick house with four bedrooms that costs a lot to heat in the winter. Oh, and we don't have central air-conditioning.

And two of my daughters are from my first marriage. And I'm Jewish. Could you please tell me how much a can of 7UP costs?"

I leave one of these kinds of messages on the voice mail of the playhouse in Brevard. As I try to explain myself and my reasons for wanting to appear in their production of *The Littlest Angel* in the role of the Heavenly Messenger, it doesn't escape my notice that I sound like a lunatic, and that only makes me ramble more.

"So I used to live in North Carolina, and I know that Brevard is lovely," I hear myself saying, and I tell them about a dining room set I once bought in High Point, North Carolina, too, before hanging up.

That went well. My call is never returned.

I compose myself before dialing the other theater, Big Top in Marietta. If I blow this phone call, I probably won't have another chance and will have to drop this redo from my do-over list. I get a human being this time, and, haltingly, I explain to her the nature of my project. She doesn't immediately hang up on me. That's a good sign. Instead, she tells me she'll pass along my message and my cell phone number to the director of the play, Annie Cook, who's in rehearsal at the time of my call.

Five days later, I get a call from Annie, who likes the idea. She actually likes it. Hallelujah (so to speak)!

"This sounds good," she says, "but I'll have to check with Nathan first. He's the one cast as the Heavenly Messenger right now, and so I have to clear it with him. But I think he'll enjoy having an understudy." An understudy for a nine-year-old.

She asks me about my availability for rehearsals.

Rehearsals? I hadn't imagined that. I thought I'd just get the part, fly down to Atlanta the night of the performance, and walk onstage and say my lines. If worse came to worst, I could always throw the box at the Littlest Angel again. Big Top will produce the play several times on the weekends at the end of November and into December, and I only need to appear in one performance to satisfy my psyche, I think.

She says she'll call me back and that she'll send me a CD of her singing the songs from *The Littlest Angel*. She's going to lower the key. "It's too high," she says.

Songs? Since when was *The Littlest Angel* a musical? I don't remember that at all. I'm quite certain that in our play in second grade, we didn't sing. If there *were* songs in our production at Putnam Elementary, the director mercifully removed them.

Unfortunately, I'm not going to have too many opportunities to rehearse with the cast before the December 2 performance. The week before, the week of Thanksgiving, is the London trip, and I have several other commitments, including my teaching schedule, that make it impossible for me to fly down to Atlanta more than once for rehearsals. But for a small part, I figure that should be plenty.

"I'll send you the Messenger pages," she tells me before hanging up. "And when you get down here, Nathan can teach you the blocking."

Messenger *pages.* I thought I only had one line. And blocking. I actually have to move around in an orderly fashion onstage? After I hang up, I start to worry that this experience might be shaping up to more of a nightmare than a do-over — appearing in a musical with elaborate staging and multiple lines and virtually no preparation. Ah well. A little panic is good for an actor.

Weeks pass, and I receive neither the promised pages nor the CD from Annie. As it gets closer to the rehearsal dates, November 7 and 8, I say to myself, *To hell with the Messenger pages* (so to speak); *I'm going to get them on my own.* I order a copy of *The Littlest Angel* off the Internet, rush delivery, and a few days later a package appears that might as well be filled with feathers, rocks, and butterfly wings. It's a play titled *The Littlest Angel,* but it's not *my* Littlest Angel. Its title is its only similarity to the play I'm familiar with.

CONSTANCE: And now this is Christmas Eve! That means it's the night when the Holy Child will be born, far down on earth, in Bethlehem.

MICHAEL (*excitedly*): We want to go!

ANGELS (*equally excited*): We want to go! We want to go! We want to see the Holy Child.

CONSTANCE: Of course, you do! But we have so much to do tonight.

MICHAEL: Oh, look at the fine men riding camels!

CONSTANCE: Yes, Michael. Those are the Three Wise men from the East!

Very exciting. Note the heavy use of exclamation points if you doubt how exciting this play is. And it only gets better — Gabriel announces toward the end that he can bring one angel with him to attend the birth of the Holy Infant. The Littlest Angel, Michael, is chosen because "only one very small angel" can fit. And so, as an added benefit, this play answers by implication the age-old question, How many angels can fit on the head of a pin?

Answer: None. How could *any* fit on the head of a pin if only one of them can fit through a stable door? And what does that say about the diet in heaven?

MICHAEL (*ecstatic, nearly peeing*): Constance, you'd better hold off on that extra scoop of heavenly hash if you want Gabriel to take you to the Second Coming!

After reading this play, I'm troubled by the number of versions of *The Littlest Angel* out there. And this version doesn't even have a part for the Messenger.

Luckily, Annie's pages *do* eventually arrive, though I'm still waiting on the promised CD by the time my two days of rehearsal roll around in November. Looking through the pages, I can't be sure of the exact line I flubbed when I was seven. I have thirteen lines in this version, and I appear onstage twice as the Heavenly Messenger, once when the Gatekeeper asks me to fetch the Littlest Angel's box from earth (the Littlest Angel tells me his house is right outside Jerusalem, near a donkey farm and an olive grove). A little later, I come running back onstage with his box and say, "Sorry I'm running a little late. I made a wrong turn at the donkey farm." And then I run offstage in pursuit of the Littlest Angel, yelling, "Littlest Angel! Littlest Angel!"

I'm not trying to shift the responsibility for flubbing my line, but I wonder if David Ransom, instead of running offstage with me in pursuit, forgot to run offstage, leaving me standing there with two useless lines. I distinctly remember him standing there waiting for me to give him the box. I couldn't very well shout, "Littlest Angel! Littlest Angel!" with him standing right there. So, instead, maybe I threw the box at him, out of frustration, yelling, "Here's your stupid box!"

Regardless, this is going to be more of a challenge than the first time — not only do I have my thirteen lines to remember, and the blocking, but also five songs to sing with the rest of the cast.

Mercifully, unlike the first version I received in the mail, this play doesn't read like it was created for finger puppets on a shoebox stage.

↶

A suburb of Atlanta, Marietta has the distinction of being the home of the Gone with the Wind Museum, which under normal circumstances I wouldn't miss. But my time is limited, traffic from the airport to Marietta is heavy, and I've got to make the most of my rehearsals, as nearly a month will pass between them and the reprise of my role as the Heavenly Messenger.

The first thing I notice on the drive from the airport is that the message "different is great" hasn't trickled down from Iowa yet. A billboard shows a smiling African American man and these words under his photo: "I changed my mind about homosexuality. And you can too!" Still, maybe I'm misinterpreting the sign, and it's not a warning *against* homosexuality but a pitch. Perhaps the worst fears of social conservatives have come true, and men living the "gay lifestyle" are now running recruitment drives with billboards. Heavens!

It would be nice, I suppose, in some circumstances, if you could just change your mind about things that are unalterable. *I changed my mind about being a grown-up. And you can too! I changed my mind about being a Yankee. And you can too!*

When I went to high school in Tennessee, with Yankee blood, I learned to say "y'all" (a construction that *everyone* should use because it makes sense) and eat grits. When I moved to Charlotte, North Carolina, in my twenties and lived there for the next eight years, I expanded my southern food repertoire considerably, learning to like sweet tea, liver mush, Brunswick stew, and both eastern *and* western styles of North Carolina barbecue. I grew disdainful of Yankees, with their own horrid accents, who made fun of southern accents or made fun of someone's intelligence by putting on a fake southern accent. When a poet friend of mine and I stopped in Darlington, South Carolina, and filled up on a buffet with everything from chitlins to sausage and gravy, I suggested he make me a laminated card declaring me an honorary southerner. But they don't take honorary members in the South, and as much as I love the many souths I've seen (the south of New Orleans, after all, is different than the south of Tennessee), I could never truly fit in.

Southerners make fun of Yankees too. After a boom of retirees from the North moving to North Carolina in the early nineties, the town of Cary, for instance, was referred to by some of my friends as Containment Area for Retired Yankees. The Civil War (or more properly down South, the War Between the States or, better yet, the War of Northern Aggression) was still being debated vigorously in the letters to the editor of the *Charlotte Observer* when I lived there. Almost every week, someone wrote in with such burning issues as, Who was the better general, Grant or Lee? And as my friends often pointed out, if you didn't bury both sets of great-grandparents in the South, you were a newcomer.

So I guess I'm forever doomed to stay as I was born, a Yankee. Still, I have enough time before the rehearsal begins to stop at Zaxby's Chicken and get my fill of chicken fingers, sweet iced tea, and Texas toast before heading across the strip mall that contains Gold's Gym, All-Star Pizza, and most important, Big Top Theatre, where I'm met by Annie, my director, who looks strikingly like Laura Bush. Apparently, I'm not the only one who thinks so. Sometimes she appears as Laura Bush for celebrity look-alike gigs. And she often plays, as understudy, "Iowa Housewife" in the long-running musical *Menopause,* in downtown Atlanta. Iowa housewife, huh? I guess the South isn't the only place that suffers from stereotyping. But I don't hold it against her. She's a Democrat, and so am I, though it's undeniable she's got that "innocuous conservative" (Laura Bush as opposed to Ann Coulter) look going for her.

As Annie and I make small talk in the foyer of the theater about other plays they're staging, my fellow cast members start to trickle in.

"See, Mom, I told you it was at four," says one boy.

Another stage mom approaches Annie and says, "I have some bad news. Sandra is going to miss a couple of rehearsals. She's going to Saint Simon's Island."

"I get to see wild horses!" says Sandra.

Annie makes a sound that's more groan than enthusiastic assent. "Oooh."

"Pay close attention today," Sandra's mom says.

Well, isn't that precious? St. Simon's Island. Not that I'm one to talk since I'm missing almost every rehearsal, but I'm not talking — I'm just thinking, *Where's your sense of commitment to the the-a-tah?* And I bet Annie's thinking it too.

Nearly everyone in the performance is a kid, with the exception of the Gatekeeper and one other angel, who are played by Cherie and Athena, two women in their thirties or early forties. The rest of the cast ranges in age from five to fifteen years old.

There are two stages, a main stage and a smaller theater where *The Littlest Angel* will be presented, but another play has our stage today, so we have to rehearse in the lobby. Before long, there's a swirl of excited kids, and a few hasty introductions are made. I shake hands with Nathan, the nine-year-old I'm understudying, as well as the Littlest Angel, in this case, an eleven-year-old girl named Susanna.

"I just can't imagine you making that mistake," she tells me, as though she's known me her whole life.

"Well, I was seven," I say.

She shrugs as if to say that's no excuse.

I also meet the Voice of God, Bill Mann, who, like Bill Greer's dad, has the kind of deep voice that we commonly associate with God, though I suppose He could have any voice He chooses: a woman's, a child's, even a squeaky, cracking teenage boy's. That would be fun. But no, somewhere it's been decreed that God has to be middle-aged or older and have a deep voice. In this case, His voice is distinctly southern, and He wears a Bluetooth earpiece for His cell phone.

"The Voice of God is from the Deep South," says Annie.

"I hope so," says Bill.

We start with "The Welcome Song," a tune with the bounciness of a TV commercial, welcoming new angels to heaven. I'm immediately lost, but I try to mouth the words, grasp the tune, and throw my arms up spasmodically a second or two too late as all the angels stand in a circle. Hands up. Hands together. Hands to the right. No, your other right!

As an angel, I'm a little morbid. While singing "The Welcome Song," I try to imagine the deaths of all of the people we're greeting so cheerily as angels. In this play, every good soul becomes a carefree angel-in-training immediately on dying. One minute, you're worried about paying your taxes, you take a bite of a doughnut, it goes down your windpipe, you choke, everything goes black, and then you hear:

Hello, welcome, hello, welcome
Welcome to this heavenly place
Pleased to meet you, glad to greet you
It's so nice to see your face!

And what do you see but cute cherubic angels, except for this one middle-aged angel mumbling and making spasmodic hand gestures, who doesn't even know the words, and far be it from you to be judgmental, but where's the quality control here?

I suppose that what I'm doing is commonly called a coping mechanism. If there isn't a heaven and a hell, you'd better invent them to explain your existence. And daydreaming while butchering the opening number is my way of coping with the fact that my first public humiliation in *The Littlest Angel* might have been nothing in comparison to what it's going to be this time.

⌒

Not only is Annie kind enough to allow me the chance to redeem myself in *The Littlest Angel,* but she's also opened up her home, which she shares with her husband and teenage son and daughter, when the daughter is home from college at least. They live near Kennesaw Mountain, scene of some bloody fighting during the War of Northern Aggression but now dotted on its perimeter with subdivisions of McMansions. As versions of heaven go, this is one, I suppose, and maybe this is where those young men on Kennesaw

Mountain went when they died, waking up not to welcome songs ("Hello Rebels, Welcome Yankees . . .") but to wide-screen TVs and three-car garages.

Of versions of heaven and hell, my favorites are the ones writers have come up with, one Catholic and one Jewish. C. S. Lewis, in *The Great Divorce,* imagines a bus ride between heaven and hell. His narrator, who has nothing better to do, gets on a bus to heaven from his bus stop in hell. In hell, you can build your house as large as you want, but the catch is that the weather in hell is a lot like England's, and the walls and roof of the houses are incorporeal, so you're not actually protected from anything. Staying in hell is your own choice, in Lewis's vision of it.

Stanley Elkin, in "The Conventional Wisdom," starts with the premise that every fundamentalist cliché about heaven is true, from real pearly gates to angels floating by on clouds and strumming harps — a kind of theme park, Six Flags Over Heaven. Unfortunately, everything you've ever heard about hell is true too, and that's where the protagonist is cast, into the burning lake of fire. An otherwise good man, almost saintly, he's sent to hell because he once had an impure thought about a woman who worked at a store he owned.

When I lived in North Carolina, I used to teach "The Conventional Wisdom" but gave up because no one thought it was funny. My students kept referring to it as "an accurate depiction of heaven and hell," and that just depressed me. Not that I think either Lewis or Elkin is "accurate," but it's natural to think of the afterlife when you're pushing fifty (and your father died at fifty-one) and appearing in a play about the afterlife. In any case, as a Jew, I'm let off the hook from giving the afterlife too much thought since there's no Jewish consensus on where you go when you die. The emphasis is on the preafterlife, and that should be my focus too. I want to get it right in this lifetime.

And in this lifetime, I'm in a play. The next day, the Wife of the Voice of God is setting up a Christmas tree in the lobby of Big Top when we arrive.

"How's the Voice of God?" Annie asks.

"Oh, God's all right," she says, hanging a colored globe.

Today, we're on the main stage, and since time is limited, we run through my scene twice, once with Nathan and once with me. Nathan takes a kind of Groucho Marx approach to the role with such lines as, "Sorry I'm running late. I took a wrong turn at the donkey farm." I've got a little more of Jack Benny in mine, a kind of exasperated Heavenly Messenger: "I hope it's not far. I've put a lot of miles on these wings today!" Complete with my chin in my hand and my eyes rolled.

After my run-through, Nathan gives me the thumbs up. "Wow, you caught on faster than me."

"I was following your lead," I tell him.

But, really, I haven't caught on. In fact, I blew my line when I came to that same part that gave me trouble the first time. I forgot to say, "Sorry I'm running late," and instead skipped to the next line, "I made a wrong turn at the donkey farm." In performance, no one would notice it, I suppose, but I want to do it perfectly this time. Still, I figure that remembering my lines is the least of my problems. Like every director in the world, Annie keeps changing her mind about the blocking, and I try to take notes on my script, but I know that I'm doomed, that there's no way that what she tells us to do today will even vaguely resemble what we do a month from now. She puts us in a star formation for one of the numbers. As I stand next to Athena, I shake my head despondently.

"It'll be a miracle if I remember this."

"Don't worry," she says. "You're with Athena. I'll just shove you around the stage."

"This is like a nightmare I have sometimes."

"It's a nightmare for me too," she says. "And this is my sixth play." It's hard for me to believe this. She exudes confidence, and I believe her when she says she'll just push me around the stage. She used to raise and break horses. She says she likes to face her fears. A couple of years ago, a horse threw her, and she broke three ribs and her tailbone, so she sold the horses and decided to seek her thrills in other ways.

The three grown-ups in this play are proving something to ourselves, something different from what the kids in the cast are doing. Dreams figure into it for all of us. Nightmares too, for some of us.

Mostly, it's about acting. Pretending to be something you're not, convincing yourself you're something, finally becoming something you always wanted to become.

The other grown-up in this play, Cherie, used to be a corporate lawyer for Coca-Cola but left six years ago. She has an excellent voice, and as the Gatekeeper she's onstage a lot. She wanted to get into acting from the start. Her mother wouldn't let her, so she became a lawyer instead.

Even Annie, our director, if given the chance, would take a slightly different path. Among other things, Annie has sold Mary Kay cosmetics, taught Suzuki piano, and written a musical that was performed at the Kennedy Center in Washington, DC, but it's only now, since she and her family moved to Atlanta three years ago, that she's focused almost exclusively on her acting. If she were to do it over again, she confides, she'd major in drama in college, not music.

At one time I wanted to be an actor too, like my daughters, like practically everyone in America. My great-uncle Bill was an actor, appearing in more Three Stooges films than anyone else besides the Stooges themselves. He and my grandmother and their other siblings grew up in Brooklyn, literally next door to the Howard brothers, Moe, Curly, and Shemp, and Moe married a cousin of ours. When I was ten, I met him at my uncle Alan's beach house, and I still have the two photos he gave me, signed "To Cousin Robin." My mother hated the Stooges, and almost no one in my extended family thought of them as actors, just as my mother, when she referred to Bill, called him a "ham actor." Ham or not, he represented the Big Time to me. He had been on *The Dick Van Dyke Show* and *The Danny Thomas Show,* and I have a recurring dream in which I'm in a waiting room, like a doctor's office, but I'm scheduled to meet Dick Van Dyke, and we're going to reminisce about my uncle. I never get past the waiting room in the dream, never actually get to meet Dick Van Dyke. I suppose that's because I allowed myself to be dissuaded from acting by my relatives, who always spoke of Bill as a failure. To them, any acting personage less than Dick Van Dyke hadn't "made it."

When I was eleven, I tried out for a theater group in Miami. This was when I was in sixth grade in Hollywood, Florida, the same age as Susanna, the girl with the lead in *The Littlest Angel,* is today.

They were putting on *Peter Pan,* and I gave a good enough reading that they wanted me to join their company, but my mom wouldn't allow it. Liberal in most ways, she had a kind of irrational fear of gay men, at least as far as I was concerned. She hated sending me into a public bathroom, imagining the "homosexuals" lurking there with recruitment pitches and incentives to join. The same went for theater troupes. In any case, she wouldn't let me act in the play, though I still held out a vague hope that somehow I'd be "discovered." Later that same day, I walked pensively around a fountain while dressed in my mod clothes, a Naugahyde vest and a sun medallion as big as my head, figuring some vacationing movie mogul from Hollywood would spot me and convince my mother to let me star in something manly and unhomosexual. Maybe a Western.

I don't blame my mother because I don't think I really wanted to become an actor. I really wanted to be what I am, a writer, and I really wanted to become a father, even though I never knew that's what I wanted until I became one. It's hard to watch your children struggle, and I don't blame my mother for discouraging me from becoming an actor (after all, she'd seen my dreadful performance in *The Littlest Angel*) or my grandmother for discouraging my mother from becoming a writer. But I'll never discourage my daughters. Izzy wants to be on Broadway, and Olivia wants to sing opera. Those are the futures they imagine and the futures I imagine too. Any cracks of doubt, I'll keep to myself.

I'm moved by how supportive and curious everyone in the cast is about my project. Nathan tells me that if he had blown his line, he'd want to do the same thing as I'm doing. And Susanna, the Littlest Angel, is delighted that one of my do-overs will be sixth grade. "I'm in sixth grade!" she tells me. Everyone here from child to adult to the Voice of God seems to want me to succeed this time, and for me to fit in, to be an honorary angel.

⌒

Practically a month goes by before I see my fellow angels again. Now I have the pages *and* the CD of the songs and a growing list of questions and concerns about my performance. Not only do I have blocking and singing and my thirteen lines to consider, but Annie's given me more lines, even solo parts to sing. That's because Nathan has been assigned a number of these random parts, places in the script that are assigned to angels designated only as "First Angel" or "Third Angel." And I'm his understudy.

By the time of our trip to London, I'm in a full-blown panic, and every time I speak to Izzy on the phone, I ask her to run lines with me while we're on vacation. I play the CD of songs from *The Littlest Angel* so often in the car that Shoshie starts to memorize the words and walks around the house belting, "The Littlest Angel is something to see!"

My children all seem born performers, but Shoshie is the hammiest kid I've ever met. At age three, she seems to think she's onstage constantly, and watching her is better than watching any play. At the airport, while we're waiting in the boarding area, she decides she wants to play charades.

"I swim in the ocean," she says.

We guess. Fish, dolphin, shark.

"I have one fin. It starts with a *p*."

"Pishy," Margie says.

"It has arms and a fin and it swims."

"A mermaid," I say.

Eventually, Margie guesses a mermaid too.

"Right," says Shoshie.

"A mermaid with a perm," I say. "A permaid."

"Hey, *permaid* rhymes with *mermaid*," Shoshie says. "Okay, now I'm going to be a giraffe, and I'm going to stand up." She stands up and says, "What am I?"

"A giraffe," says Izzy.

"You're good, Izzy!" Shoshie says.

Usually, Shoshie is a great traveler. She's been traveling internationally since she was three months old. Some people don't think you can or should travel with small kids, but I'm not one of those people. We had no choice with Shoshie — she was born in the Philippines while I was on sabbatical there finishing up a book. This was fine by Margie, as her family is there, and Margie trained as a pediatric nurse, so she knows a thing or two about taking care of young children. We returned to the United States when Shoshie was three months old, in the midst of the SARS scare. When we landed in Taiwan to refuel, all of us, including Shoshie, were wearing surgical masks, and this is the only time I can ever recall Shoshie screaming on a plane. She was inconsolable on that brief flight from Manila to Taipei — not because of her face mask but due to a head cold — and after that she settled down and has never been bothered by a flight since.

All this changes when we reach London. Apparently, she forswore her Terrible Twos and banked them for this moment. Her Tantrum Threes. All through the trip, she whines about wanting this toy and that toy, and she doesn't want to go here and won't go potty when we leave the hotel, but then suddenly needs to go on the Tube. She's so whiny that we all need Shoshie breaks. I make the mistake of telling Margie and Izzy that it's probably my karma. When I was eleven, my mother, sister Nola, and I traveled to London. My sister had been overseas, but this was my mother's first trip as well as mine, and I was a bigger brat than Shoshie. At least I was old enough to know better, but I whined the entire trip about wanting this toy and that, mostly little metal soldiers.

"So, it's your fault," Margie says.

"If you believe in karma."

"It's your fault. Okay, you take care of her."

Still, no one can act bratty day in and day out — although if there were a Guinness category for that, I might have been a strong contender. And Shoshie is much cuter than I ever was, even when she's acting bratty. After a particularly long day of traipsing through Westminster Abbey and Harrods, Shoshie sighs loudly as we exit the Tube station near our hotel.

"Hiya, hiya!" she yells to passersby. "Give me a nickel, give me a dime. Be my honey baby, all the time!" Then she throws her head back and stretches out her arms.

"Where did she get that?" I ask Margie.

"Maybe preschool."

Back at the hotel, she starts jumping on the foldaway bed, says it's her stage, and that she's going to perform. She tells me to get off the stage.

"What's your first number?" I ask.

She puts out her hand and yells, "Four!"

Although we miss having Olivia with us, the trip gives me a chance to spend time with Izzy in a way that I don't always have an opportunity. When Olivia was fourteen, I took her to the Paris Opera, but Izzy's not the opera type. She prefers musicals, so the two of us go one evening to see *Wicked*. She's already seen it once in Chicago, but she's nearly ecstatic about seeing this production, as it stars Idina Menzel, the original Wicked Witch, Elphaba. We've got nosebleed seats and have to rent opera glasses to see the stage, but it hardly matters to Izzy. At intermission, we're both feeling a bit giddy. Maybe it's the height. We start discussing names because of Idina Menzel's name. My niece is named Adina, but I've never heard of an Idina.

"I bet there's someone named Mississippi," Izzy says.

"Yes, but someone married who doesn't use the designation Ms.," I say. "Mrs. Ippi."

Izzy and I both have sodas. She's sipping through her straw, and she gives me a sideways glance and lets out a small sharp laugh. I suddenly have the childish desire to make her laugh in the middle of a sip.

"Ms. Sourri," I say, and she laughs again. "Mr. Rhee," I offer. "Sir Pent. Sir Ten."

She sits back and gives me an appraising, you're-nuts look, shakes her head, puts down her drink, and pretends to look through her opera glasses, but I know I've got her. She's giggling. The lights flash that intermission is just about over.

She reaches for her drink.

"How about Sir Will Thatbeall?"

My timing is off. I should have let her take a drink first. She lets out a laugh so sharp and loud that the man beside her jumps.

"How about Sir Wouldyoulikefrieswiththat?" she says, and cracks herself up.

There's not much time left. The audience members are settling into their seats. She puts her straw to her lips and takes a sip. I strike.

"And what if someone asked him that?" I say. "Sir Wouldyoulikefrieswiththat, Would you like fries with that?"

She nearly chokes but doesn't. Instead, she drops her drink on her lap, and it spills over her dress. "Oh!" she says.

"Shhh!" I say. "It's about to start again."

Mission accomplished. Luckily, she was almost done with her drink anyway.

As the next act begins, she leans over and whispers to me. "Sir Isthatforhereortogo, Is that for here or to go?"

↶

When we return to the States, Olivia tells me it's a good thing she didn't go to London because after her performance in *The Wizard of Oz*, she was slammed with a succession of ailments around Thanksgiving: pinkeye, an ear infection, and multiple colds. I guess I can't really share her conviction that it was best she didn't go. I would have liked to have had her along. She probably came down with her colds because of all the stress she was under, at school, in the play, and, I have to admit, from just knowing she had disappointed me and wasn't able to travel to London with us. So I keep my mouth shut. Sometimes it's best for parents to be Seen and Not Heard, or, if you're on the phone, Sensed and Not Heard. Even over the phone, we can sense each other's disappointment. We don't need to verbalize it and make it worse.

Now it's my turn to see how I handle the stress of performance. My do-over as the Heavenly Messenger is only a week away after our return from England, and there's still so much to do before I'm ready. For instance, I need white pants! I have a white shirt, but the last time I had white pants was in 1975 when my grandmother bought me an all-white leisure suit at a place called Schmoracks in Long Beach, New York. I wore that suit only once — into Manhattan. Even in 1975, this all-white leisure suit looked unbearably ugly. The fabric was textured in rivulets and looked vaguely reptilian, except for the fact that the suit was blindingly white and I know of no such reptiles. The jacket had snap-on buttons, and the pants flared. When I took the Long Island Railroad into the city wearing the suit, everyone seemed to be staring at me, though I chalked it up (after all, I looked like a stick of chalk) to my adolescent self-awareness.

Before starting my do-overs, this was as close as I had come to appearing naked in public. At Penn Station, I continued to attract the stares of otherwise inwardly focused New Yorkers and excited tourists. Had I stayed in one place, I might have become a landmark, a beacon. But I kept moving until I reached Times Square, where two pimps and several prostitutes started hailing me loudly: "Hey, Shiny! Hey, Shiny!" Unaccompanied by a Bee Gees sound track, I tried to look unconcerned as I strutted past this gauntlet. But the experience traumatized me, and I never wore white pants again.

Not only do I have to find white pants again to regain angel status, but I have to find them close to Christmas. Still, I have faith that I'll find something that will work, and I go to a local department store and browse through the athletic section, figuring I can find some white jogging pants. No go. And too late I've thought of ordering karate pants. The show is in a couple of days, and there wouldn't be time to have them delivered. I rummage through rack after rack of clothing — nothing. And it strikes me that even if I were to find something white, it would have to come in my size approximately. There's nothing. Not in the men's section. Not in the sale racks. I'm about to give up when I lift my eyes to fluorescent heaven and say, "Please let me find some white pants." I can't say the heavens open up exactly. I don't hear the Voice of God. But I part a group of clothes stuffed together on a bulging sale rack, and lo! White pants! Some of the whitest pants I have ever beheld. Undeniably white. A pair of Dockers a size too big in the waist but the right length exactly. They've been marked down to fifty cents. From now on, I will recall this episode as the Miracle of Finding the White Pants at Kohl's.

When it comes to heaven, it's probably a mistake to act cocky, as I find out two days later, the day before the play, as I'm getting ready to fly to Atlanta. A major snowstorm has socked in Chicago, and it looks as though I'm going to miss tomorrow's performance. It's too far to drive to Atlanta, so I call Annie and we talk about the possible alternatives.

"At least I'm an understudy," I say, though I'm really disappointed and want to keep trying to find a way down to Atlanta.

"We can't help acts of God," she says

"If there's an act of God, this is the right play for it," I say.

At the Cedar Rapids airport, I'm issued a succession of airline tickets, until finally I'm booked on a flight that leaves at 7:00 p.m. If this doesn't work, that's it for this week. The earliest departure the next morning would arrive in Atlanta too late. I'd miss the rehearsal Annie has scheduled, and there's no guarantee I'd even make the play.

Again, I call Annie. "It's an angel show," she says. "You'd think we'd have connections."

"Call the Voice of God," I suggest.

But it's no good. I'm not getting out tonight. Finally, I give up, and we agree to try again in a week. Thankfully, there are multiple performances.

That night, I'm sitting despondently on the living room couch. There's a knock at the door. A college-age man, clean-cut, stands there sheepishly.

"I know this is a strange question, but did you find a Santa Claus in the rafters of your house?" he asks.

Yes, that is a strange question, and I contemplate widening my eyes in mock horror, slamming the door on him, and threatening to call the police. Too late. Margie has heard the question and has come in from the other room to see who's asked it. She smiles at the boy and invites him in, so I guess I have to let him pass.

He introduces himself as Jeremy Negus, the grandson of the elderly couple from whom we bought our house. The Negus family owned our house for eighty years. The old man had been born here and only moved out when he needed the care of a nursing home. You'd think that people who had been in a house for eighty years would leave something behind, but they stripped it clean. Isabel found two old belts in the attic, and that was it. But oddly enough, the Neguses left behind a big lawn ornament in the rafters of the garage: Santa and his reindeer. They weren't life size, but they were close — and old. They dated from the sixties at least, maybe the fifties, and I figured they had to be worth some serious money. For two years I contemplated hauling down Santa and bringing him to an antique consignment shop where the owner told me he'd be happy to sell them for me, based on my description. Now I sense it's too late.

"We wondered about those," Margie tells him cheerily. "They're still in the rafters."

"It's yours now," Jeremy Negus says. "If you want." Suddenly, I feel as though the play has changed, and I'm now in *A Christmas Carol.* "But it's been part of our family . . ." I wait for him to add, "Mr. Scrooge," but he doesn't.

Instead, Margie chirps, "That's okay. We're Jewish."

"It's yours," I say, saddened to see Santa go.

And, of course, I'm coming down with something, losing my voice. So when Isabel and Olivia call me after dinner, I can barely squeak out a sentence, though I try to recount to them the events of the day.

"Maybe it's for the best," Olivia tells me. "Maybe you're being saved from a horrible plane crash."

"Or maybe I'm being saved for yet another horrible plane crash," I tell her.

"There you go," she says. "That's a cynical way of looking at it."

I suppose that's true, but perhaps I could be forgiven for feeling a bit cynical today. I've missed my plane. I've lost my voice. I didn't get to be an angel in a Christian play. And I had my Santa repossessed. All in one day.

↶

The following Friday morning I fly into Atlanta without a hitch and spend the rest of the day and evening frantically practicing my lines and listening to the play's songs in my hotel room. I *think* I have my lines down, but I'm still unsure about the blocking and my solo parts in the songs. This is bound to be a disaster. Maybe the universe was trying to tell me something last week when it took away my voice, my ability to travel, and my Santa. But, like most humans, do I listen when the universe speaks? No. This is finally what gives us our common humanity, an intrinsic inability to take a hint.

That night, I dream I'm being quizzed by Dick Van Dyke — the first time I've met him in a dream. We sit around a long table, and he asks me, "What do you do after you finish brushing your teeth?"

They're hygiene questions. Simple enough. "I go downstairs and find a snack in the refrigerator," I tell him.

Wrong! Not only am I messing up the answers, but I look down at my white shirt and notice I have a stain on it.

Hmmm. This is why I hate dreams, because mine are so ridiculously transparent. I'd like to chide my subconscious for its lack of ambiguity, to tell it to at least throw in something that would seem a little less obvious.

When I arrive at Big Top the next morning for dress rehearsal, Annie hands me my wings and halo. There's a little loft backstage where the boys change, and she sends me up there with the other boys, Nathan, Danny, and Erik.

"Welcome to the lair of the mole people," Nathan tells me. He's in a manic mood today, cracking jokes and talking about *Borat,* which he's just seen and loves. *Borat* seems a little advanced for a nine-year-old, but Nathan seems unfazed.

"Some people think it's anti-Semitic," he says as he places his wings and halo on a shelf and grabs his white shirt and pants. "But I don't. Sacha Baron Cohen is Jewish too."

"Too?" I ask.

"Yeah, I'm Jewish. I didn't think it's anti-Semitic. It's irony!"

That *is* irony. My fellow messenger, forty-one years after my performance as the Heavenly Messenger, turns out to be Jewish too. Historically, I guess, Jews make pretty good messengers, so it makes sense. After all, Muslims call us the People of the Book, and there's certainly no scarcity of Jewish writers, actors, and comics, all Heavenly Messengers in one form or another. Susanna, the Littlest Angel, I find out later, is Jewish as well. We almost have enough members for a Little Jewish Angel Club. A quorum, even, if we add Jesus!

I turn my back to the boys and change as quickly as possible, feeling a bit self-conscious being a grown-up changing with kids. But the boys, all between nine and eleven, are a lot less uptight than I am. Why adults insist on seeing children as angelic has always baffled me, even when I was a child.

"Don't look at Nathan's one-eyed monster!" Danny yells to Erik.

"Yeah, Nathan likes to go commando," Erik says.

"No one look at me," says Nathan. "I don't want anyone seeing my John Thomas. That's from Monty Python and *The Meaning of Life*."

Nathan proceeds to entertain us with an entire battle scene from the movie, and then he segues into the Ministry of Silly Walks skit from *Monty Python's Flying Circus*. He's a great mimic, as it turns out, and has us all in stitches.

"Let's go, boys!" we hear Annie call from below, and so we grab our wings and halos and run downstairs.

With only a few minutes to go before the dress rehearsal, the Littlest Angel comes up to me and says, "It's a good thing you weren't at last week's performance. The Gatekeeper dropped her stomach."

I figure "dropping your stomach" is showbiz lingo for forgetting your lines, but no, she literally dropped her stomach. In the beginning of the play, she's supposed to be fat from eating so many cookies baked by the Heavenly Baker, and by the end of the play she's lost weight. But last week, she had one of those *Littlest Angel* moments of shame, of the variety I experienced four decades ago. Her pillow dropped out of her shirt and fell onstage. She lost her concentration then and even forgot to introduce the first song, and so it was skipped.

Of course, I *wish* I'd been at that performance. Then I'd be fine with making a mistake of my own because no matter what I did, it wouldn't be like dropping my stomach onstage. Unless I threw up, which in any case, is a distinct possibility.

And then we're on. True to her word, Athena pushes me around the stage during dress rehearsal. This time, the Gatekeeper's stomach doesn't drop, and she introduces the first song. We sing "The Welcome Song" and then comes my first solo in "Have You Met the Littlest Angel?" during which a mob of disgruntled angels complain about the Littlest Angel's antics. One of the angels sings, "She's swinging from the Golden Gates. They're swaying to and fro."

I'm supposed to chime in, "They're breaking underneath her weight. Oh no! Look out below!"

I open my mouth, but instead of me, Nathan sings the lines. I've been upstaged. Am I disappointed? Am I disconsolate? Au contraire.

I feel like dropping to my knees and thanking the Lord. Of course, had I been thinking straight, I might have wondered what Nathan was doing in the Lair of the Mole People, changing into his angel outfit. If I was *his* understudy, what was he doing there at all? Maybe Annie changed her mind about me taking on all his parts and forgot to tell me, or maybe she saw the panic on my face and made a quick call: Nathan, get over here pronto! I'm still onstage in my role as Heavenly Messenger, but Nathan has all the extra lines Annie assigned to us.

In any case, I stumble through the dress rehearsal, shoved this way and that, led around the stage not only by former horse breaker Athena but also by a blur of confident young thespians, who all seem to know where they're going.

Even their gentle ministrations do no good. Once again, I botch a line. When the Gatekeeper tells me my assignment, I'm supposed to say, "I'm outta here!" But instead, I say, "I'm on my way!" and about four lines too soon, as the Littlest Angel is telling me where her house on earth is located. Then, as I'm exiting, my wing gets caught in the curtain and a few of my feathers tear off.

By the end of rehearsal, I'm more convinced than ever that I'm going to fail this one again.

Afterward, the Voice of God comes over to me. "My part always gets me," he says, and sure enough his voice seemed to crack during his speech to the angels.

"Silence!" he tells the angels toward the end of the play, and they all bow down, some prostrating themselves. When Bill Greer's dad said it, the scene reminded me of *The Wizard of Oz*, right before Toto pulls back the curtain on a balding, unimpressive man who needed to yell to make everyone afraid of him and leave him alone. That's one reason I wanted to look up, I think. Who was this bully? To make us more awestruck, no one ever saw Bill Greer's dad except for Bill Greer. We all knew it was a radio announcer and not really God, but we weren't allowed to speak of this.

This southern version is more soft-spoken. When he says "Silence," it's more like a parent saying "hush" to a fevered child. "God doesn't have to yell," Bill says. "It's like they say in the military. An officer's wish is an enlisted man's command."

The angels are all backstage as the theater starts to fill that afternoon, a clutch of them playing a card game called Egyptian Rathole. Their lack of concern contrasts with my absurd amount of concern. *This isn't a real test,* I keep telling myself. *It means nothing.* But my subconscious will have none of that. Apparently, I've still got that stain on my white shirt, and Dick Van Dyke is watching. I pace the wings and read and reread the George Burns quote hanging on the wall: "The most important thing in acting is honesty. If you can fake that, you've got it made."

I ask Cherie to run lines with me, one last time, and I botch them again.

"Remember to take a few deep breaths before you go on," she advises. "And think of visuals for your lines. Above all, don't make eye contact with anyone in the audience or it might throw you off."

"That's what happened to me the first time," I tell her.

We're all crowded backstage now, half of us by one exit, half by the other. I imagine myself a World War I soldier about to charge out of the trench along with my fellow doomed compatriots. I see myself cut down by machine-gun fire not two steps out of the trench. This is likely not what Cherie had in mind when she told me to think in visuals. I feel suddenly floaty. My limbs go soft, almost numb, and I'm heavy lidded. I wish I could take a little nap on the nice hard stage. Just curl up. Wake me up when it's over, guys.

Onstage Annie gives a curtain speech. "Today we have with us a very special angel," she begins. I don't hear the rest. I'm at peace with my fate, whatever it is.

And maybe I still don't know all the hand movements, and maybe during the song "Did You Hear?" I forget half the words and could be renamed the Mumbling Angel, but these are ensemble parts, and I fake it well enough. When it comes to my own lines, I sail through this time. When the Gatekeeper tells me I have to go back to earth to fetch the Littlest Angel's box, and I say, "Oh no, is it truly necessary?" I get a laugh from the audience. And again when I say, "I'm outta here," this time in the right spot.

And when I come to the spot that gave me so much trouble the first time, I run onstage out of breath — hardly acting, I'm hyperventilating — and I yell at the retreating figure of the Littlest Angel, of David Ransom, of my uncle Bill, of Dick Van Dyke, of my own young aspirations to be an actor, "Littlest Angel! Littlest Angel!" but they're all, of course, long out of sight.

And when it's my turn to give a gift of my own, I take a small box off the shelf, but a young girl with bright eyes and dark hair takes my gift and gives me a bigger empty box. "Here, take this one. It's much nicer."

"You've been upgraded," Athena confirms.

After the play, Cherie gives me a hug and so does Annie, and when I take the stage for my bow, the audience cheers. In the halls of the theater, men and women approach and congratulate me, many of them the proud parents of my fellow cast members. Receiving their compliments is the next best thing to receiving the belated congratulations of my own parents.

Timing is everything, as any actor will tell you. The next morning, back in my house in Iowa City, basking in the glory of this do-over, Margie knocks on the door of my study, holding something small in her hand and gazing at it the way the Littlest Angel is supposed to gaze at his treasures once I've retrieved them, in disbelief and no small measure of happiness. And she says those two words that fill me with another kind of stage fright: "I'm pregnant."

CHAPTER THREE

CAMP ECHO

Summer Camp Do-Over

ORIGINAL AGES: 7, 9, 12, 13, 18
DO-OVER AGE: 48
ORIGINAL LOCATIONS: ATLANTIC BEACH DAY CAMP, ATLANTIC BEACH,
LONG ISLAND; CAMP CATAWBA, BLOWING ROCK, NORTH CAROLINA;
GRANITE LAKE CAMP, MUNSONVILLE, NEW HAMPSHIRE; CAMP ECHO,
WARRENSBURG, NEW YORK
DO-OVER LOCATION: CAMP ECHO, WARRENSBURG, NEW YORK

No one paid attention to kids when I was growing up, not parents,
not teachers, not counselors. Childhood was something you went
off and did until you got over it. And camp was one of those places
to which kids were exiled, almost as a form of punishment, a ware-
house where you suffered while your parents went on that Norwe-
gian cruise. Camp was anything but fun, unless you define fun as

forced marches, prison food, and Darwinian social dynamics. In some ways, I've always considered myself a failed camper. I was not a great physical specimen as a kid, not quite a sissy but one who had to use his brains to deflect a bully's animus and divert his attention: "Psst. I'm not the one you want. There's a sissy over there."

At Atlantic Beach Day Camp when I was seven, I organized a pickpocket ring in lieu of swim time. I'm not sure where or how I learned to pickpocket, but it seemed almost second nature to me, and before long I had taught a number of my fellow campers this skill. Over two days, we filched combs sticking out of back pockets, wallets from the pockets of our counselors, baseball cards, whatever we could find. We buried most of it. At age seven I had no notion of what to do with these things. I simply liked the thrill of taking things undetected. But eventually we *were* detected, and the head counselor lined us up by the swimming pool and told us he knew there was one "bad apple" among us. If the ringleader stepped forward, he promised to let the rest of us go.

This seemed like a bad deal to me. Good for everyone else, but not good for the bad apple. Me. A fat kid named Eric stood trembling beside me. I nudged him and whispered, "Tell him it's you."

"What?" Eric asked. I might have been a bad apple, but a fat kid was even lower on the camp food chain, and we both knew it. "Tell him you're the ringleader, and you'll be a hero."

Eric looked disbelieving, but I nodded stoically as though I were his commanding officer offering him a suicide mission that would save his men and redeem him in our hearts.

Eric raised his hand feebly and in a weak voice uttered the words. "It's me. I'm the ringleader."

The head counselor glared and jerked Eric forward by his man-sized Atlantic Beach Spartan T-shirt. "The rest of you get out of here," he told us. "And don't let me catch you doing anything like this again, or you'll end up like your little buddy here."

Yes, it was a harsh lesson for Eric, but his sacrifice had not been in vain. For the rest of the summer, we sang songs in his honor and told of his valor.

Well, not quite. We actually never mentioned him again, and I at least learned a valuable lesson. If you're cunning enough, you can avoid responsibility for your actions. Not a good lesson but valuable in the cutthroat world of summer camp.

My next camp was a sleepaway experience in North Carolina at Camp Catawba when I was nine. What I remember from this summer camp is the cruel society of boys, torturers of little animals, always trying to get an edge on their fellow campers through the well-placed taunt or blow. One day a group of my fellow campers threw a knife at a stunned bullfrog in the middle of the main path while counselors walked by, unmoved, the knife edging closer and closer until one camper stuck the knife in the bullfrog's back and its heart seemed to jump out of its mouth. That was camp play. That was praiseworthy.

The camp's neighbors were a "hillbilly" clan named the Yams who purportedly shot saltpeter at campers who strayed onto their land. We lived in fear of the Yams, who had attacked the camp — so the story went — the year before. Whether this story was true or not, Camp Catawba was full of dangers. Once I chased a garter snake onto the Yams' property. I climbed back through the barbed wire fence in a flash when I realized where I was and tore my hand open in the process. I was so afraid I'd be punished for my trespass that I didn't tell anyone about my hand, and it soon turned infected and had to be lanced by a doctor in nearby Blowing Rock. At Camp Catawba too, I learned to swim in a fashion, pushed in the deep end one evening as I tried to relight a floating candle, one of many candles we had placed in the pool as the climax of some end-of-summer camp ritual. It was either doggy paddle or die, as no counselors noticed that I had fallen.

Granite Lake Camp, my last, was equally grim, with one bright spot, the camp plays in which I always appeared: as Linus in *You're a Good Man, Charlie Brown* and as the lead in a Sholom Aleichem play, *A Tale of Chelm*. The former was certainly the highlight of my acting career and probably the highlight of my camping career as well. I was *meant* to play that role. Like Linus, I was a cerebral thumb-sucking kid, and my older brother Jonathan filled the Lucy role for me. But other than drama, this camp was just as dreadful as the others. I assiduously avoided sports, except Ping-Pong at which I oddly excelled.

I refused to do anything my counselors wanted, regardless of any consequences they offered. I even made one of my counselors snap — a quiet young man from Taiwan, who chased me around the outside of the cabin one day, screaming "I gonna *kill* you!"

I say that Granite Lake was my last camp, but that's not exactly true. I was also briefly a camp counselor at Camp Echo in upstate New York when I was eighteen. My bad-camper karma caught up with me here when I was assigned to a group of the brattiest ten-year-olds imaginable, worse than I had been. I remember the kids in my bunk placing bets on how long it would take to get rid of me. They liked the other counselor in the cabin; his name was Joel, and he listened without protest as they guessed whether I'd last a day, two, or a week at most. I was their third substitute counselor two weeks into the summer, and I had no idea how to handle the kids who refused to obey me regardless of any consequences I offered. When I complained to one of the senior staff, he'd poke his head into my cabin, do a General George Patton impression for a minute or two while the kids looked at him beatifically, and then he'd say, "See, you just have to be firm, Robin," and then he'd close the door and the kids would riot again.

One day the head counselor told me to get the kids to swim no matter what, but one kid refused to go. Somehow I missed the irony of this at the time. Frustrated, I pulled him off his bed and led him down the stairs of the bunk, and then he dropped to the ground limp and expressionless, so I pulled some more. I dragged him about ten feet toward the lake when the head counselor marched up to me and said if he ever saw me lay a hand on a kid again, he'd fire me. The kid looked up at me with a smile, snapped his fingers, and pointed in "gotcha!" fashion.

I quit on the spot.

But it was to Camp Echo I would return if I was to return to any of my camps, because the rest were now defunct. Echo would serve as the echo of them all, back as far as my first camp debacle at age seven. I don't like to think I hold grudges, but I do. I have a grudge against my camp experiences. I have a grudge against that particular child who bested me thirty years ago. He and his bunkmates haunt me, all of those Hobbesian kids (nasty, brutish, and short) who resided in Bunk B5-2 at Camp Echo in 1976.

Admittedly, my reasons for wanting to go back were a bit immature. A part of me wanted to use my unfair advantage as a forty-something male to make a big impression on a cabin of ten-year-olds. I wanted to beat them at swimming, baseball, Ping-Pong, capture the flag. Pathetic? Undoubtedly. But these kids were going to have to get used to other people pressing unfair advantages on them as they grew up. They might as well learn that lesson sooner rather than later.

When I called Camp Echo, I reached the owner and director, Marla Coleman, whose family had owned the camp for the past five years. Marla liked the idea of my return as a camper, but she needed to clear a few things first. "You'll probably want to bunk with the older kids?" she said.

"No, I'd really prefer to bunk with ten-year-olds. You see, when I was a counselor at Camp Echo thirty years ago, I was in charge of a group of ten-year-olds. I want to experience camp from their perspective."

"Okay, I can see that," she said. "But I'm sure you can understand that a grown man wanting to bunk with a group of ten-year-old boys might raise some questions. So we'll need to complete a background check, the same as we'd do for any counselor."

"I'd be concerned if you didn't," I said.

Fortunately, my background check didn't pick up the rubber lobster incident with Mrs. Collins, my pickpocket ring, or the reason I had quit Camp Echo thirty years earlier. My inner thug had always operated below the radar. I was in.

↶

The background check figures as the easiest part of going back to Camp Echo. The hardest is leaving my daughters for a precious week — I have them with me half the summer, and the only time I can schedule the return to Camp Echo is during their visit with me. At least everyone has things to occupy them. A bookworm, Olivia will spend most of her time reading in her room. Isabel and Shoshie will spend a lot of time together playing games or watching videos, or Margie will take them all downtown or to the mall to window-shop and eat. Isabel is determined to win the part of Lucy in her middle school's fall production of *You're a Good Man, Charlie Brown,* and so she's brought the script with her as well as the music on a CD. She spends much of the day on the sunporch marching around to the rousing show tunes that make up much of the musical. I suggest we run lines together since I had played the part of Linus at Granite Lake when *I* was twelve.

Isabel makes a good Lucy, assertive and certain of herself. She wants to grow up to be a Broadway actor. Olivia wants to be an opera singer. I've always tried to quietly support the dreams of my children. I once took them to a Broadway show in which my friend had a major role. After the performance, he took us onstage and told Olivia and Isabel to sing. Shyly, they sang a couple of notes, and he told them that now they could say that they had sung on Broadway. A couple of years later, we were in France for part of the summer, and I was able to take Olivia to the Paris Opera for her fourteenth birthday. It wasn't perhaps the *most* appropriate opera for a father/daughter: Richard Strauss's *Elektra,* sort of the flip side of the Oedipus story. But it was the only opera in town, and, anyway, it was in German with French subtitles projected onto a screen, so we didn't understand a word. But we were happy just to be there.

As for me, besides an actor, I have wanted to be a doctor, an archaeologist, an anthropologist, and a diplomat. In second-grade art class, we had to make dioramas of what we wanted to be. I told my art teacher that I wanted to be a paleontologist, and she told me she wasn't sure I could be that until she went home and looked up the word. The next day she told me, okay, I could be that if I wanted.

The only problem was that I had no interest in building a diorama, so I convinced my classmate, Tad Grover, that he wanted be a paleontologist too and that he should also do most of the work on the diorama (with such a helpful demeanor, it's no wonder he became a minister instead). I summed up my dream in an accompanying booklet in a more succinct style than I currently possess:

I want to be a paleontologist. A paleontologist has to find dinosaur
bones. He has to go many places in the world. It is very hard to
do the work that he has to do. If you were a paleontologist, you
would go to places like deserts and Africa. You would be looking
all day with hardly a bit of sleep. You would be tired. Would you
like to be a paleontologist?

Although I didn't become a paleontologist, I still like to dig up
the past and travel. As for my second-grade classmates, I don't think
any of them became exactly what they wanted either, or their goals
inevitably shrank or broadened. Crysteen Cooper wanted to be a
mother because "mothers have fun." Gretchen Eldridge wanted to
be a teacher because her mother was a teacher. Mark Frink wanted
to be a scientist. Roger Gilders wanted to be a swimmer. Bill Greer
and Liz Stumpf both wanted to work at the radio station WOUB.
They planned to work right next door to each other so that they
could "send important messages to each other, and other messages
that are not so important, such as, 'Are you feeling well?' or 'Is anything wrong with your machines?'" Jim Heady wanted to be an
astronaut. Ann Holmes wanted to be a veterinarian. Gary Keller
wanted to be a fireman. Donna Mae Seelhorst wanted to be a horse
trainer. Tony Turnball wanted to be a television star *and* a camera-
man. And Lee Whanger wanted to be an airline pilot.

I know all this because at our elementary school reunion Liz
Stumpf gave me a copy of the little booklet we made in second grade
about our future professions. My memory is good but not *that* good.

Shoshie says she wants to be lots of things. Most recently, she
said she wanted to be a golf course. When I told her she would probably prefer being a golfer to a golf course (less wear and tear), she
agreed, and added that she also wanted to be "one who sells people
cars what needs them," as well as "one who gives money to people
what needs cars." And she's the one I'm banking on to take care of
me in my old age.

Mostly, as we grow older, we learn what we can't be, not what
we can be. If Isabel wants to be a Broadway actor, let her try. If I
want to be ten for a week, then Camp Echo is my big chance. But

Olivia, at fifteen, is in full-throttle embarrassment over the fact that I, her father, am going to be spending the better part of a week bunking with a bunch of ten-year-olds at summer camp.

"No, don't get the SpongeBob jammies," Olivia tells me one afternoon a few days before my departure as I browse a department store's shelves for my sleepaway clothing. "They'll hate you and never speak to you! *I know kids!*" Ostensibly, she's acting as my childhood consultant. If I printed up a business card for her, it would read:

Olivia Hemley
Childhood Consultant
Avoid Embarrassment as You Relive Your Misspent Youth
"I know kids!"

Isabel is a little more forgiving of my many faux pas. She suggests that I should do a belly flop into the lake.

"No, don't do that," Olivia says. "That would be stupid."

I respect Olivia's opinion, but the entire project, from her perspective, is alarming. Why would I want to make a fool of myself by acting like a ten-year-old? Don't I realize I'm forty-eight, a father of three, a man of responsibilities? I guess I haven't moved on. Perhaps if I'd learned better lessons as a camper, I'd have made a better counselor. Perhaps if I'd been a better counselor, I might be a healthier adult, a better father.

↶

"The boys are waiting anxiously for you," Marla, the owner and director of Camp Echo, tells me before letting me out of her golf cart in front of Bunk B5-2. Really? They're anxious to spend the next few days with a forty-eight-year-old man? Maybe they're thinking I can help them find a way to escape.

I've arrived on Visitors' Day. Marla thinks that Visitors' Day is most appropriate for my return, as this day is already a little unusual for the campers: parents descend on Camp Echo, bearing armloads of candy that would otherwise be forbidden. The younger siblings also have a chance on this day to spend the night with their older brothers and sisters. Some campers attend camp half the summer.

Other kids attend the whole summer, and Visitors' Day is the demarcation, another good reason for me to be reintroduced into Camp Echo today. I'm a new kid, though not your typical new kid.

As I enter the bunk, a faint whiff of parent scent still lingers — they've vacated this spot a mere thirty minutes before my arrival. I, of course, drove myself here, the only camper to have done so. A pile of parting-gift junk food sits like a sacrifice to the camp gods in the middle of the cabin floor: gummy things in all their myriad shapes and colors, Skittles, red licorice, cotton candy, Nestlé Buncha Crunch, Swedish Fish, Doritos. More junk food spills cornucopia-like out of two Styrofoam containers, one with candy lettering spelling BUNK JUNK, the other labeled with a magic marker, GO METS. This Willy Wonka portion of sugar-coated love and expiation remains the only telltale sign that the parents of these ten-year-old boys exist.

I think I'm in the same cabin I was in thirty years ago at Camp Echo. There are only two cabins occupied by fifth graders: Caribou, B5-2, and Bison, next door, B5-1. It's either this cabin or that. I remember only six boys and two counselors (including me) bunked in my cabin then, but there are ten kids and two counselors in this, plus one kid brother who's sleeping over to get the feel of camp life. The boys stare at me and tell me their names and say hi in that friendly, uncomplicated way that ten-year-old boys have about them. I say hi back and the counselors introduce themselves, my counselors, both young enough to be my children. There's twenty-one-year-old Craig Warwick, from Birmingham, England, at least a head shorter than me but three times as muscular. No one calls him Craig, but "Snoopy," his nickname. This is his third stint at Camp Echo. He's one of the 35 percent of Camp Echo's staff of 220 who hail from various English-speaking parts of the world other than the United States. Brad, son of one of the camp doctors, has the bunk across from me. He's eighteen, younger than my students at the University of Iowa, but I automatically see him as an authority figure, and I wonder if he automatically registers me as a subordinate. It's Snoopy and Brad I'll answer to over the next few days.

Everyone wants to know if the camp looks different from the way I remember it thirty years ago. I remember the cabins. I remember the lake. I remember the footbridge across the lake. The most senior staff member, Jay, is in his thirtieth year — he arrived a year after I left. People tell me over the next few days that it's too bad that we missed each other, but I'm thinking it's a good thing, though it's absurd to think he would remember me in any case. The rest of the place feels as new to me as it must have three decades ago.

⌒

On my first day at camp, Tony, a slightly chunky kid who would have been beaten up for his chunkiness in my day, invites me to play catch with him at Twilight. Like everything else at Camp Echo, Twilight is scheduled, a certain time of the day when the 350 boys (and the girls on the other side of the lake) are free to play within sight of their cabins and their ever-vigilant counselors. We toss a rubber ball and a hardball, and Tony keeps praising me for my throws and my catches, most of which are off the mark — and I'm thinking, *What kind of boy is this? Campers praise one another at Camp Echo?* That just seems sick. This must be a new version of Ten-Year-Old Boy, introduced during the 1980s or 1990s after my version was phased out.

Soon we're called back to our bunk to get ready for dinner. A water fountain sits beside B5-1, and I go out to fill my bottle, but another one of my bunkmates, a darkly tanned boy named Vince who wears a turned-around Yankees cap, tells me there's a better water fountain behind our row of cabins with colder water.

"Robin, where are you going?" says eighteen-year-old Brad, who's sitting on the porch regarding me cannily as I head off.

"I —" I start to say, and point.

"Is it necessary for you to go to that water fountain?" he asks in his best counselor voice, friendly but firm. I didn't know how to handle campers when I was a counselor, but these days each counselor receives at least a week's intensive training to deal with all eventualities, even bad apples like me.

I put my head down, Charlie Brown–like, and trudge back to the less-cold water fountain in front of B5-1.

Growing up involves many lessons, but as a grown-up it's easy to forget the lack of power and choice I had as a boy. Obviously, I'm not a boy anymore. I'm six-one and weigh 185 pounds, but I'm wearing a Camp Echo T-shirt, and my group has been told that I'm to be treated like any other camper. As I trudge to dinner, I get double takes from campers and counselors alike. Most people don't know what I'm doing here.

I'm standing in line with my ten-year-old bunkmates outside the dining hall when a group of thirteen-year-olds surrounds me. "Are you a new counselor?" one boy asks.

"I'm a new camper. I'm in B5-2."

"With the fifth graders? What, were you held back twenty grades?"

Moving 350 campers and 220 staff members into the dining hall is done in shifts, and you wait with your group to enter, much the same way the airlines board passengers. The salad bar is definitely new, and campers have more food choices (kids on special diets are accommodated too), but camp food hasn't changed much in the past thirty years. Spaghetti and meatballs, chicken pot pie, grilled cheese and curly fries, chicken tenders, and, one day, their opposite: "chicken toughs" I call them — chicken breasts of a variegated Southwestern adobe color. The tables in the dining hall are about as big as the one in Leonardo da Vinci's *The Last Supper* and hold as many campers and counselors — our side of the hall fits nineteen such tables. Pitchers of water and high-fructose, colored juice sit at either end of the table. I grab water as soon as I sit down. Green juice that tastes like the blood of a gummy bear is not my idea of refreshment. Our counselors, in their blue staff shirts, sit at either end of the table, and we campers sit in the middle. We only have half an hour per meal, so we have to eat quickly, though it's hard to concentrate on eating because things are always being passed this way and that: Hand me a fork, please! Hand me a cup. Snoopy and Brad make us say thank you and please.

Then, *Quiet please!* A chant begins as loud as a jet engine:

Dedication to Danny Wasserman
Don't let that Sally Frost
Get an inch above your knee

"It's usually a little less hectic here," one of my bunkmates confides. "Everyone had sugar today." Another B-52, as I've started to think of them, turns to me and shouts, "Hey, Robin. Shake your booty!" I don't trust this request. I haven't quite accepted where I am yet, who I'm with, what I'm doing. What would I look like, a forty-eight-year-old shaking booty in front of a dining hall full of kids? I shake my head instead.

Another boy turns to me and puts his finger to his nose. "If you see this," he says, "do it too."

Snoopy sees him instructing me and says, "What are you doing? Giving away all our secrets?"

Presently, Snoopy puts his finger on his nose, and I put my finger on my nose and so does everyone else, until one lone camper remains who hasn't yet put his finger on his nose.

"You! You! You!" They chant at him, and he smiles broadly, and I'm thinking, *You what? You nincompoop? You idiot? You blind fool who can't put his finger on his nose fast enough? Is that all?* In my day, we knew how to humiliate each other properly.

My first night at camp, we have a big event scheduled: Echo-Mania! It's like WrestleMania (you have to shout it!), I'm told, though I have no idea what that is either. I assume it has something to do with wrestling and mental illness, which seems logical to my sports-hating mind. My guess seems correct, as a wrestling ring, covered in a thick coating of lime Jell-O, has been set up in one of the camp's outdoor pavilions, and the wrestlers are costumed teams of counselors, staffers, counselors-in-training, and some of the older campers. My bunkmates sit down toward the front with the other fifth and sixth graders. The older kids sit on bleachers behind us. We've brought the candy that our parents gave us, but I have no candy because my parents are dead and I'm a new kid, so my bunkmate Vince offers me some of his Bunk Junk, and I settle in for the show. It lasts over an hour, and I'm of course delighted to see people fall into Jell-O. Repeatedly. But by about the seventeenth group of wrestlers slipping and sliding around in Jell-O, my attention starts to wane. I look behind me, and many of the kids in the bleachers also have glazed looks.

My own bunkmates are fidgety. A beetle has somehow crawled into our midst, right in front of my foot, heading toward Vince.

"Just a little beetle," I say and I flip it over onto its back, not out of cruelty but compassion. There's no way this beetle is going to survive a journey through this crush of campers, so it's best to let him ride out the show on his back, little legs churning. *Don't wear yourself out, little beetle,* I'm thinking, when one of the kids flips him over again, and he resumes his journey to Vince's back. Vince has turned around and regards the bug warily. Some lime Jell-O lands on us, some of it on my shirt, and I'm thinking, *Will lime Jell-O come out?* Another bunkmate tastes the Jell-O on his shirt — it's only been smashed by a hundred sweaty bodies — and says, "Yep, it's lime Jell-O, all right." I flip the beetle on its back again, and my bunkmates stare at it until one of them flips it over again, and it starts off as fast as it can. The boy who tasted the lime Jell-O grabs a bottle cap from the ground and staves in the beetle's little head. He gives me a big grin.

After EchoMania! we trudge back to our bunks for Lights Out. I have a choice. I could stay outside with the counselors and chat after Lights Out, or I could go turn in with the rest of the "boys." I'm not sleepy, and the camp is in the middle of a heat wave of one-hundred-plus-degree temperatures. Unfortunately, the bunks haven't changed. There's no AC, and that bunk smell of old towels and sweat pervades the cabin, all compounded by the heat wave. Lights are out at ten, though Brad allows the bunk "flashlight time" for the duration of one cut from a Red Hot Chili Peppers CD. Although I'm sorely tempted to join the counselors outside, to be true to the experience I climb up to my coffin-sized bunk above Gary, the other new kid. I do not even have room to toss and turn that night as I try to get to sleep. The best I can do is scootch a little.

↶

My visit has not met with universal approval from all quarters of Bunk B5-2, I learn from Snoopy the next morning. The bunk leader, a boy named Jason, has been quiet since my arrival, obviously acknowledging the new Alpha Boy. Me. Or I'd like to think it's me. At least I'm in no danger of getting beat up anymore. This is the kid I would have been terrified of when I was ten — he has the haircut and the look of a little Roman centurion. "Yesss! There's cooking today!" he yells when Snoopy tells us of some of the choices on the day's schedule. I like cooking too, but I never would have admitted it within earshot of a centurion boy when I was ten.

"Sounds delicious!" says Gary, the new kid like me, with a sweet voice, who would have been beaten up twice, once for being a new kid and once for having a sweet voice.

The cabin comedian, Dale, has blond hair and a mischievous grin. He sometimes wears a top hat around the bunk (he might have wound up in a body cast for that alone in my day). "You just missed Top Hat and Tiara Day," he tells me. But, happily, I haven't missed Luau Day! That's this morning. Oh joy.

"I think it's time you and I had a heart-to-heart," Dale tells me while we're sitting on the cabin porch waiting for Snoopy and Brad to lead us to breakfast on the beach of Camp Echo's man-made lake.

"Why?" I ask, thinking he's going to make fun of the yellow luau shirt that Marla had to lend me, and then he bursts into a song from *The Lion King*.

He proceeds to interview me with a tennis racket, handle side up, about all the things I've forgotten to bring to camp. "Robin forgot his lacrosse stick," he tells the viewing audience. "I don't even think he brought a towel, did you, Robin?"

"I didn't get a packing list," I say weakly.

"Interesting," he says, arching his eyebrows. "Well, back to you, Bob and Sarah!"

The only thing I didn't forget to bring is a folding chair, which I now carry proudly to the beach for Luau Day festivities. But when I unfold it, I realize that I brought Shoshie's tiny folding chair by mistake. I sit in it petulantly for a few minutes before getting up and offering it to one of my bunkmates. And I must have packed one of my older daughters' toothpaste tubes. This morning when I brushed my teeth, the toothpaste was bubble-gum flavor.

When it's my bunk's turn to eat, I take a plate and grab a bagel and lox. (What? You expected kalua pig and poi?) The humiliation today will take the form of a bunch of Hawaiian-ish games devised by the counselors-in-training. Snoopy wears his grass skirt around his head. He looks like a cross between a rugby player, with his solid body and crew cut, and some kind of fetish dug up from Easter Island. But I'm fond of Snoopy. Everyone is. He's firm with the kids and metes out appropriate consequences and praise with a fair hand and a maturity that I obviously still lack. I say I lack it because of the following inci-

dent. When coconut tic-tac-toe proves to be as boring and predictable as regular tic-tac-toe (the difference is that coconut tic-tac-toe involves a floating tic-tac-toe board into which campers lob coconuts), some counselors-in-training get the idea to play Coconut Nuke 'Em. The name alone should alarm the grown-up in me, and yet I passively take my place on one side of the volleyball net with my team. The goal of this game is to chuck a coconut over the net at a ten-year-old, call out his or her name, and watch him or her attempt to catch or dodge the round missile. Thankfully, after only a few minutes of this and no head traumas, the camp photographer, Amanda, puts down her camera and says quite firmly, "We're not going to do that anymore."

I have a headache and tell Brad I'm going back to the bunk to get some aspirin.

"We're going to have to have a consult about that," he says, and crooks his finger for me to step aside with him. He tells me that I'm not allowed to have any medicine in the cabin and that as a camper I can't go there alone, so he recruits a sixteen-year-old counselor-in-training to escort me.

Some of the group head to the dining hall for lunch while I'm gone — the rest would rather hang out in the bunk, including Brad. I'm hungry again, but lunch for me is not a priority for Brad, and so I stay back with him and the rest of the group.

The reason no one's hungry today might have something to do with the fact that they've been eating candy since nine this morning. We're told that we have ten minutes to eat the rest of our candy and chips.

"If I find any hidden candy," Brad says, "there will be consequences."

In the spirit of cooperation, I decide to give Tony a hand. He's busy stuffing his mouth with red licorice. I take some and stuff it into my mouth too. "This is the worst three minutes of my young life!" Dale shouts, candy flying down our throats as the end draws near.

In the seconds before everything left is placed into a black plastic garbage bag, Tony holds eight licorice sticks in his hand and tells me he's going to cram them all into his mouth at once when the countdown reaches one second. It's like a threat, like he's holding a bomb and not eight licorice sticks. His eyes are mad. The frenzy has taken hold of me as well. I grab handfuls of Cheetos and a candy log and a gummy ice cream cone, and gorge. Then I go outside and wait, orange Cheeto dust all over my white camper T-shirt.

Tony comes hulking down the steps with a blue lollipop in hand, a big grin, and a blue tongue. "They didn't say we couldn't bring candy along with us," he says.

"You should go fill up your pockets then," I say.

His eyes light up, and he does just that. Three of my other bunkmates come out with big wads of chewing gum in their mouths. Chewing gum is *completely* against camp rules — Brad doesn't seem to enforce this particular rule, but Snoopy invariably tells campers to throw their gum away if he catches them with it. "Isn't that against the rules?" I say, and they put their fingers to their mouths and say, "Shhh!"

The warmth of conspiratorial acceptance washes over me.

↶

If Camp Echo were a country (it does have its own flag, which is raised and lowered with the U.S. flag every day), Marla would be the country's information minister. Throughout my stay, Marla appears ubiquitously to give me her spin on my camping experience. A past president of the American Camp Association, she and her family run Camp Echo like a cross between some small enlightened European principality (say, Liechtenstein) and a cruise ship.

She tells me that camps have only recently learned what business they're in. "They used to think they were in the recreation business, but they're really in the youth development business." Like so many other institutions of contemporary childhood, camps now serve a developmental agenda and have their own value systems. At least this one does. There are ten Echo Values posted outside of my bunk, reinforced every day by counselors and staff, culminating in a Sunday night torch ceremony in praise of individual campers who have exemplified one of these values over the past week. Marla has given me my own laminated sheet of Camp Echo Values.

SELF-RELIANCE
COURAGE
PATIENCE
COOPERATION
COMMITMENT
RELIABILITY
COMPASSION
REASON
CREATIVITY
SELF-IMPROVEMENT

There were no Echo Values when I was here last. But, in hindsight, they might look like this:

INTIMIDATION
HUMILIATION
CRUELTY
BOREDOM
IMMATURITY
SADISM
INDIFFERENCE
EMBARRASSMENT
SELF-PRESERVATION
TOUGH LUCK

Another clue that that this might not be the same place I left thirty years ago are the water fountains scattered strategically around the two hundred acres of Camp Echo. I certainly don't remember those, but I'm grateful because of the heat wave. At meals campers line up without stigma or comment to get meds. That's new too. In fact, everything seems new, from the water park on the lake (which I sample one afternoon despite my lackluster swimming ability) to the gaga court (gaga, Marla explains to me, is a kind of low-impact dodgeball) to the attitudes of the administration.

I grew up without anyone helping me along. No Echo Values in camp. No I-Care Rules in kindergarten. Positive reinforcement hadn't even been invented when I was growing up! I remember my great-uncle worrying in front of me that I was a sissy. My grandmother told me I'd get leprosy if I didn't take a bath. My mother told me girls wouldn't like me if I didn't gain weight. I remember one kid in fifth grade we called Boomer. He'd make little bombing noises throughout class. Once he peed out the bathroom window on kids playing kickball. Another time he grabbed our teacher, Miss Cotton, and pulled her across her desk. Boomer was either being yelled at by the principal, ridiculed by the other kids, or manhandled by a teacher or two. Today Boomer would be medicated and in therapy. Maybe me too. Back then, family, schools, and camp worked hand-in-hand to make us little arts and crafts basket cases.

Almost from the outset, I've got the hang of being ten again. "Regressive pull," Marla says it's called. The idea is that a grown-up in the midst of a bunch of ten-year-olds will start acting as a ten-year-old. Counselors and staff members are warned against it, but Marla says that I'm showing it has its positive side too. I guess that becoming a child again is like riding a bicycle. Somewhere deep inside, I've memorized the patterns and behaviors of childhood, both good and bad, and when I put my feet back on the pedals, off I fly.

While mountain biking, I chat with one of the instructors, Danny from Scotland. I ask him where he's from, and he tells me he's from a place near Glasgow.

"Is it anywhere near Stirling?" I ask.

"Oh, you've been to Stirling?" he says.

I once almost went on a faculty exchange to Stirling but didn't. I've never even been to Scotland. "Yes," I say.

"Ah, you saw the monument to William Wallace then?"

"Yeah, great," I say, and then I take off on my bike, flabbergasted that I just lied to him. What just made me do that?

Regressive pull, man. Shout it out!

Life comes down to choices, but at Camp Echo they're mostly not irreversible, and they're given the friendly name of "options." At breakfast lineup every day, you're given your Options Card, and as you file inside you place your card in a slot designating your chosen option. There's horseback riding, hockey, three-on-three basketball, arts and crafts, cooking, ceramics, woodworking, mountain biking, swimming, fishing, golf, aqua park, yoga, soccer, tennis, Frisbee, and, *Oh my god,* tryouts for the musical *You're a Good Man, Charlie Brown.* What can I do but try out for the play and consider this a good omen, that of all the plays they could put on at Camp Echo, they've chosen the same play I once appeared in at Granite Lake Camp, the same play that Izzy will try out for at school. That afternoon, I write home excitedly to Margie and the girls. I want to write them, but I also *have* to write to my family if I want dinner. And I do want dinner. All this activity makes me hungry. I borrow a sheet of football stationery from one of my bunkmates and write:

Dear Isabel, Olivia, Shoshie, and Margie:

How are you? I am fine. I am writing during Letter Writing Time at Camp Echo because I can't get into dinner unless I've written a letter. I didn't have any paper, so I borrowed this cool paper from one of my bunkmates. I have the top bunk. It's hot! Today, I went mountain biking and made a checkerboard in woodworking. Tomorrow, I go to the trapeze and do horseback riding. This is just like the letters home I used to write from camp. Send candy!

Love,

Dad

XXOO

P.S. I'm going to try out for "You're a Good Man, Charlie Brown."

P.P.S. I miss you!

So far, as a grown-up, I have had my share of awkward moments at Camp Echo, but none quite approaches the strangeness of sitting in a hot hall with a group of fifth- through ninth-grade boys and girls waiting to try out for a play I was in when I was their age. The drama coach, Diane, gives us all a script of the first act and tries to gauge our Echo Value of Commitment. Fifteen boys and as many girls sit in folding chairs expectantly, and then there's me. A part of me believes, quite psychotically, I suppose, that I might actually find a way to be in this play.

Diane runs through the main songs of the play, "The Baseball Game" and "Happiness," and she tells us to sing along if we know the songs. I have not sung either song in nearly forty years, and yet they both come back to me instantly, and I sing right along with her and the other campers. A boy in front of me keeps looking back, checking out the old dude belting out the songs in a voice stronger and deeper than anyone else's. I don't care. Diane seems impressed by our effort, and then she auditions us separately, asking us to stand at the front of the room and sing the last verse of "Happiness." As with everything else, we go up by grade. When she comes to fifth-grade boys, it's only Dale and I who stand. Dale goes first, and I'm so nervous I can't even hear him. A couple of the girls' counselors look at me with dropped jaws, as do the campers. But I've come this far, haven't I? Diane asks me to sing next, and I oblige, singing in my clearest tenor. When I'm finished, the front row bursts into applause, and I say, "Thank you," and sit down. That's enough for me. I'm going back to my bunk. I thank Diane and the other staff and then I leave the building and head back.

"Camper," I hear someone shout behind me. I turn around. It's a counselor I've never met. "Where are you going? You can't leave without a buddy." I turn around and wait with the rest of them until we find a counselor who'll accompany me to my cabin.

Later, Dale returns to the bunk, and I ask him how it went.

"I got the part of Linus," he says.

"You did? That's my part!" His eyes widen in alarm. But I don't mean it the way it sounds. I'm really happy for him, I say. Really *really* happy! He nods and walks away from the crazy man. But by the next day, he's telling everyone that he got the part I had when I was in camp, and on our breaks we run lines together.

Camp administrators and propagandists will tell you that camp is a family, but that's not true. The individual bunkhouses are families. B5-2 is a family, happy and well-adjusted for the most part, due largely to the efforts of their hardworking counselors. Camp Echo itself is a country, a kingdom, a feudal society that demands complete compliance and obeisance, but that's not bad. Ten-year-olds, older kids, and maybe even I, need structure. It's the regimentation of camp that strikes me the most. The wildness of being a child constantly clashes with the camp's need to control this wildness. Where are our civil liberties? I'm a more compliant camper than I used to be. At Granite Lake Camp, I caused a stir in 1969 by refusing to put my hand over my heart for the Pledge of Allegiance. At Echo, I put my hand over my heart *and* say the pledge too. I want to be a good camper, but I'm always lagging behind. "Robin, we're waiting for you," Brad is always telling me, the last one out of the bunk for nearly every activity. I'm in my own world. That hasn't changed.

But sometimes even the carefully controlled and monitored environment that is contemporary camp life breaks down in the face of the inner pandemonium that's at the secret center of every child's savage heart.

There is a lady, let's call her the Drum Lady, who visits our camp. She teaches our bunk how to pound on drums and release some of our wildness, both natural and sugar induced, but control it at the same time. She did it at orientation with the counselors, "and it worked very well." Hmmm. She does it with B5-2 one afternoon, and it works less well. For the most part, the bunkers follow her hand signals. She gives us three. Raising her hands means that we should increase our pounding. Lowering means we should decrease. And the most important: swiping her hands the way an umpire does to call a base runner safe means to knock it off. But sometimes the kids turn inward. They don't look at her. They follow their wildness fully and pound and pound and pound and seem as though they will never stop.

That night, she hands out percussion instruments to the *entire camp,* 350 campers. She seems not to grasp something that I do about the difference between grown-ups and kids: there's a difference between grown-ups and kids. Before long she has 350 drummers pounding. She raises her hands, and they thump furiously. She lowers her hands, and they thump furiously. She makes that Safe motion, and they thump furiously. I have never before heard anything so loud as 350 campers thumping drums. Talk about Echo-Mania! Talk about tinnitus! I have two drums. I'm banging the hell out of my drums when a kid not in my bunk turns around and gives me a what-do-you-think-you're-doing look. I give him one of my drums. The Drum Lady is signaling the runner Safe Safe Safe Safe, and she has a wild, teeth-bared smile and a panicked look on her face. So she goes to a keyboard set up against the wall of the pavilion and starts pounding on it and shouting into a microphone over the drumming, and I know there's some music there, but it's so distorted it sounds like a raptor shrieking, and I know there are words but they are incomprehensible. All I can make out when she screams is "Here comes the chorus!"

Shriek! Shriek!

Only later do I learn that the Shriek Shriek of the Drum Lady on her keyboard was supposed to be the camp song.

Finally, the senior staffers raise their hands to signal silence, and the counselors raise their hands, and slowly the campers calm down, but there's still pounding going on, and so Herb, one of the senior staffers, steps into the middle of the circle and shouts, "Put the instruments down, and put your hands on your head!" He repeats this a half dozen times. And about a hundred of them do it, like prisoners in the aftermath of a riot. They put their instruments down and their hands on their heads. I put my hands on my head too, and then I take them down slowly, edge up against the wall, and stand, willing myself to be a grown-up again.

But sometimes that simple fact (I am a grown-up) momentarily escapes me. Or maybe I let it escape and happily watch it float off like a lost balloon in the sky: Bye-bye, simple fact. Have a nice time!

On the way to lunch one day, the darkly tanned Vince who wears a turned-around Yankees cap runs after chunky Tony saying he's going to kill him. I should point out here that while I'm not in favor of Vince killing Tony, at least Vince seems more like the kind of boy I'm used to. Vince's only weapon is a leftover palm frond from Luau Day, so I'm not too worried. Then Vince sits on Tony, who's laughing.

"Do something, Robin," Tony says through his laughter. If I were my old kindergarten teacher, Mrs. Collins, I'm sure I'd sit on him too.

"Sorry, I'm just a camper," I say.

"Boy, I wish you were a counselor right now," he says.

Vince lets Tony off the ground and starts kicking him in the butt as Tony walks with me. "Come on, Vince," I say, but Vince ignores me and starts beating Tony in the face with the palm frond. Tony covers his eyes and starts crying. I go over to Tony and ask him if he's okay. Vince is concerned as well. Once Vince determines that Tony is going to be fine, he starts kicking him in the butt again.

Normally, as a grown-up, I would have stopped this before now, but regressive pull has me in a headlock, and Vince and Tony have accepted that I have no authority here. So have I. Later I ask Tony if he's okay. "Sure," he says with a big grin. "Vince and I always fool around like that. We're friends."

Learning skills is a big thing at Camp Echo, what Marla calls Level I skills and Level II skills. Level I skills involve learning things like how to swim in the deep end of the pool. Level II skills involve learning things like not beating someone in the face with a palm frond or sitting on them. Even if you mean it as a friendly gesture.

I think that at the age of forty-eight, I'm finally getting a handle on Level II skills, but Level I skills, at least when it comes to swimming, still give me problems. Swimming. My old nemesis. In this, I have no options. But camp is all about getting out of your comfort zone, as Information Minister Marla will tell you. One day at swim time we're told we're going to play water polo in the deep end of the pool, so I get in with all my bunkmates, when Snoopy calls me and the other new kid, Gary, over to the side of the pool. "Guys," he says. "You're going to have to take a swim test before you can go to the deep end."

The swim test involves swimming two laps of the crawl, followed by treading water and floating on our backs. I can float on my back. I can tread water. I can do the sidestroke. But I cannot do the crawl. What Marla says is that campers are encouraged to think of their fears and hurdles as: "I cannot do it . . . yet!" So, okay, I walk over to the shallow end of the pool repeating in my head, "I cannot do the crawl . . . yet!"

Gary and I get in our respective lanes and off he goes, and I start doing something crawlish looking, my arms slapping the water, my head twitching from one side to the other, water getting in my mouth, choking me, and I look up and see Gary torpedoing across the pool. I hear Snoopy yelling encouragement. And I stand up at the other end of the pool completely winded and whine, "I've got water in my mouth!" *Goddamn it,* I'm thinking. *I cannot do the crawl . . . at all!* But Gary is already across the pool, so I catch my breath a moment and then plunge back in. I'm just barely competent enough at swimming to pass, and after I've floated on my back and treaded water, the lifeguards place a little blue plastic band with my name on my wrist, my ticket to the deep end.

Except for doing the crawl, I admit, I've come to like this place. I find myself reliving camp in a way I'm not prepared for. I've tried on a new kind of boyhood, XL, and it fits. I'm made to feel good about myself at Camp Echo by Snoopy and Brad. I'm encouraged to try new things, and I try them.

One morning I climb a sixty-foot ladder to a tiny platform, where I'm supposed to swing out on a trapeze and fall on my back into a net below. Slowly, I climb. I have a fear of heights that at sixty feet does not feel unreasonable. A staffer tells me to rub my hands in a chalk bag so I can hold on to the trapeze, and I'm fine with that, but when I actually grab the trapeze bar and feel its heft, I panic. "I don't think I can do this," I tell him. "I want to go down."

My bunkmates stand below, Snoopy shouting for me to press on, and all of a sudden I'm in midair, swinging. It's always Snoopy's voice I hear — and it doesn't seem forced or fake. He's the counselor I wish I had been thirty years ago, and the counselor I wish I had had as a camper. I'm infatuated with him in the way that ten-year-old boys get infatuated with their counselors. The problem is that I'm not ten. I'm forty-eight, the father of three girls, a college professor. Infatuated with my counselor and still swinging in the air.

"Okay, on the count of three, I want you to kick up your legs and let go of the bar," the instructor says, and counts one . . . two . . . three, and I'm still swinging, and so he tells me this time he wants me to pay attention to the letting go part.

And I do.

CHAPTER FOUR

THE YEAR OF BULLIES

Sixth Grade Do-Over

ORIGINAL AGE: 11

DO-OVER AGE: 48

ORIGINAL LOCATIONS: SLIPPERY ROCK, PENNSYLVANIA; HOLLYWOOD,
FLORIDA

DO-OVER LOCATION: LONGFELLOW ELEMENTARY, IOWA CITY, IOWA

On the bulletin board of John Long Middle School in front of a fal-
con clutching an American flag (pesky birds — they're always making off with American flags for their nests; them and eagles) is a

photo of Isabel Hemley as Lucy Van Pelt. Izzy has dyed her hair black for the part and is dressed in a stiff oversized dress that gives her the appearance of a cartoon come to life. As both her dad and a former cast member, it's my duty to show my support for her, and so I have driven four and a half hours with Margie and Shoshie to see her perform.

Izzy called me a couple of days ago after the first performance and reported how it went.

"The performance went so well," she said. "'She was amazing,' Mom overheard some guy say about me. Someone else said, 'That kid with the black hair is really going somewhere with this!' And guess what, Dad? No one made one mistake!"

Almost breathless, she was excited about the performance but also about us attending the play. "Not many of my friends have met Shoshie," she says. "Not many have met you either."

Shoshie's turn to be breathless came in the hotel room as we changed for Izzy's play later that same week. Jumping on the bed, Shoshie kept screaming "cockle doodle doo!" as Margie tried to help her into a new blue dress, and she's still bouncing up and down as we enter John Long. "I don't want to see you jumping anymore," Margie says, her mood soured by Olivia's declaration that she's not going to sit with us during the performance but with her friends instead. Isabel will spend the weekend with us at the hotel, but not Olivia because she has one of her many practices to attend. At this point I'm fatalistic about it, even though we haven't seen her since September. I suppose this is one of those "face the facts" moments, though Margie doesn't seem so resigned to facing facts or she wouldn't bother to feel my hurt. I'm probably as close as I've come all year to facing facts. Torn between melancholy and pride, I try to concentrate on Isabel's performance, purchasing her several of the carnations that are being sold at a table up front, scribbling a congratulatory card, and asking that the flowers be delivered backstage.

I suppose that almost all parents want to live vicariously through their children, though one of the major realizations that any parent must have is that their children are not mere extensions of themselves. But seeing Isabel perform that night does fill me with a strange sense that I'm watching myself perform alongside her. Songs I haven't heard in almost forty years come back to me like a foreign language I've neglected to practice. The boy playing Snoopy in this production can hardly carry a note, just like the boy who played Snoopy in my production at Granite Lake Camp, but like my Snoopy this Snoopy has the manic energy, comic timing, and general joie de vivre to carry off the part perfectly. The boy playing Linus dances with his blanket, as I danced with mine, to "My Blanket and Me." I've never been crazy about "Happiness" — the song, not the concept. For me, this is where the play teeters on the syrupy sentimental, when what I love about the musical is that in most other places it enshrines childhood without lying about it. Lucy perpetually threatens Linus. Schroeder perpetually rejects Lucy. Charlie Brown is the fall guy we all knew and were at some point or another. But "Happiness"? Well, it spawned a whole line of sappy greeting cards in the 1970s and 1980s that almost ruined *Peanuts* for me as a respectable commentary on life. Still, I succumb completely, giving myself over to a wash of sentimental gooeyness when I hear my daughter belting:

> *Happiness is knowing a secret, sharing a sandwich, getting along . . .*

Getting along. The logistics here are awkward. Although people speak of blended families, you can't simply push a button, blend, and have everything come out all right. Sometimes things don't work out for the best. You flub a line. You drop the ball in the big baseball game. You try to move on, but there's still bitterness. Your older daughter disappears into the parking lot where her mother waits at the far end in the car.

Back at the hotel room in Milwaukee, Shoshie hangs on her older sister, grasping her around the neck, the waist, asking to have a piggyback ride. Izzy's dead tired but indulges her adoring younger sister. Too exhausted to eat at the Thai restaurant that's one of our favorites in downtown Milwaukee, we instead order room service and talk about family resemblances, wondering if Izzy and Shoshie look at all alike, especially around the chin, our way of blending, of saying when things and people get mixed up, sometimes the results are beautiful.

Back in Iowa City on the day before I start sixth grade, I call my daughters in Grafton and get Olivia. We talk for almost an hour — she dispensing advice in her own Lucy Van Pelt fashion on the ins and outs of sixth grade. Olivia enjoys giving advice, like Lucy, but there the similarity ends. In this family dynamic, Isabel is by far the more intimidating. When she was younger, Isabel could bully Olivia with a well-aimed pinch on the arm, and Olivia, a decided pacifist, could never protect herself against her younger sister. But I can easily imagine Olivia, like Lucy, sitting in a homemade booth behind a sign that reads THE DOCTOR IS IN.

"The whole point of dodgeball," Olivia says, "is to get out as soon as possible. I tell my friends to hit me, and then we sit on the sidelines and talk."

"You don't try to win?" I ask.

"No, Dad. Of course not."

Despite an armload of useful advice from Olivia, I'm still as nervous that night about going to sixth grade as I was about kindergarten and camp. For me, sixth grade was the year of bullies, a year of boy versions of Lucy Van Pelts pelting me, first in Slippery Rock, Pennsylvania, and then in Hollywood, Florida, where I moved to spend the second half of the school year with my grandmother. In part, I fled Slippery Rock to escape the bullies, a group of boys in my neighborhood and school who taunted me for being Jewish, for being from New York, for joining (briefly) the Boy Scouts. One night they ambushed me on my way back from scouts and beat me — they were mean, but luckily for me they were also stupid. They pummeled me with inflated inner tubes almost too big for them to handle. So it was kind of like being beat up but kind of not. It didn't leave a mark on me physically, but they scared me. I quit the scouts and stayed in my room when I wasn't in school. One day I tried to memorize Hamlet's "To be or not to be" speech but only got a few lines in and gave up in favor of watching *Dennis the Menace* on TV.

While the bullies didn't follow me to Hollywood, my school in Florida had a few of its own, including one boy on whom I put a curse. I couldn't handle him physically, so I figured maybe I could summon some kind of dark force to overcome his meanness. Unfortunately, he found my curse (of course I'd written it down) on

the floor and approached me. "Did you put a curse on me?" he asked and showed me the incontrovertible evidence.

For the record, I'm good at fleeing, not fighting, but he was blocking the exit.

Instead of beating me up, he meekly asked me to take the curse off him. He had found the note before recess and had followed me back in, ready to clock me in the nose, when a roof tile let loose and hit him on the head. After he got up off the ground and shook off the pain, he changed his mind.

Temporarily. He didn't beat me up. He respected my "powers" that much, but for the rest of the year he did everything else that bullies do to intimidate, short of using physical force. Well, a few wedgies. And some noogies. And a few "Indian burns." But no concussions. No broken bones. No missing teeth or bloody noses. Just a lot of names. A lot of chairs pulled out from under me. A few thumbtacks on my seat. This was all payback in his mind. Not fatal, but fair is fair in the brutal economy of bullies. Kid stuff. If I put another curse on him, he warned, he'd have to get serious.

I usually gave him my lunch money too. So, yeah. Sixth grade. Bring it on.

↶

The morning of my first day back in sixth grade, Margie drives me and Shoshie to our respective schools, as she did when I went back to kindergarten, though this is a different school in Iowa City, Long-fellow Elementary, which, like Horace Mann, is only a few blocks from my home.

I have the urge to flee when I see the crowd of elementary school kids staring at me as I walk toward them with my book bag. *Stay cool, Robin,* I tell myself. *You can take any one of them in a fair fight, maybe two or three at a time.*

I'm greeted almost immediately by a boy with long blond hair who separates himself from the line of sixth graders around the front door.

"Are you Robin Hemley?" he asks. He introduces himself as the coolest kid in sixth grade and high-fives me. High fives actually were invented after my childhood, so I've never quite accepted them or got them down. My high fives generally miss the mark and seem slow and overdetermined, as though I'm about to start a round of patty-cake. Every time someone high-fives me, I feel as though I'm being tested on my precision and the quality of sound as palm meets palm. The worst is when I try to initiate a high five with someone, and they just look at my hand hanging in the air as though I'm waiting to be called on.

So concentrated am I on my high-five accuracy (I'd give myself a 7.5 on this one) that I immediately forget the name of the kid who just introduced himself. I chide myself to pay more attention. All kids take their age seriously and think of themselves as much older and wiser than kids merely a year behind them, but nowhere is this more evident than in those top-of-the-food-chain grades, most commonly fifth or sixth grade in elementary school (depending on whether sixth graders attend elementary school in a particular school district or start over as the lowest rung of middle school), eighth or ninth grade in middle school, senior year in high school. Those grades come with big attitudes. They're the mafiosi of the educational system, if I remember correctly, and you don't dis a fellow sixth-grade boy without paying the price.

But there's no time to worry about retribution now, because I'm herded with the rest of the sixth graders up the stairs to my new classroom where I meet my teacher, Liz Monroe, who seats me next to Amanda, grade school royalty, a future prom queen, who in my day was known as Ann Holmes. She gives me a cool don't-try-anything-funny look and straightens out her desk as I'm handed an assortment of intimidating history and English books, given a schedule and a daily planner, and introduced to the class, a combined group of fifth and sixth graders, and then bustled off with everyone else to the first subject of the day, math, taught in the room next door by Mr. Pirelli, a teacher nearly twenty years my junior.

As we're sitting down in our desks (these are nice and roomy compared to kindergarten desks), the long-haired boy who high-fived me comes up to me and says, "Do you remember my name?"

"Um."

He gives me a look of disgust and then sits down across from me, staring hard as though he hates me now, which he probably does. His name, I now learn, is Perry, but his real name is Torment. He's a fixture in every fifth- and sixth-grade class the world over, just as Ann Holmes/Amanda is a fixture in every class too. In Tracy Kidder's 1989 study of a fifth-grade classroom in Holyoke, Massachusetts, *Among Schoolchildren,* the teacher, Mrs. Zajac, had a Perry in her class too. His name was Clarence, and he was a puncher, a sulker, and a disrupter. "Every year you get one," she bemoaned. "And every year it's the same." I haven't been doing do-overs long enough to track them, but I imagine eventually Perry and Amanda will wind up together in high school, get married or not after an unwanted pregnancy or two, and then settle down to a life full of regrets that they can trace back to the day they crossed me.

Mr. Pirelli, on the other hand, is a model of perspicacity. (Look it up. It will be on your spelling quiz.) Mr. P seems to take his students as they come, and today we're learning about probability. According to our book, a sugar-addled kid named Jack has struck a deal with his mom regarding how many times in a month he's allowed to eat a cereal called Cocoa Blasts for breakfasts. His mother, who apparently encourages all sorts of bad habits in her son, gives him a coin to flip. Should we really be teaching probability in sixth grade? Seven years from now, we're going to find Perry gambling away Baby Perry's formula money at the craps table in the riverboat casino in Dubuque.

Mr. P passes out quarters and breaks us into groups. "Please

91

give me my quarters back," he tells us. "That's half a year's salary. If I don't get them back, I'm going to sell your gym shoes on eBay."

I'm in a coin-flipping group with Amanda, and immediately there's a dispute over how to flip the coins. Amanda is in favor of the flip-and-slap-on-the-back-of-your-hand technique, while the rest of the group except for me (I tend to side with Amanda; I like the extra flourish, but I'm silent in payment for her earlier coolness toward me) wants a simple coin flip, nothing fancy. Amanda is distraught at the thought of getting rid of this variable, but she's overruled and we flip until we arrive at the conclusion that Jack will eat Cocoa Blasts a total of eleven times out of thirty-one days in the month of July.

Perry is definitely the kid to watch out for, the one I would have feared and hated in sixth grade originally, though I'm supposedly older and wiser now and I think I can handle him. And I *should* be at least as mature as Shoshie whose voice resounds in my head, "*Hate*'s a bad word, Daddy." But at the door of math class, as we're filing back to our homeroom, Perry blocks my way and says, "Can I call you Robin Hood?"

"You can call me whatever you want," I say, horrified a moment later that I just said that.

There's no such thing as a level playing field in sixth grade — this exchange would have been my undoing the first time around. Robin Hood was the least of it. *Flat Man and Ribbon. Robin is a girl's name. Rub on. Robin Hood and His Fairy Men.* And it gets worse from there. Use your imagination. Or better yet, don't. One nickname morphed into another until it was impossible to track its pedigree, and it simply turned into a crude insult. The same thing happened to most of us, except perhaps for the Perrys of the world, who, come to think of it, probably have no regrets, get elected to high office, or become presidential advisers.

One thing I like immediately about Ms. Monroe is that she doesn't coddle or condescend to the kids in her class. Like Mrs. Statler, my do-over kindergarten teacher, Ms. Monroe was recommended to me as an exceptional teacher. She's fourteen years older than me, and next year is her last as a teacher, but, unlike with Mrs. Statler, we haven't had a chance to meet before this. I'm new to her and she's new to me, and she tells my classmates now that I'm a special resource for them since I'm a writer. I kind of wish she hadn't said that. But in some ways, this is a mission impossible. As much I'd like to blend in and be just another sixth grader, who am I kidding? Wouldn't Perry have verbally torn me to shreds just now when I told him he could call me whatever he wants if I were *really* in sixth grade?

Going into reading, I'm feeling a bit depressed, thinking that maybe kindergarten, the play, and camp will stand as my only triumphs. It's not as if I blend in here. I'm hard to miss. It's as if I'm wearing my pajamas to school. Or naked. Maybe I'm the only one who really thought I could do these things over, though, on the other hand, maybe I'm the only person I need to worry about. Who cares what anyone else thinks?

As luck would have it, I'm put in the same reading group as Perry. The class is broken into several groups, each reading a different book. Mine and Perry's is *Tuck Everlasting,* about an unfortunate family that has stumbled on a kind of fountain of youth and drunk from it. As a result, they can never grow older than they were when they first sipped the water. Ms. Monroe is wild for this book. She's taught it every year for eighteen years. When she discovers I've not yet read the book, though I know Olivia has and that both she and Izzy have watched the movie, Ms. Monroe tells me it's one I definitely need to read. If not for the fact that she's taught this book for eighteen years, I'd suspect she'd chosen it specifically for me, given its theme as a cautionary tale of staying the same age forever.

There are ten of us in the group — we're seated in a circle around Ms. Monroe in a corner of the room while the rest of the class sit at their own desks reading silently to themselves, waiting for their group to be called to the front. We've read the first two chapters of the book, and Ms. Monroe wants to gauge our comprehension. Right now she's talking about similes and metaphors.

There's something a little stagey about really good teachers — they keep themselves amused as they go along, doing a kind of running commentary, as much for their benefit as for their charges. How else could one survive thirty or forty years in the school system and not go crazy like my kindergarten teacher?

"What do you think of when you think of August?" she asks.

"Cold," says Perry.

"Perry has a bad case of Monday morning," she informs our group, and we nod. Perry smiles and flicks hair from his eyes.

"Anyone else?" she asks. "What do you think of when you think of August?"

Another boy raises his hand. "The end of the world," he says.

Ms. Monroe blinks and then bursts out laughing. I'm a bit slow on the uptake here, but Ms. Monroe and my classmates get it immediately, of course. Beginning school in August equals the end of the world. "Perfect," she says.

Next, Ms. Monroe asks the group what words in the book are giving them problems.

"Bovine," says a girl named Samantha.

"*Bovine* is a word I don't hear on the playground every day," Ms. Monroe agrees.

"Melancholy," offers another kid.

"I have a word," says a boy named Richard. "I think it sounds like possum."

"What?" Ms. Monroe asks.

"Boss um," he says.

"Show it to me."

"Bosom," she says and laughs. "Bosom." After she explains to the group what a bosom is, the group has a sixth-grade moment and breaks into giggles, including the boy who thought it was a "boss um." Before stepping into this classroom, I would have thought it was nearly illegal for a teacher to laugh at a student, that a Self-Esteem Alarm would be sounded and a shock team of child psychologists would descend on ropes from trap doors in the ceiling to soothe the trauma-stricken student, and that the teacher would be hauled away in a hair shirt and chains. Apparently not. I look at Perry to see his reaction — in sixth grade I would have immediately formed an alliance with Perry to make fun of Bosom Boy for the rest of the day, maybe the rest of the week, to take the heat off of my "You can call me whatever you want" remark, but Perry seems ready to let the moment pass, as all of them do. Maybe he's thinking, *But for the grace of God, I would have said "boss um" too.*

Ms. Monroe's class is a combined fifth- and sixth-grade class, and so most students have her for two years. A fifth grader with unruly blond hair and a serious face straight out of *Peanuts* comes up to me as Ms. Monroe finishes with my group and calls up the next one. He's carrying a book on King Tut, and he says, "Excuse me, sir. Has anyone ever figured out how to read hieroglyphics?"

"Why yes, they have," I say and tell him briefly about the Rosetta stone.

This innocent boy is Bret, a fifth grader who will attach himself to me for the rest of the week the way Stefan did in kindergarten and the way Marcy did to Peppermint Patty in *Peanuts*.

"Does anyone in America know how?" he asks.

"I believe the information on how to decipher hieroglyphics has filtered to America," I tell him. "By now."

He nods. "Do you know how to play harmonica?" he asks with the same degree of seriousness.

"No," I answer to this random question. "Do you?"

"No," he says. "But I know how to make nice sounds. I can show you at recess," and he pulls out a harmonica to show me as though it's a hot watch.

After this first of many odd exchanges with Bret, I return to my desk, where I quietly read *Tuck Everlasting* for the remainder of the period, happy to be left by myself for a little while. But I daydream too, finding it hard to pay attention to the story. What kind of boy was I? I wonder, looking around the room, trying to find a match. I certainly wasn't Perry, but I wasn't Bret either. When I shamelessly asked one former classmate at the Putnam Elementary School reunion what he remembered of me, he said, "Nothing terribly specific. I think you and I were kind of similar kids. We didn't stick out from the crowd too much. We weren't leaders. We were followers. We went along for a good time and kept our heads low."

A follower? I definitely remembered him as that. He was a bully magnet: sweet face, girlish lips, delicate eyes, a little buzz cut, and clothes right out of a JCPenney catalog. The kind of kid who wore checkered blazers over white turtlenecks. Even *I* picked on him. My parents once called me into the living room when I was in second grade and spoke sternly to me (a first, I believe) about calling people names. I had made fun of his last name repeatedly, and they told me that this behavior was hurtful. I took these proto-I-Care Rules in stride and never made fun of him again. When I saw him decades later, I never would have recognized him. He had changed in the years as much as I had. He looked fit and healthy and still had a thoughtful, serious demeanor, wore his hair longish, and was now a major sound engineer for a number of famous musicians. Still, the fact that he saw us as two of a kind bowled me over. *Me* not a leader? Maybe I wasn't a leader on the playground. I wasn't the fastest kid in our class, not a prankster, not a troublemaker, but I thought I had *some* elementary school clout. Apparently not. In my own mind, I was a leader: a paleontologist who never slept; Silver Surfer, the galaxy-surfing nemesis of the Fantastic Four; Barnabas Collins, the time-traveling vampire from the show *Dark Shadows;* Peter Tork of the Monkees (my favorite), who played the inept fool of the group. But I was definitely *not* Davy Jones, teenybopping British idol of prepubescent girls everywhere. In other words, I was an ordinary boy, who simultaneously kept his head low *and* in the clouds.

↶

In social studies, we're studying the ancient world, specifically the land of Canaan. We each have our own unlabeled maps, and when I glance over at Amanda (to cheat, of course), I see that she has mislabeled the Dead Sea and the Sea of Galilee. Naturally, I should let it go. I should let her get it wrong. If I were a sixth-grade boy, my kind of sixth-grade boy, I would let her get it wrong and revel in the fact that I knew the right answer and she didn't. But almost against my will, something rises in me and I tell her she's got the two seas switched.

"Oh," she says, and gives me an appraising look, then takes her pencil and starts erasing her answers.

"What's this then?" she says, pointing to a small body of water above Galilee.

"The pool?" I say.

"The Pool of Amanda," she says.

"The Dead Pool," I say.

The book we're reading from is called *History Alive!* but, like

most of these texts, it should be called *History on Life Support!* It's
not much different in tone from the history books we had to read in
my first sixth-grade experience, as stimulating as a test of the Emergency
Broadcast System:

> In Unit 1, you learned about early hominids and the empires of
> Mesopotamia. In this unit, you will explore three civilizations that
> arose in Africa and Southwestern Asia. They were the *Egyptian,*
> *Kush,* and *Hebrew* civilizations.

Unit. What a word. Who wants to learn a unit? Not me. I've always
loved history, but not the way history is taught, with the emphasis
on rote memorization rather than the stories of the people. In
high school, I read popular histories of the Civil War by Bruce Catton;
I Claudius, Robert Graves's version of the Roman empire; and
The Guns of August, World War I as told by Barbara Tuchman as if
they were comic books (I read comic books too, of course). They told
stories as much about people dreaming and scheming and dying as
they did about civilizations arising and dying. Catton and Tuchman
wrote about why something happened, not only the date on which it
happened. Blame it on the standard curriculum and part of the No
Child Left Behind mentality that makes school all about quizzes and
tests rather than actually caring about the subjects being taught —
just passing them. Don't blame it on the teacher.

Thankfully, Ms. Monroe knows how to spice it up. She turns
this unit into a *Jeopardy!*-style quiz show.

We're divided into groups. I'm in a group of four with Amanda,
a big kid named Ray, and Amanda's sidekick, Sandy, who sits on the
other side of her. Amanda raises her hand and asks Ms. Monroe if
she can be Alex Trebek, the one who reads everyone's questions, but
Ms. Monroe quashes that.

"No, every group will appoint someone to read the group's
questions."

"But I don't want to be an ordinary person," Amanda whines.

I sympathize. Maybe Amanda is the person I identify with most
in the class. Maybe she's the kind of boy I was.

I nominate her to be our group's answerer/questioner, and the group nods in agreement.

After we write our questions on index cards, we pass them up to Ms. Monroe, who flips through them and decides which ones to read.

"The answer is, 'These are six physical features of ancient Egypt,'" Ms. Monroe says.

We huddle and offer our answers. I say, "The Mediterranean," but I'm quickly overruled.

"That's *way* up there," says Ray.

It turns out I'm right, and I feel pride both that I got the right answer and that they didn't believe I had the right answer, which I think means they've accepted me as an equally fallible sixth grader and that they feel comfortable around me. But that's probably a false assumption. Most kids don't think grown-ups know much. And mostly we don't, at least not the facts found in *History Alive!*

Happily, one of our group's questions is chosen by Ms. Monroe: "The answer is 'These are the main sources of fresh water in the region.'" It's kind of a tricky one because it includes a sea, the Sea of Galilee, the Jordan River, the Nile. Not the Pool of Amanda.

Ms. Monroe picks up another card and laughs. "Topography," Ms. Monroe reads. "The surface features of a place or religion such as mountains or desserts."

We all laugh, and Sandy leans in and says, "I feel sorry for the person who wrote that question."

Yes, where is that trauma shock team? Well, at least it was anonymous ridicule, or semianonymous. The rest of that person's group would know, of course, but not the whole class. It could be a lot worse. When I was in seventh grade, one of my favorite teachers, Mrs. Wilson, made a point of telling the class that I was the *only* person in the entire class who missed the gimme question on a multiple-choice test she gave. The question was "Who is Mrs. Wilson?" and one of the answers was a famous actress. I've never taken tests well, and instead of thinking of the obvious my mind flashed to a Folgers commercial of the time in which some lady named Mrs. *Olsen* pronounced in a Swedish accent or maybe Swiss or Liechtensteinian, "Folgers . . . it's the richest kind!" I must have panicked, and I simultaneously forgot my teacher's name and transformed

Mrs. Olsen into Mrs. Wilson, figuring my teacher, what's-her-name, wanted us to know our TV commercials.

But I wouldn't consider the incident a biggie, just as I'm sure the kid who wrote *religion* when he obviously meant *region,* and *dessert* when he meant *desert* probably won't suffer night terrors because of it. You might as well learn to tough out your Charlie Brown moments early and get on with it. But there are certain kids, like Perry, who turn ridicule around the way Gandhi met violence with passive resistance.

When Ms. Monroe asks us why nomads move around, Perry raises his hand urgently.

"Because they're mapping," he says.

"Wrong!" she says, barely registering his answer, and calls on someone else. If I could, I'd send Perry off to Camp Echo to learn some Echo Values or demote him to kindergarten to learn the I-Care Rules. Here in sixth grade, there are also worthy suggestions for behavior. They're on the hall walls. "Honesty is the Right answer." "It takes a world of Difference to make a Difference in the world." They're nice thoughts, but the older we get, the more they blend in and become simply another kind of wallpaper.

⌒

We're learning the recorder in music class. The recorder, an instrument that was invented in the Middle Ages solely to be played badly by ten- and eleven-year-olds. During the Children's Crusade, hordes of ten- and eleven-year-old boys, some younger, most bearing only recorders, were hurled en masse against the Saracen infidels, who panicked and abandoned their positions to the strains of something resembling the song "Greensleeves."

This is all to say that we were "learning" the recorder in my elementary school, and we're still learning it forty years later. And with just as much aplomb and skill as the kindergartners banged on their drums: *Bring out your dead! Bring out your dead!*

I stand next to a circle of girls and try to follow their movements with my fingers. When people want to say something sounds bad, they often resort to the formula: "It sounded like a [blank] in pain." Alternately, it's "in heat." But my recorder does not sound like an animal in pain or in heat. More like an impatient animal at an intersection telling another animal to hurry up and move. A kind of hoot/squeak.

My teacher, a cheerful young woman who studied music in Africa, chides me. "Don't get bummed out! Keep a positive attitude."

Okay, then. So I blow full tilt on my recorder — a composition I call "Road Rage in the Game Park" (it's supposed to be "Twinkle, Twinkle, Little Star"), and the girls next to me shrink away and stop playing as they consider the fury of my recorder.

"You've done such an awesome job on the recorder," the teacher tells me and moves me hurriedly to the xylophone.

The class discusses songs we can sing. We can sing "Frosty the Snowman" but not "Rudolph" because it mentions Christmas.

"What if we were all Christians?" the boy who suggested "Rudolph" asks.

"But we're not," says the teacher.

This ultra-awareness of difference has changed since my day, and I have mixed feelings about it. Singing "Rudolph" does not really make me want to become Christian, although maybe I should reconsider. Would you believe that hundreds of thousands of atheists and agnostics alike have turned to Jesus after hearing the song "Rudolph"? And would you believe that "Santa Claus Is Coming to Town," when played over a department store loudspeaker in Tel Aviv in 1997, was responsible for the instantaneous mass conversion to Christianity of seven hundred Jewish shoppers? The words "Gonna find out who's naughty and nice" are what did it. And would you believe that "The Little Drummer Boy," if played in its eight-hundred-and-seventy-three verse entirety, actually has the opposite effect and is the *largest single factor* in the recent mass exodus from the Catholic Church?! Would you believe it's the pope's favorite song?

Good. Neither would I.

I sang in a church choir briefly, before we moved from Athens, Ohio, and the songs we sang neither made me believe or disbelieve. Like Bret with his harmonica, I merely wanted to make nice sounds. *Rum pum pum pum.*

On the other hand, as the only Jewish kid in my first sixth-grade class, I was frequently singled out. Slippery Rock was a small coal-mining town with a state teachers college where freshmen all had to wear beanies that looked like yarmulkes (for one blissful moment, I thought I'd landed in the only Jewish coal-mining town in the world). But the town was decidedly not as tolerant a place in 1969 as Athens was. One of my classmates told me he could no longer play with me because his mother told him I was a Christ killer. This news surprised me as I had no memory of killing Christ.

"I did not," I said. "You did." I wasn't sure he had killed Christ either, but even at eleven I knew that people often blamed others for the things they were most guilty of.

The school play that year was *The Grinch Who Stole Christmas*, but a grimmer and more puritanical version that had some kind of fallen elf, played by me, aka Christ Killer Boy, kidnapping Santa so that Christmas wouldn't take place. I was too dim-witted to realize that this public performance was the town of Slippery Rock metaphorically stoning me and my family, but my mother wasn't. She sat horrified in the audience as I minced around in my green tights and my devil horns, shouting, "You tink you can outschmart me? Vell, ve'll see who gets to outschmart who, Mr. Ho Ho Ho!" Within days of the curtain closing on the play, my mother had made arrangements for me to live with my grandmother for the rest of the year in Hollywood, Florida.

↶

I can tell you this definitively: sixth grade is a lot harder than kindergarten. There's still recess to look forward to, but by day two I'm already sinking fast. I've forgotten to do my math homework, and I'm in a bit of a panic. Not all my homework, but I forgot to do a few of the questions on probability. I'm torn between finishing my homework and figuring out the probability that I'll walk home rather than get picked up by Margie after school. We had a spat this morning because I didn't want to be late to school, and I thought she was dawdling. I don't like to be late, and she doesn't like to be rushed, so when she let me off at the corner where all the other kids were being let off by their guardians and parents, not spouses, she said, "You walk home."

"Fine, I will," I said and got out of the car without looking back.

Just like the five-year-old me. *Fine. I'll run away.* I act my age 70 to 80 percent of the time when I'm in public, but when I'm at home, the percentage plummets. When my mother was alive, we'd repeat conversations we'd been having since I was ten.

"Will you mail this letter for me? Make sure to put it in the out-of-town slot."

"Mom, I'm twenty-five. I think I can distinguish out-of-town from local."

"Will you get me a newspaper from the machine? You know how to operate it, don't you?"

"Mom, I'm thirty-one. I still remember how to put a quarter in a slot."

"I'm just checking."

When I was twenty, my mother sent a complete stranger into a public restroom to "just check" that I was all right.

"Your mom is worried about you," the complete stranger said from the other side of the bathroom stall. I contemplated never coming out.

Margie claims I act the same way toward Olivia and Isabel, waiting for them outside of airport restrooms. When she catches me, I deny it.

"I wasn't worried. I just wanted to make sure they knew where we're sitting!"

But I guess we all infantilize others and ourselves. We grow physically, but who we are inside has no fixed age.

"Think about it," as Mr. Pirelli says while talking about probability. "The past predicts the future."

In the case of rushing to finish my math homework, this is an indisputable fact.

"Is it equally likely that the Steelers will win, tie, or lose on any given day?" he asks us.

One boy says it's equally likely.

"Well, the Steelers suck this year," says Mr. Pirelli. "But not always. Maybe another year. Remember. The past predicts the future. Okay, now let's supply our own likelihoods."

"I like gummy bears!" Perry shouts.

"Explain yourself," says Mr. Pirelli evenly.

"The red ones," Perry says. "Not green . . . so much."

Mr. Pirelli shakes his head, dislodging Perry from it, and passes out marshmallows for us to flip.

"I would highly recommend not eating them," Mr. P says. "I changed diapers this morning. And I pet my dog." He makes sure to touch each one of the marshmallows, but Perry challenges him.

"I can wash it off."

While the rest of us flip our marshmallows and record how many times they land on their sides and tops, Perry rolls his on the table until it looks like an off-white slug.

"Hey, Perry licked his marshmallow," Amanda reports.

Perry is unrelentingly gross. It becomes even clearer to me today that he's the kid I've come to meet in battle, that he's the sixth-grade nemesis I need to overcome. Somehow, I've got to best him, not care about him, move past him, but I can't seem to find a way to do it.

If Perry had a bad case of Monday yesterday, he's delirious today with a systemic case of Tuesday. After math class, Perry pauses at the door and squares off with one of the other boys. "Doug is a bug! And he's a geek. Oh yeah!" When we gather in our *Tuck Everlasting* group, Ms. Monroe notices that Perry doesn't have his book. She asks him where it is.

"It's in my backpack," he says dully, not looking at her.

"You need to bring it to reading every day."

"I read it."

She repeats herself, and he trudges away to reappear minutes later, still with no book in sight. Meanwhile, Ms. Monroe instructs us on discussing the book on our own as a group. Andrew is the Literary Luminary for today, the Big Cheese of the discussion group. He's prepared questions about various passages in the book he'd like for us to take a second look at. A girl named Jenny is Investigator. Jenny is one of the class stars, a quiet, tall girl who seems equally capable in every subject. She's researched the life of the author. Doug is the Connector. He looks for themes and ideas and characters that are connected. And Perry is the Illustrator. He's illustrated a scene from the book, and we're supposed to guess what it is. As he takes his place again, Ms. Monroe turns to Doug.

"Make sure he doesn't talk about his picture."

As soon as she leaves us, Perry shows us his illustration. "It's Tuck in his bed," he says.

The others groan. "I bet it's Tuck in his bed," Jenny says.

Throughout the rest of the discussion, Perry keeps burping, loud and smelly burps.

"That's totally disgusting," Jenny says.

Doug (the Bug) fans himself. "That smells horrible."

"I brush my teeth," Perry says.

Today I don't have to worry about him, but tomorrow I have to be the Literary Luminary, so I'll have to keep an eye on my foe, Perry the Noxious. Later in the day, there's a lull as the students perform an experiment with battery cells and magnets. Ms. Monroe and I chat, not about Perry, but about what it means to sit in a classroom all day as a sixth grader. She tells me that there are kids in this classroom for whom sitting here all day is "abusive."

"Is the goal of teaching to widen or narrow the gap between the fast learners and the slow learners?" she asks me.

I sense my eyes bulging because I know the answer isn't pretty. And I know the answer has something to do with me.

The answer is to widen the gap, which she says widens by two-thirds times the age of the child. So the gap widens each year. If you try to teach the other way around, the fast learners are bored, and no one gets very far. This, I'm thinking, is the educational system in America in the twenty-first century. It might be a battlefield, but the approach is the opposite of a triage unit (sorry, that ugly word). Instead of treating those who need the most help, you treat the healthy ones and let the wounded die. As I'm pondering this, she points out the different types of learners in the class. A huddle of fifth- and sixth-grade girls stand around her desk, measuring wire and cutting it for the next experiment.

"Those are the helpful ones," she says. "The future teachers of America."

Of a boy named Samuel she says, "He's got a lopsided brain like mine. Verbal but can't do a multiplication table. And Doug over there has a laser brain. Give him a math problem, and he can do it. And then there's one child here who *lives* for the time during the day when he's pulled out of the classroom and taken to a rudimentary program that actually teaches him at his own level. The rest of the day he's lost."

I suppose I was most like Samuel and Ms. Monroe, someone with a lopsided brain. After the sixth grade, I never really understood math again, and the gap widened and widened, like two trains traveling at different speeds between St. Louis and Chicago. Like the age of eleven times two-thirds of forty-eight.

↶

Margie, with Shoshie in tow, waits for me in our car in the lineup of cars at the end of the day, as orange school buses stream from the parking lot and children burst from captivity out the front doors. "I thought you weren't going to pick me up," I tell Margie as I get in. She doesn't say anything, but gives me a sideways glance that shouts quite clearly, Grow up.

Well, okay, I'm trying, really I am. But the next morning I walk to school, not because I'm still pouting but because it's a clear, frigid day in the single digits, and I want the exercise, and the cold air clears my head. I arrive in time to see parents dropping off their kids or walking them to the door. Then the bells ring again, and the doors are locked, and for the rest of the day the land of children sees no visitors except for me.

Today is a day of minor defeats. First, Ms. Monroe catches me doing my math homework during reading, and, if this isn't embarrassing enough, I misspell three words on our spelling quiz. Okay, they're plurals, and I *do* know how to spell the plural of *volcano*. I *know* the plural has an *e* in it. Look, I even won our sixth-grade spelling bee in my school in Hollywood, Florida, but for some reason, my brain fritzes and I resist the urge to look over Amanda's shoulder. We have to mark our own quizzes, and when Ms. Monroe comes by, I hand her my quiz with the three words that I got wrong circled, no other comment.

She smiles and puts a fist in the air. "Yes!" she says, pulling her fist down.

Well! If my parents were alive, I'd certainly have them say something to her about this during the next parent-teacher conference. But as it stands, I have to sit quietly and take my lumps.

"The usual male problem," she says. "I can't read your handwriting."

At recess I get into trouble too. I join a bunch of fifth and sixth graders who have no interest in the football game the sixth graders have going in another part of the playground; we're playing Zombie. Zombie is my kind of game, though the rules are voluminous. There's the one Kid Who Explains All the Rules. He's a type, you know. In grade school and junior high, he was my best friend. Verbal, ironic, big but not pudgy. His name was Glenn when I knew him. His name is Marcus at Longfellow. He's also my daughter Olivia. The Kid Who Explains All the Rules is not actually interested in playing the games he explains because by the time he has finished explaining all the rules, recess is almost over. In Zombie, the rules mostly involve how you become undead and how you can become human again.

Despite the rules, Zombie is mostly chaos. We run and shoot each other with highly inventive weapons. Bret has his nice-sounding harmonica, which doubles as a zombie shooter. I'm armed with a nuclear-tipped slingshot (it's the only thing that's even slightly effective against Zombie hordes, as it turns out). As Bret and I face down the Zombies massed around us, arms extended, a personage more fearsome than anyone undead lumbers over, waving her arms: the dreaded Playground Lady.

"No pretend weapons! No pretend weapons!" she shouts.

Oh. I guess that makes sense. I slowly put down my pretend slingshot. Unlike Herb at Camp Echo, she doesn't make us put our hands on our heads.

So we decide on hide-and-seek and listen to Marcus explain the rules of a highly evolved game of hide-and-seek that somehow includes a time-warp component.

Sounds like a lot of fun (I've always been a sucker for time warps) but, sadly, as Marcus is explaining how we time warp during hide-and-seek (my mind flashes to *The Rocky Horror Picture Show,* but I'm sure that's not what he has in mind), the bell rings, and it's time for art.

In art class, we're doing calligraphy, creating our own alphabet fonts. I'm at a table with Perry, Amanda, Amanda's sidekick, Sandy, the studious Jenny, and Marcus. Sandy's alphabet is smile based. Jenny has eyes all over her alphabet. Perry has settled on snakes. As the teacher hands me some paper, she looks me in the eye and says in a voice that is definitely not friendly, "I'm going to have a hard time taking this seriously."

I don't know what it is about art teachers. I'm always having run-ins with them about imagination and creativity (of all things). In art class at Putnam, I once made a time machine out of a big box to which I affixed Styrofoam knobs. My art teacher, the same one who wouldn't let me be a paleontologist until she looked the word up, insisted that my time machine wouldn't work.

Still, under the illusion that this was indeed art class as I had been led to believe and not *I'm Just Waiting to Retire* class, I insisted the machine *would* work, and though I knew in my heart that both I and my feeble cardboard box were doomed, I decided to send Ann Holmes back in time. Perhaps, in a fit of magical thinking, I hoped that the universe would take pity on me and do the impossible, as a gesture of sympathy. Ann stepped inside, I turned some knobs, one of which broke off in my hand, and announced, "I have done it! I have sent Ann back in time. Voilà! She is gone."

"No I'm not," she said from inside the box. "I'm still here."

That day, the teacher verbally swept the construction paper–covered art room floor with me.

Although today's art teacher hasn't said as much, she's said enough to completely undo me. I'm not sure why she has to be such a killjoy, but I'm also surprised that so far, she's the *only* adult I've encountered with this attitude. Everyone else seems to get it. And that in itself seems a minor miracle.

I try to shrug it off and settle down to creating my alphabet. A number of my classmates finished their alphabets last week and now are moving on to "marbling" them.

"I'm going to call one group at a time over to look at my marbling," the art teacher says. "Just don't touch anything."

I decide to pattern my alphabet after palm trees. Each letter will have some part of a palm leafing from it.

When I reach the letter *D*, Perry stops his own lettering and bends over the table to look at mine. I brace myself.

"That's pretty cool," he says.

The rest of my group looks at my alphabet, and they all agree. My art class triumph. Not impressing my teacher but my classmates.

Jenny and the rest of us start giggling because she's putting eyes everywhere.

"Ooh! That's wrong," she says. "Quick. Give me an eraser."

Halfway through the period, the art teacher comes over to me, and we start chatting about my project, not my palm tree alphabet, but my do-overs. Actually, I don't have a problem with this, even though she's blowing my sixth-grade cover for the moment. I guess I've made her curious, and, to be fair, what I'm doing *is* pretty odd when I think about it. I don't blame the art teacher for feeling a tad uncomfortable. Perhaps I've misjudged her. Soon we're chatting like old friends, and she tells me about her sixth-grade teacher, a woman who wore one black glove and banged a ruler with it. A terrifying figure. "She made me cry every day," she tells me. On the other hand, Mrs. Norman, her kindergarten teacher, used to give Pez candy to the kids.

"She was great," she says, and I believe her, feeling as though I've made a convert, though I'm not sure exactly to what.

↶

I know I'm not really a sixth grader, and my classmates know this too. But we forget sometimes, and it's good to forget. Sometimes I'm an observer. Sometimes I'm a participant. Sometimes I'm an oddity. But most of the time, I seem to fit in somehow, and these are the moments I relish, even when I'm playing the fool or basking in the imaginative worlds of childhood.

One day I pair with Bret, who is a fifth grader in this mixed fifth- and sixth-grade class, and we both read to a first grader.

"What's your favorite animal?" Bret suddenly asks the boy, apropos of nothing.

"Mouse that goes eek when you press its tummy," the boy says.

Bret nods and frowns as though he's a pundit posing tough questions to a political candidate. Now that the boy has been freed from his book by this interruption, he starts talking to Bret about marshmallows bursting into flames and then segues into a tale about his brother who pointed a disintegrator ray at a fence and burned the fence down.

"I didn't know they called them disintegrator rays anymore," Bret says. "I thought they call them flamethrowers nowadays."

Bret turns to me. "I had a flamethrower, and it was a lot like he described it but not so small. The size of a rifle."

I suppose if I were my old art teacher, I might challenge Bret and call him and the little boy liars. If I were the Playground Lady, I'd tell them they cannot talk or even think about disintegrator rays or flamethrowers or rifles. I would tell them that they cannot push on mouse's tummy and make it go eek because that's cruel. I would pile rule upon rule on them until they understood that the world is made of cement, not air and water.

Bret hasn't learned that yet. Perhaps Perry has, and that's what makes him such a young cynic. But Bret's world is still full of miracles. One day at lunch, he tells me that plants have many more feelings "than previously known."

"One plant died of spite for its owner who said it was ugly," he tells me. "It was watered every day, but it still died of thirst. They hooked up a lie detector to a tree and said they would cut it down. The needle went wild."

Then he tells me about "The Miracle of the Cherry Tree." The tree was planted many years ago by the former owners of his family's house. It never gave fruit in all its years, but this year it gave three cherries.

"It's a miracle," he concludes, and who am I to argue with him, to tell him of the laws of probability, which, anyway, he'll learn next year as a sixth grader from Mr. P?

⟳

Despite minor setbacks, I consider my second Assault of Sixth Grade a qualified success. Although I don't *have* to turn in my homework, I manage somehow always to finish it, though sometimes at the last minute, and sometimes when I should be doing something else. By the end of the week, I'm even getting stars on my math homework. I redeem myself in spelling too. Bret and I go over our misspelled words together, and on my second quiz, I ace them. Alas, music is a wash. If my recorder were not a loaner, I'd take it out to a crossroads at midnight and bury it, the way they used to do with witches, so it would never find its way back to me again.

Although Amanda was aloof when we met, by the end of the week we're buddies. As she and Sandy are preparing the results of their battery-and-paper-clip science experiment for the class, she erases her name and Sandy's on the transparency sheet for the overhead projector and writes, "Sandy, Robin, and Amanda." And she trusts me enough to share the results with the class when one day she and Sandy must leave class early. She hands me the transparency sheet as though I'm about to go off on a deadly mission — which I am, since I haven't a clue what their results mean and am terrified of presenting "our" results on the overhead projector in front of the class.

"You're going to have to go up for us, Robin," she tells me. "We have Safety Patrol."

Happily, class is over before I have to humiliate myself.

I still don't like PE, but I hold my own running laps and dribbling a basketball. During indoor recess, I learn how to time warp in the game Clue, as modified by my new best friend Marcus. Every game should have a time-warp factor.

During reading time on my last day, I sit at my desk surreptitiously doing my math homework as Perry sits nearby on the floor, firing spitballs at Marcus while questioning him on what he knows about Jerry Lee Lewis. It's not a random question. Jerry Lee Lewis is the subject of the biographical report he's supposed to write for Ms. Monroe, and firing spitballs while quizzing Marcus is his form of primary research.

"Have you heard his song 'Great Balls of Fire'?" he asks Marcus.

"No," Marcus says, swatting his cheek where a spitball has stuck.

"I have," I say, wanting to take the heat off Marcus for a moment so he can concentrate on his own report.

"Do you know he married his cousin?" Perry asks me.

"Yeah, she was thirteen," I say.

"I know," he says. "Why did he do that?"

I want to say because he was weird, but instead I tell him I don't know.

"It's pretty weird," Perry says.

"Yeah. It was a long time ago."

"I know. 'Great Balls of Fire' was his best song."

"Do you know any of his other songs?"

"No," he says. "Can you help me with my paper?" He gets off the floor and pulls up a chair beside my desk, and I put away my homework. Perry goes to his desk and brings over a couple of books on rock and roll.

"Anything strike you as interesting here?" I say, asking him to read one of the passages on Lewis.

"In 1976 he shot his bassist in the chest," he reads.

"Not everyone shoots their bassist in the chest," I say. "That's pretty interesting."

"Yeah," he says. "He got in a lot of trouble."

"Why don't you write about that?" I say. "Why don't you write a paragraph about getting in trouble?" Perry knows a lot about trouble and so do I. Maybe we're more alike than I thought.

He goes off to his desk, and a minute later I see him writing intently in his notebook.

Doug approaches me then and asks, "If you could live forever at a certain age, would you?" He's Investigating, pencil poised.

"No," I say without hesitation, and once again take out my math homework, keeping my head low and glancing now and then in the teacher's direction to make sure she's not looking my way.

CHAPTER FIVE

FRAT BOY

Sigma Alpha Mu Do-Over

ORIGINAL AGES: 11, 14
DO-OVER AGE: 48
ORIGINAL LOCATIONS: ATHENS, OHIO; COLUMBIA, MISSOURI
DO-OVER LOCATION: BUENOS AIRES, ARGENTINA

When I was eleven in Athens, Ohio, I saw a group of college students standing on a corner of Court Street downtown, armed with a bullhorn, approaching stopped cars and pedestrians with cups for collecting money. At first I thought they were war protesters, but, if so, this seemed like an unusually quiet war protest. Where were the riot police and the tear gas canisters? If it had been a war protest, I would have kept my distance, as instructed by my mom. A couple of weeks earlier, John Kortlander's dad had been gassed as a bystander at one of the protests. And a girl's eye had been knocked out by a rubber bullet. Normally, Athens seemed like a safe enough place when I was a kid, but when I saw loudspeakers and students gathered, I knew this wasn't a good sign. These students had shorter hair than most of the protesters, and, odder still, they had constructed a small stage near the Civil War monument, and on the stage a young man repeatedly bounced a basketball while sitting in a chair below a banner that read: BOUNCE FOR BEATS!

Sufficiently curious, I jaywalked over to the stage and asked a pimply boy with black curly hair what was going on.

"We're raising money for the American Heart Association." The boy explained that they all belonged to a fraternity, Sigma Alpha Mu, or the Sammies as they were known, and that part of being in the fraternity involved community service. The fraternity had chosen the American Heart Association as the charity it wanted to raise money for, and they were doing it by trying to set a new world record for *The Guinness Book* by bouncing a basketball. "Bounce for beats. Get it?" he said.

I got it. Activism. Community Service. The Greater Good. All of those things made sense to me. In my own small way, I wanted to be involved. I wanted to be a part of something larger than me. "My father died of a heart attack when I was seven," I announced somberly and hung my head. It's not that I didn't feel bad that my father had died of a heart attack when I was seven, but saying "My father died of a heart attack when I was seven" was a kind of invocation, a shtick. The words hardly had meaning for me anymore, though they had a profound effect on a lot of grown-ups. Saying them was like turning into a superhero.

Look, walking down Court Street, it's . . . My Father Died of a Heart Attack When I Was Seven Boy.

How can he act so happy?

He must be really brave.

I wonder how he'll get by in life without a dad.

That's some special kid!

"Wow, really?" said the pimply boy now. "Oh, I'm sorry." And his expression was one of wonder, as though I had just caught a bullet between my teeth and spat it out.

When I was My Father Died of a Heart Attack When I Was Seven Boy, I could get almost anything I wanted. It was worth toys, candy, gum, ice cream sodas, banana splits, amusement park rides, and lots and lots of sympathy. Everybody loved this guy!

"Can I help you collect money?" I said. I told him that I was an expert UNICEF collector, though I skipped the part about skimming money for candy bars. Anyway, I was beyond all that now. I really *did* want to help out. My father *had* died of a heart attack, and what better way to honor him than to collect money for the American Heart Association.

I always enjoyed being part of the excitement, and this seemed exciting to me, watching someone bounce his way into *The Guinness Book of World Records,* while a group of young men and women milled around the streets asking for donations, and one of the Sammies exhorted passersby to give some change for the cause. He brought me up on stage too, and he gave me the microphone, and I told Athens about how people shouldn't smoke and how they should think about their kids before they light up another cigarette. I was pretty effective, really. People practically threw money at me and seemed more interested in me than the poor guy with blackened hands ceaselessly bouncing a basketball on stage. I stayed with the Sammies collecting money until I had to go home that night, then returned early the next morning and stayed for the entire day with hardly a break. The guy bouncing the ball didn't break the record. Somewhere in the middle of the night, he lost his concentration and the basketball caught a bad bounce and shot off the stage and into the street. But I collected more money than any of them and didn't skim a penny. When the fund-raising was over, the Sammies told me they wanted to show their appreciation by taking me out for a dinner.

They told me they were going to take me to the best restaurant in town. There *were* no good restaurants in town, so Pizza Hut would have to do. Even so. A large sausage pizza sounded fine, and on the appointed evening my mom dressed me in a coat and tie, and I waited by our picture window for the Sammies to pick me up. I had never felt that honored before in my life. A whole fraternity thought enough of me that they were going to take me out to dinner. My mother took a picture of me in my suit, and I waited for the Sammies to show. After half an hour she took another picture, but I had a hard time smiling. I waited another half an hour and then another, until it became obvious to my mother that no one was picking me up. Had they mistaken the time, the night? Had some important fraternal emergency arisen? I never found out. They never called me. That night I was demoted from superhero to just another stupid kid who believes grown-ups when they make promises. I had always been taught to keep my promises, and mostly I did. It had to be some mistake. I just couldn't imagine that a group of nice guys who would spend their weekend collecting money for the American Heart Association would want to disappoint a cute eleven-year-old kid like me.

"I could take you to Pizza Hut," my mother offered.

"I'm not hungry," I told her and took off my tie. "I think I'll just go to bed."

"Maybe they got mixed up," my mother said.

"Maybe," I said, and I went to my room and closed the door. "There aren't many eleven-year-olds who can do what you just did," the boy who had tried to bounce the basketball for the world record told me, and that's what I heard him saying as I closed my eyes and slept and grew a little bit older.

↶

The next time I encountered the Sammies was three years later, when we had moved to Columbia, Missouri, where my mother was teaching at Stephens College. One spring day, I was walking downtown when I saw a familiar banner: BOUNCE FOR BEATS!

Maybe a more cynical kid would have paid attention to the old saw "Once bitten, twice shy," but I felt a surge of excitement when I saw the banner and ran up to the stage as though seeing a group of long-lost friends. If anything my initial experience with the Sammies had made me more of an activist. After moving to Columbia, I started an environmental group for kids. We met every Saturday in a room of a drug rehab center. This was the Age of Acronyms. Not only did my little group have the cute acronym of SPEC, standing for the more grandiose title Society for the Prevention of Environmental Corruption, but I had attracted the attention of a national youth group named YARA (Young Americans for Responsible Action) and had been invited to go to Washington, DC, to lobby for environmental legislation that summer. I went and had an office in the National Press Building. That summer was the opposite of my do-over project. Instead of being an adult among children, I was a child among adults, and plastered with George McGovern buttons I rode the elevator every day in the National Press Building.

But my second encounter with the Sammies happened several months before my stint with YARA in DC. Once again the Sammies were going for a world record, and once again the Sammies let me collect money. This time I became almost a mascot for them, and I made friends with most of the members of the chapter. I worked night and day collecting money but wasn't so selfless as to forgo mentioning how the Sammy chapter in Athens had let me down three years before. This time I wanted my fancy dinner. I didn't actually ask them to treat me to dinner, but I dropped plenty of hints in my pathetic guise as My Father Died of a Heart Attack When I Was Seven Boy.

The boy now going for the record was Terry Dietz. I remember his name still because it rhymes with Bounce for Beats! I don't remember if he actually broke the record, but everyone involved, including me, had their photo in the paper after the event, and I felt fulfilled and semifamous. This time the Sammies took me out to dinner at a real restaurant, and they told me to order anything from the menu I wanted, so, of course, I ordered the epitome of haute cuisine in 1960s and 1970s America, "surf 'n' turf"— a beef fillet and a lobster tail.

After dinner, they told me they had a surprise for me. One of them went out to the parking lot and returned a few minutes later with a certificate proclaiming me an honorary member of Sigma Alpha Mu. They also gave me my own fraternity pin and taught me the secret handshake.

"When you go to college, show this certificate to the local chapter," Terry said, "and they'll make you a full-fledged Sammy."

At that moment, I could think of nothing cooler than being a frat boy. I was certainly the only frat boy at Jefferson Junior High, and I wasted no time in telling everyone in school that I was a Sammy. Most didn't care except for my best friend, Glenn, my version of the Kid Who Explains All the Rules. He was speechless for once and wanted to know how he could become a frat boy too.

"I guess you'll have to wait until college," I told him smugly.

The only other person who cared was Susan Fitzpatrick, my girlfriend of two weeks, whom I pinned. She gratefully accepted my Sigma Alpha Mu pin and then lost it the next day. A serious bump in our relationship and perhaps in part responsible for our eventual dissolution as a couple.

For the rest of my time in Columbia, I hung around with the Sammies whenever I had the chance. They were all nice guys — one of them, a boy named Mark, used to drive me around on his motorcycle on weekends. Now, few parents would allow their children to ride unsupervised with an adult male for entire days, but we didn't know about background checks back then, and even though my mom was homophobic, she trusted the Sammies, and they were, indeed, all trustworthy as far as I was concerned.

By the time I started attending college in 1976, becoming a frat boy was no longer a goal of mine. I was trying out a new role as Studious Young Man, Poet Extraordinaire, and Japanese Scholar, and this role didn't seem to mesh with fraternity life. I was also a resident of the *one* dorm at Indiana University most like a fraternity: Dodds House, filled with the biggest assortment of fraternity wannabes that you could collect under one roof. They were proudest of the fact that they were the only group of non-Greeks that had ever won the Little 500, the annual bicycle race made famous by the late 1970s film *Breaking Away*. Half of them flunked out their first semester playing euchre and smoking their bongs instead of studying. For some reason, they liked me, but they hated my roommate, Dan, and in an attempt to flush him from the dorm put toothpaste in our lock, set fire to our door, and taunted him in the halls. If this was fraternity life, I wanted no part of it.

After my first year in Dodds House, I transferred to an apartment in town, and I waited until my junior year before curiosity led me to make a tentative call to the Sigma Alpha Mu chapter on campus.

I explained my story to the boy on the other end of the phone in the same excruciating detail as I later explained my desire to be in *The Littlest Angel* to the playhouse in Brevard, North Carolina, thirty years later. "Hi, my name is Robin Hemley. I was born in New York, and my father died when I was seven. I'm Jewish, and I study Japanese and write poetry . . ." And so on.

The boy listened patiently and didn't hang up on me. They were a small fraternity as fraternities go and probably desperate for members.

"Why don't you come over for dinner on Saturday night?" he said.

I showed up on Saturday evening — there were only about ten boys, and they were having spaghetti on dirty dishes. Someone threw me an Old Style beer and told me to sit down at the table. "So, tell us how you heard about the Sammies," one of them said to me.

I told the story again. I had long since passed the cute stage and couldn't pass anymore as some selfless kid, the mascot of Sigma Alpha Mu.

"I've never heard of an honorary member," the head of the chapter told me. "You mind if I show the certificate to our national headquarters?"

"I guess not," I said. There was a knock then, and eight women entered the front door and came into the dining room. They were all dressed as Native Americans — four riding piggyback on the other four.

"We throw heap um big party!" said one of the girls, a blonde with a perm and a bow and arrow. "We send smoke signal to Sammies, but it no work um, so we travel many moons to invite um to harvest moon dance."

The four maidens descended then from their mounts and withdrew from their satchels ears of Indian corn to which they had tied invitations. They made their way around the table and bestowed an ear of corn on each of the boys, except, of course, me.

That was fine. Something about this display confirmed my worst suspicions about fraternity life. At best, it was in bad taste, and fledgling poets like myself abhorred displays of bad taste. After the Indian maidens departed, so did I. I thanked the Sammies for the spaghetti and left my certificate with them.

That was the last I saw of my certificate and the Sammies for the next thirty years.

I suppose there are a lot of things I left behind in my youth that are more valuable than that certificate, practically speaking. My comic collection, for instance — from time to time, I mourn the fact that I sold it at the Chicago Comic Convention when I was nineteen. Today it would be worth a couple hundred thousand dollars. Or the paintings I inherited from my grandmother, lost in the move when I left Iowa City after graduate school. But there is something especially symbolic for me in the loss of my honorary Sigma Alpha Mu membership. This wasn't simply a matter of belonging to a fraternity but also about my youthful idealism and activism. The years since college have seen me become a little more of a cynic, a little more unsure of my ability to make a difference in the world with my actions. All the Scarecrow needed was a diploma to give him the piece of himself that was missing. I thought all I needed was a piece of paper too.

Unfortunately, there isn't a Sigma Alpha Mu chapter on the University of Iowa campus where I work — not since 2004 when the struggling little chapter there died. A colleague of mine, who teaches composition, remembered having its beleaguered president in one of her classes, a kid with the most insistent smile, a stateless king who seemed completely incapable of accepting his fate. The Sammies aren't the only Jewish fraternity, and the other Greek organization for Jewish men on campus, Alpha Epsilon Pi, had simply outmaneuvered the poor Sammies. This sad tale of their dissolved chapter just made me like the Sammies more. But how was I going to earn back my honorary membership?

I suppose I could find another chapter, even drive several hours south to Columbia, Missouri, to see if the chapter there was thriving. Another option was to check the Internet. Here, I found that the national organization was active. At least they had a Web site, and community service still seemed to be at the heart of their mission. Apparently, the Sammies' idea of community service had changed a bit over the years — I didn't see "Bounce for Beats" listed but, instead, a medical mission to Havana, Cuba, open to Sigma Alpha Mu members, alums, and their families. Mojitos and Romeo Y Julieta cigars! Xavier Cugat, Ricky Ricardo, and conga lines! A new Che Guevara T-shirt! In middle age, this seemed like the perfect brand of community service for me.

I wrote to Roger King, the executive director of Sigma Alpha Mu, explaining my project, and I followed up with a phone call — actually a series of phone calls. It took about a month of calls and letters before I could get hold of Roger, who was constantly on the road. What did fraternity presidents do on the road? I wondered. Make surprise keg inspections? Check the taps of individual chapters to see they if they met fraternity regulations? Finally, I reached him, and he told me I'd have to clear the trip with one of the national board members, David Goldfarb, who was in charge of the trip — to Argentina, not Cuba. That had been last year's trip. They'd had a great time, he told me, and had delivered some much-needed medical supplies to the Jewish community in Havana. I didn't know much about Argentina, but I wondered if the Jews of Buenos Aires really needed charity. Maybe they did, but Buenos Aires just seemed like such a glamorous destination. Havana had its own allure, of course, but it was easier for me to imagine the humanitarian angle of a trip to Havana. When I thought of Buenos Aires, I imagined tango and gauchos, Evita, and one of my favorite authors, Jorge Luis Borges. I wondered where the Sammies would visit next? Ibiza? The French Riviera? Maybe if I waited a year, the Sammies would go on a humanitarian mission to assist the beleaguered Jewish community of Monaco.

When I spoke to David Goldfarb, I told him my story and said that I wanted to earn back my honorary membership. Of course, I didn't expect any free rides. I'd pay my way just like a regular member — the trip, which would last ten days, wasn't cheap, and the fee included a donation to the Jewish community.

"I can't see any reasons you shouldn't come," he told me. "I don't have any objections, but Sigma Alpha Mu has never given an honorary membership in its hundred-year history. Some fraternities hand them out all the time to celebrities. We make a point of not doing that."

I didn't want to be argumentative. "You gave *one* honorary membership," I told him, though unfortunately I had no proof.

"We can't always control what our local chapters do," he said.

At least I could go on the trip, but this other information seemed like a major setback. Somehow I'd have to convince them that I was worthy of their making an exception to the rules. If I'd only kept that certificate, I could have shown it to them and appealed to them to honor it, but it was gone forever. In a way I felt they were standing me up for dinner again. I was unrealistically confident — I certainly wasn't cute anymore, but I still possessed some of my old superhero charm. I'd do good deeds in Buenos Aires, live by the Sammy creed, whatever that was, buy my own basketball, and become a kind of Sammy X-Man, a mutant, an Honorary Sammy of the variety that appears only once every hundred years.

⌐

Waiting at the gate to meet up with the Sammies before boarding our flight to Buenos Aires, I'm starting to feel self-conscious in my pinstripe suit. I probably look like the Heavenly Mobster, but I got talked into the suit by a tailor in Vancouver a couple of years ago. I should wear a suit to make a good impression, shouldn't I? On the other hand, it's really uncomfortable, and I *am* flying to another continent, and I *am* meeting former frat boys. It's a small group going — David and Roger, and several other alums and their spouses. It's too late to change now, so I sit at the gate and watch CNN while I'm waiting for the Sammies to show up.

Wolf Blitzer is interviewing David Duke, former Grand Wizard of the KKK and former state representative from Louisiana, concerning his attendance at a conference sponsored by the Iranian president, who today has announced, once again, that the Holocaust never happened. Holocaust deniers, in my view, are much like alcoholics. The more they deny, the more certainly they need treatment.

"I resent your characterization of me in your introduction," he tells Blitzer. "You referred to the KKK eleven times, and that was over thirty years ago." He goes on to accuse Blitzer of being a former communist and a Zionist and rails against "the Zionist media," claiming "we're in Iraq because Israel wants us to be there."

Blitzer fires back. "Last time I checked, the president wasn't Jewish. The vice president isn't Jewish. The Speaker of the House isn't Jewish. Are you saying they're all tools of the Zionist media?"

It strikes me that Duke and I share at least this much in common — we'd both like to move past things that happened thirty years ago. But there are some things that shouldn't have the option of a do-over. Membership in the KKK comes to mind, as does the Holocaust.

I'm saved from further depression via the Zionist media when David Goldfarb approaches me, and we forgo the secret Jewish head butt and booty grind in favor of a simple handshake. David, of course, is dressed sensibly in sweats and tennis shoes. Soon we're joined by other Sammies and their wives. There's Bert, a radiologist from Denver, and his wife, Janet, an architect. Bert and Janet, early fifties, are both fit and trim and have a friendly, assured demeanor. There's also Owen, a gynecologist from L.A., dressed in a Sigma Alpha Mu sweatshirt, and his wife, Harriet, both in their thirties, jovial and wisecracking from the start.

"A kid comes home and tells his mom he's got a role in the Jewish school play," Owen tells us, and says, "'I get to play the husband.'"

"'You go back,'" says the mom, "'and demand a speaking role.'"

The couples all know each other and were together on the Havana trip last year — they remark on how much weight David has lost.

"Forty pounds," he says proudly. "Weight Watchers."

All of them are so friendly — they treat me like a fellow Sammy. Unfortunately, it soon becomes apparent, when one of them asks me what chapter I belonged to, that they think I *am* a Sammy. No one mentioned to them what I'm doing here. So I tell each of the couples in turn. Happily, they all seem unfazed, except for Harriet, who seems astounded I'm forty-eight.

"I would have sworn you're in your early thirties," she says.

"Hey, you want to be an honorary Sammy. You have my vote," says Owen.

I like this couple.

"We don't have honorary members," David says.

Oh you, I'm thinking. *Always with the rules.* Just like kindergarten and summer camp.

"But why didn't you just go do 'Bounce for Beats' again?" Owen asks me.

"Chapters still do it?" I ask.

I don't get my answer because I'm introduced to Roger, the executive director. Roger is a big guy, probably the youngest in the group, and he seems to carry the weight of the organization on his shoulders — he's serious and soft-spoken and seems somehow more "official" than anyone else. The fact that he's a frat boy at heart is evidenced mainly by the Hawaiian shirts and straw hats he likes to wear. I'm also introduced to Phil, another wisecracker like Owen.

On the plane, I sit next to David, who tells me that for him, being on the board of Sigma Alpha Mu is a kind of do-over too. Twenty-some years ago, he was a regional governor for the Sammies, and one day he was supposed to pick up a board member at the airport, a supreme court justice from the state of Nebraska who insisted on being addressed as "Your Honor." David forgot all about it, and the judge was furious. Three months later, he received a letter from HQ telling him "your services are no longer needed." A couple of decades passed, and he received a call that they needed a regional governor again. Now he's treasurer of the fraternity.

As it turns out, "Bounce for Beats" is only one of several projects the Sammies have done. For a while, their partner charity was the American Heart Association, but now it's the Alzheimer's Foundation. Each chapter — there are sixty-five — is asked to do two service projects a year.

"Some chapters might still do 'Bounce for Beats,'" David tells me. "But not many."

Although I feel a little guilty going to Buenos Aires instead of standing on a street corner in the Midwest watching some schmuck bounce a basketball while I accost passersby for quarters, I still think I've made the only logical choice. At my age and weight, it's unlikely anyone is going to see me and think, "Oh, look at that darling man lumbering toward me like a Saint Bernard yelling 'bounce for beats!'" And no one would give me the time to explain what I was doing hanging around with a bunch of eighteen-year-olds: "Hi, my name is Robin Hemley, and I'm a divorced and remarried professor with three kids, two from my first marriage, one from my current marriage, and one in the oven." I think that's about as far as I'd get.

So, on that level, the do-over would be a failure. And even if the fraternity bought me surf and turf and made me an honorary member again, I'd know that Sigma Alpha Mu doesn't *give* honorary memberships. And what am I supposed to do with *that* information? No, the only hope I have of being granted an honorary membership, and a sliver at that, is to go on this junket, amid the officers of the national organization. Nothing less will do. The larger question remains, Why do I want it so much? It has something to do with a sense of belonging, tying myself back to my youth, certainly, but not only that. While it was coincidence perhaps that led me forty years ago to a street corner where I helped out a Jewish fraternity, the Jewish part of this isn't lost on me now. When David and I discussed the trip on the phone, he halted and stammered a bit. "You know, part of this involves going to synagogues . . ."

"I'm Jewish," I said, cutting him off. My name never gives me away.

"Oh, you are," he said. "Well, then." Yes, well, then.

The flight is easy, and in Buenos Aires, we're met at the airport by our guide, a small dark-haired Argentine woman named Sonya, who brings us to our hotel, the Plaza downtown. It's Gringo Central, a bustle of tourists with North American accents milling under chandeliers or sitting on antique furniture waiting for the rest of the group or asking the concierge the best place for a juicy steak or a tango show or gawking at high-priced leather on display behind glass and precious stones in the adjacent jewelry store. We've arrived in the early morning, and Sonya gives us some time to rest before taking us on a city tour, the highlight of which will be the March of the Mothers in the Plaza de Mayo, in which mothers of those who were "disappeared" by the military dictatorship in the early 1970s and 1980s remind the country of that dark period, known as the Dirty War.

At the appointed time, we're joined in the lobby by two more in our party who traveled on their own to Argentina: Bruce, a widower in his late sixties, and Rachel, also widowed. They're one of those wonderfully romantic stories, a couple who knew each other in college, who came together again only after their partners passed away. It's a do-over for them too, and the best kind, a rediscovery of their youth with someone who shared it.

We go first to La Boca, a traditional immigrant and artists' neighborhood on the waterfront, filled with colorful buildings and murals, but a place unsafe at night, Sonya tells us. It's clear that Sonya disapproves of the new immigrant population, Peruvians, at whom, whenever mention is made, she scowls. I am a "bleeding heart liberal," which in my case means that if a Peruvian attacked me, I would think of all the underlying social and political reasons he needed to rob me, and I would be thankful at least that he wasn't playing that god-awful flute that Peruvians keep inflicting on us in public. I don't know what it's called, but it's some version of the recorder and just as odious.

My views become even clearer when we visit a café where Bill Clinton once stopped for a coffee. Not only is there a photo of Clinton grinning amid the locals but a plaque commemorating the memorable coffee stop too.

As we're examining the photo, one of our number exclaims, "Figures he'd be here. It's where the babes are, the ladies of the night."

Oh my god. I'm among Republicans. This shouldn't surprise me, but it does. And not everyone is Republican, certainly, but some in the group are undoubtedly. They might all be Sammies. We might all be Jews. But that doesn't mean we're alike at all. Of course, this is the most obvious revelation in the world, but one that's easy to forget. Sometimes it feels good to be part of a group, sometimes not so good. Sometimes we get to self-identify as members of a fraternity. Sometimes others decide to which group we belong (Jews, for instance, or Tutsis or Gypsies), whether we want to be identified as part of the group or not. Sometimes the barrel of a gun pointed at our heads tells us to what group we belong.

I could forgive the remark about Bill Clinton, but then this same person disappears for half an hour and returns with snow globes. Since when do you go to Argentina to buy snow globes? That's what I think of when I think Argentina: tango, beef, snow globes. And I could even forgive the snow globes, but now we're going to be late for the March of the Mothers. And this *is* something I associate with Argentina, this group that has marched for justice for thirty years, this and the word *disappeared* that Argentina made into a transitive verb.

Today, though, perhaps it's not such a bad thing that we're a little late. When we arrive, we're greeted by a bit more mayhem than is typical of your average March of the Mothers. First of all, there's a cordon of riot police, never a good sign. Sonya quickly assesses the situation and tells us that the throng of people marching and chanting in the center of the plaza are not the usual marchers but a labor union that has decided to stage a protest. She can't vouch for the marchers, and she doesn't like their look or the police cordon, so she tells us to leave anything valuable in the van with the driver, including my Big Honking Camera — not her exact words. We park across the street and walk through the police line, through the raucous union march, to a less central part of the Plaza de Mayo. Here the old women are gathered with a small crowd of supporters. You can tell who the organizers are, not only because they're so old but also because they wear their determination, outrage, and grief in the form of white scarves with which they cover their heads.

In the days of the dictatorship, the mothers marched every day, but now they march only on Thursday afternoons for half an hour. Some of the marchers were disappeared like their sons and daughters, and one of them, Azucena Villaflor, whose remains were identified by a forensics team in 2005, was cremated and interred where the union members are marching so loudly today. For years, the mothers have marched in silence, and on any given Thursday you will find them still silent but not today.

Today an elderly man holds a bullhorn for a white-scarved old woman who addresses the crowd, but she hardly needs a bullhorn to be heard. She points her finger in the direction of the union marchers and scolds them like an angry mother to a thoughtless child. "They know this is our day," she tells us. "We are here every Thursday, and they have never once marched with us in solidarity."

Her anger will never be spent. I know it's directed at the marchers and not at the marchers. It's directed at history, at a homecoming that will never happen. As with most atrocities in the world, the killers have never been brought to justice — in fact, the president of Argentina during the 1990s, Carlos Menem, pardoned the worst of them. Thirty thousand people, mostly students, were disappeared, tortured, and murdered. Jews made up only 3 percent of the overall population but represented 15 percent of the disappeared.

This wasn't the only time in Argentine history that a group was set upon and exterminated. In the 1880s President Julio Roca declared that the native people living in the south of the country were not human and sent the military to wipe them out. He announced he was going to show the United States how to do it. Every soldier had to bring back a body part. "This was a very dark part of our history," Sonya tells us. *At least it's known,* I think to myself. That's not much consolation, but it's something. That's in large part why the mothers march for their lost sons and daughters, so at least they're not forgotten for a while.

The mothers march again in silence, and we follow in a snaking line as another old man carries a blue flag of the Plaza de Mayo Madres. Their numbers are dwindling now, these women in their late sixties and seventies. I count only three wearing the white scarves. Across the street, past the police cordon, stands La Casa Rosada, "the Pink House," and the balcony where Eva Perón once addressed the masses. I'm not trying to make a point by mentioning this. I'm not a fan of the Peróns either. Juan Perón made one of my favorite authors, Jorge Luis Borges, a poultry inspector, as an insult to him, and bombed the house of Borges's sister. Every government has its excesses. But it stands there, that balcony. It can't be ignored. It's part of the tour.

⌒

The next day, I have breakfast with Bruce and Rachel from Chicago. They're the only two people on this trip who don't yet know about my project. So I explain to them my goal to become an honorary Sammy again.

Bruce has been quite friendly until this moment, and he's not unfriendly now, but his smile disappears and he leans across the breakfast table and says in a firm and resolute voice, "Won't happen."

"I'm hoping the fraternity might make an exception for me," I say.

He shakes his head and stirs his coffee. "Listen," he says, his voice softening. "That chapter had its heart in the right place. And I commend them for that. But they didn't have the authority to make you an honorary member."

I suppose it's not the lowest point of my life. There are a lot more important things to worry about, but still it's a disappointment that everyone (except for Owen, who isn't on the board) tells me my cause is hopeless. I'm not one to give up easily, but I'm not sure what else I can do. If they don't give honorary memberships, I can't get around that fact.

In the elevator after breakfast, I run into Roger. "So I guess there's no chance of me becoming an honorary member?" I ask.

"It's just not something we do," he says. "But we have initiated faculty members as full members at campuses where we have or have had chapters. We can talk about it."

We can talk about it? Yes, let's talk about it now. I want to grab him and pull him back into the elevator, but he gets off at his floor, and I have to swallow my puppy-dog enthusiasm. I never would have expected the possibility of becoming a full member of Sigma Alpha Mu via my faculty position until this moment, and he hasn't made any promises. And I could see being a faculty liaison if the chapter still existed on my campus, but it doesn't.

And really, do I want to become an actual member of a fraternity? In general I'm still not terribly fond of them — as a breed. I live close to campus, and many a football weekend, frat boys throw beer cans in my front yard and do primal screams at two in the morning.

I'm a hypocrite, I know. I shouldn't condemn fraternities as a group. It's just that I've never thought of being a *full* member of SAM — it's a commitment. Last night David told me that if he broke down in a strange city, he could always call a Sammy for help. He told me that the Sammy chapter at Iowa folded because they didn't have the savvy, they weren't aggressive enough, and they accepted anyone. If I became a Sammy now, I would essentially *be* the chapter at the University of Iowa.

⌒

Buenos Aires is a city of fashionable boulevards and shantytowns, of soccer stadiums and cafés and public parks and leather stores and a monument near our hotel dedicated to the young men lost to England in the fight for the Malvinas, what the English call the Falkland Islands, the monument guarded by two wilting Argentine marines under the intense heat of the Southern Hemisphere's summer. It's a city of dog walkers and fashionable dressers and beggars, a place of immigrants from Italy and Germany, very white and a little afraid of the latest immigrants, the Peruvians, darker and poorer than the Porteños, as the people of Buenos Aires call themselves. It's a city of "express" kidnappings, in which victims are kidnapped for the afternoon, their families extorted for whatever they can give, and the victims then released, shaken but alive. Strangest of all for me, in December it's a city full of menorahs, decorating bus stops and park benches — Hanukkah, or "Januka," seems to have equal billing with Christmas, perhaps explained in part by Buenos Aires' Jewish mayor but also by the largest Jewish population in Latin America.

This morning we travel to AMIA, the Jewish cultural and community center that was bombed in 1994. Two years prior Islamic Jihad bombed the Israeli embassy in Buenos Aires, killing twenty-nine and wounding 242. Some blamed Hezbollah and Iran for the AMIA bombing. Some even blamed former Nazis. Police were put on trial for involvement in a cover-up and were found not guilty; the judge in charge of the investigation was impeached in 2005; and prosecutors formally charged Iran with the crime. Still, all that remains certain is that eighty-six people died in the AMIA blast.

The attacks might have happened last week given the bunker mentality of the Jewish community of Buenos Aires. Our van is not allowed to stop in front of AMIA — we must park a distance away. Cameras monitor us and men in bulletproof vests with walkie-talkies solemnly greet us. We're let into the building two by two — actually, there are two buildings and, in the center, a courtyard dominated by a flashy sculpture by the Israeli artist Yaacov Agam, commemorating the attack. Personally, I hate Agam's work (although I can hear Shoshie saying, "*Hate*'s a bad word, Daddy"). You look at the mammoth sculpture one way, it's the Star of David. You look at it another, it's a rainbow. You look at it another, it's a menorah. Clever but stupid ("*Stupid*'s a bad word, Daddy"). Six delightful angles in all! A cousin of mine visiting Chicago when I lived there purchased one of Agam's pieces for ten thousand dollars at a Michigan Avenue art gallery and dragged me there to admire it, which I dutifully did. Look at it one way, it's the Star of David. Look at it another way, it's the Israeli flag. Couldn't he surprise us a little? Look at it one way, it's a menorah. Look at it from another angle, it's the Wailing Wall. From a third angle, it's a kosher dill.

Sadly, scale makes no difference when regarding an Agam painting or sculpture. Our group runs around the sculpture like squirrels around a tree, taking pictures from the various angles, and I do it too. I don't know why. I think the Snapshot Impulse is controlled by the most primitive part of our brains, the reptilian part: eat, sleep, have sex, take snapshots in front of big things.

Except for the Agam sculpture, I can't imagine wanting to blow up anything at AMIA. The organization's services are many and free and don't serve only Jews. In fact, 30 percent of the victims of the bombing weren't Jewish. Our guide, a young woman named Eva, gives us the grand tour, showing us everything, even inexplicably an air-conditioned room that's remarkable apparently only because it's air-conditioned. We nod appreciatively at the air conditioner as she explains in halting English, "Some of the people who meet here like the air conditioner on, and some don't. So they argue about it."

"*That's* the Jewish problem," says Harriet.

The group needs a bathroom break. Eva tells us about the bathrooms as though they're part of the tour. "We have bathrooms for men, women, and handicapped," she informs us in her tour guide voice, simultaneously lilting and bored.

"Also Jews and non-Jews," says Harriet.

"Circumcised and uncircumcised," says Owen. "With illustrations."

One of the givens in being part of a group is that you sacrifice a certain amount of control in your life. If there's such a thing as control. Some people think it's an illusion, like an Agam. I think this is one reason I like Owen and Harriet so much — that Jewish brand of irreverence. Owen and Harriet radiate irreverence: you can make me be part of a group, but only as long as I don't have to act like I'm in a group. I, on the other hand, am a little stunned at how meekly I go wherever the group goes and do unflinchingly whatever is on the itinerary.

Now on the itinerary we are supposed to have lunch with a hundred elderly Jews who speak only Spanish and Yiddish. It's not this that upsets me but the prospect of institutional food once again.

At lunch we're greeted with applause and a hearty meal of pizza stuffed with egg and tomato, Tang in green pitchers, and rice. Owen, ever affable, and the only one among us who speaks passable Spanish, addresses the old women and men, who greet his speech with enthusiasm, as they greet all of us. Then we join in a rousing chorus of "Happy Birthday" (or "Feliz Cumpleaños") for an elderly man named Nicholas, who stands in front of us, a cap on his head at a jaunty angle, holding a cane with both hands as though he's about to do a tap dance with it.

At my table we try to communicate as best we can. We're all Jews, but beyond that, what do we share? A woman beside me, chasing a piece of tomato around her plate with a fork, abandons her mission momentarily and leans across the table. "Do you speak Yiddish?" she asks in Spanish. That much I can understand.

Well, yes, I do, but only a little. I can say in Yiddish what my uncle Morty once taught me on my grandmother's porch in 1980 after my brother's wedding: "May you give birth to a trolley car." "What does a pig know about noodles?" Or "May you have two beds and a fever in each." Yiddish curses are the best, mean little metaphors and similes that take a moment to ponder if not savor. Still, I refrain from telling this sweet old woman to "place your head in shit and grow like an onion," as it goes against the spirit of our mission.

She pats my hand and tells me that I remind her of her grandson. *Nieto.* I remember the word from college Spanish.

Few in our group have fared better than I. Across the table Rachel from Chicago asks a woman in halting Spanish what our lunch with the egg stuffing is called. I lean in expectantly, waiting for the name of some Argentine specialty.

"Pizza," the woman answers.

Roger reports after lunch that his experience was similarly confusing. "I sat with a group of lovely ladies who didn't speak a whit of English," he reports. "And a gentleman who either asked if I'm Jewish or where I buy my pants."

After lunch we fulfill the community service part of the trip. We're taken to a kind of cashier's office where David presents the check from SAM to AMIA, a spectacularly anticlimactic moment that I record for posterity with many absurd photos of David shaking hands with an AMIA functionary while he hands over the check. Afterward, we move outside and take more pictures of the dramatic moment. Staged, yes, but then so was the second flag raising at Iwo Jima. We haven't brought a fortune. In fact, we probably could have raised more if we stood outside bouncing a basketball, but it's symbolic, right? Maybe it will buy a few more air conditioners the old people of AMIA can argue over, and, if that's the case, then we will have served our ordained purpose within the Jewish community here.

At the AMIA gift shop, I buy an Agam bookmark. Look at it one way, it's the letter *chai,* which symbolizes life in Hebrew. Look at it another, it's an upside down *chai.* Okay, maybe it's not an Agam, but I can dream, can't I?

It takes a while to herd us all together so we can leave: bathroom, gift shop, check presenting. Everyone is off doing something, and that leaves me in the lobby looking at a photo exhibit that has something to do with the disappeared, though I'm not sure what.

One photo in particular arrests me (no pun intended). A group of fifteen or so young men and women in their twenties stand in a line perpendicular to the person taking the photo. In front of them is a pile of guns. One woman is smiling. I walk over to Sonya, who's conversing with someone from AMIA, and ask if she would mind translating for me. She comes over and reads the inscription. "Uh-huh, yes," she says, nodding. "Well, the caption says that the military massacred all but three of these people. And the other three later disappeared."

I study this small group until it's time to leave. Who knows, who cares, whether they were Jews or non-Jews? Who knows what they left behind? All I can do is gawk at them in wonder in the way that the living always study the dead, in search of clues or consolation.

↶

As with everything else involving the Jewish community in Buenos Aires, we're not even allowed to stand in front of the synagogue on this first night of Hanukkah — and a security man tells Sonya to turn off her cell phone. He doesn't know us and regards us suspiciously before allowing us in. Still, the payoff is worth the trouble.

The synagogue is one of the loveliest I've seen, not the modest affairs I'm used to that resemble ranch houses about the size of Taco Bells. This is a grand old synagogue, at least a hundred years old, a large chandelier hanging from a high ceiling and a half dome with a stained glass Star of David in its center. The room, including the balcony, is filled with at least 250 people. The ark of the covenant is hidden by a red velvet drape and a large electric menorah. It's not only Hanukkah, but the Sabbath, and a girl of about twelve lights the *shabbos* candles.

The service itself is like nothing any of us in the group has experienced, a kind of concert that doesn't involve the congregation at all. Instead of everyone singing the prayers together, a man and a woman belt out the tunes to a piano accompaniment, holding their mics, raising their arms dramatically, one song bleeding into the next, a cross between a Broadway show and a gospel service, but without the fainting or talking in tongues.

Our tour guide, Sonya, sits beside me. Sonya's mother was Jewish and died when Sonya was only an infant. She was raised Catholic by her father and grandmother. She's very much a practicing Catholic, has never in fact been to services in a synagogue, though she's married to an American Jew from New York. Even so, she's less lost than I am because the prayer book, the siddur, is in Spanish and Hebrew, and she at least reads Spanish. I think of the children of the disappeared ones. When one of the students was pregnant, the military would wait until the woman gave birth, murder the mother, and give the child to military families to be adopted — children raised by the very people who had murdered their parents. This doesn't describe Sonya's childhood, but watching her makes me think of how difficult it is sometimes to know into what group you fit. Orthodox Jews would still consider Sonya a Jew, but not so my daughters, whose mothers are not Jewish.

I was shaped, in part, by the idea of not belonging, of being "an individual." The problem with this is there's no such thing in the grand scale. You think you're special, but you fit one demographic or another. There must even be a nonconformist demographic. The filmmaker John Sayles once wrote a marvelous story with this premise, titled "The Anarchists' Convention," about a group of aging anarchists, mostly Jewish, holding a convention for their dwindling numbers in a New York hotel. If you've ever been to a convention or a conference of people who do the same thing you do, you'll almost certainly be struck by how many of them actually look like you or your friends and dress like you too. You think you recognize them all. It's depressing, really. And then there are people who don't look like you but share your name. I always thought I'd never meet another Robin Hemley, my last name being a rare one. But once, I found a Robin Hemley in the phone book on the East Coast. I could never reach him, and later I found out why. On the Internet he was listed among a group of parents who hadn't paid child support, a deadbeat dad. *That* was depressing. Then a woman in Australia e-mailed me out of the blue a year ago. Her name was Robin Hemley, and we started a correspondence that lasted a week, after which her sister suddenly e-mailed me and told me this other Robin Hemley had just suffered a brain aneurism and died. That stunned me. It was like meeting a long-lost twin and then having her snatched away. If the universe had a message here for me, what was it? *Know thyself? But for the grace of God . . . ? You think you're in control of your life, but you're not. You're reading* way *too much into this, you schmuck?*

Of course even the nonconformists conform, as made clear in Monty Python's *Life of Brian* when Brian, standing on a balcony, confronts an enormous crowd that believe he's the Messiah. Exasperated, he yells out, "Are any of you individuals?"

"Yes," they scream en masse.

From a corner of the crowd comes one lone voice, "I'm not."

Sometimes I don't care. This week I don't care if I'm an individual or a member of the most nonexclusive of male fraternities, accepting all men without regard to race, creed, or political affiliation: the Assholes. In my case this week, a cigar-smoking asshole. A bad boy. Enough already of human suffering and pride. Enough with the big stuff. Just bring me a Romeo y Julieta cigar and a shot of Havana Club on the rocks.

This, I have to admit, is my favorite part of the week. Not the singing ponytailed rabbis and the cantors who look like soccer stars and probably are. Not the kvelling bar mitzvah boys or the baby-naming ceremonies or the lighting of the Hanukkah candles. The best part of the week is going out to a cigar joint with my, well, kinda sorta fraternity brothers and talking the talk.

We've found a place off the tourist strip of Florida Avenue, run by a guy who has that same kind of old *Miami Vice* rabbi look, except he's no rabbi. You can tell from just one look, he's a bad boy too. And even though Buenos Aires is the latest in a string of cities that have outlawed smoking in drinking establishments, he shows us to a private room upstairs, bare except for a TV and a bar, where an old woman pours us simple drinks, the simpler the better.

It's here, in these relaxed digs full of smoke and men away from their wives and significant others, that I learn all about . . . Who am I kidding? We're middle-aged guys. We don't tell dirty jokes. We don't compare penis sizes or talk badly about women we've slept with. We don't even talk sports stats (thank God). If we're assholes, we're boring assholes. We talk about snoring, sleep apnea, disability, and flex accounts. Heaven help us — we're in the flex account stage of life.

"You know what I was watching on TV last night?" I say during one of these sessions, just to change the subject.

"Porn?" Phil asks. There now! That's more like it. That sounds more like a frat boy. I like all the Sammies I've met, but I love to hang out with Phil, who serves perfectly as my fraternity alter ego, the frat boy I wish I could be. He told a cabbie to go "Lefto! Lefto!" when we were heading back to our hotel one night, and he brushes off beggar children like bullets off of Superman's skin. We're certainly on the opposite ends of the social and political spectrum — an avowed conservative, he's perplexed by liberal arts majors and professors like myself who stamp out such "useless" degrees. But he'd also make a good life counselor. Like my counselor Snoopy at Camp Echo, he exudes a kind of strength of character that perhaps he gained in part from his stint with the Sammies.

"Yeah, BBC porn," I say. "Actually, it was a show bringing together a number of the current Nobel laureates for a discussion of the world's problems. They seemed as flummoxed as the rest of us."

"We've had about seven Nobel laureates," Roger remarks casually.

I study him to see if he's joking. "Seven Nobel laureates?" I ask.

"Yes, six or seven."

"Why didn't you tell me?" I ask, as though they were purposefully keeping this valuable information from me.

"And a lot of authors," he says. "Philip Roth is a Sammy."

"Philip Roth?" How could they keep this from me?

That seals it. It's my destiny to be a Sammy, I decide. It's *"bashert,"* the Yiddish word for everything from finding the right parking space to the right mate. If Philip Roth is a Sammy as well as six or seven Nobel Prize winners, I want to be one too. The Sammies are also well-represented at the top of the corporate ladder: The owners of Victoria's Secret, Men's Wearhouse, both Sammies. The head of GEICO Insurance is a Sammy (imagine the GEICO gecko wearing a yarmulke). The NBA Commissioner, David Stern, is a Sammy, and so is Congressman Tom Lantos. And so is at least one convicted felon, junk bond king Michael Milken. I'm glad Milken is on the list, as well as disgraced former AIG CEO, Hank Greenberg. It's difficult to explain, but I find it comforting to see the fallen among the mighty alums. I'd be too frightened to join otherwise. I'd feel as though I'd joined the Stepford frat or some kind of, gasp, conspiracy (you never know — David Duke or the president of Iran might be looking over your shoulder . . . stay calm and act natural) and not a group of imperfect men like myself. A frat just isn't a frat without a little trouble. Witness, for instance, that only Lloyd's of London will insure Sigma Alpha Mu. "Not many insurance companies will touch a fraternity," Roger tells me. Witness that part of Roger's job involves trying to bail out chapters that have landed in one kind of fix or another.

↶

I'm starting to feel like everything in Argentina is an Agam. Look outside the van as we pass the small plot of land the size of two porta-potties lying end to end, and it seems unremarkable. Look at it again, and it's suddenly Jewish: the smallest public plot in the city, Baron Hirsch Square, named after a Jewish noble who helped bring Jewish émigrés to Argentina.

I'm not complaining. I'm on this trip for the duration. But sometimes it feels like hazing, as when we travel on an unbearably hot afternoon to the apartment of an artist whose works have titles such as *La Explosion Numero Uno* or *July 18th, 1994,* the date of the AMIA explosion, with bits of books burned in the explosion worked in to the composition. Great stuff. Don't get me wrong, but sometimes you don't want to be depressed by all the reminders of the people who hate your kind for reasons you'll never fathom. Sometimes you just want to see a goyish gaucho gallop a horse past you, or two Catholics doing a tango. And we *do* get to see these things, but I want more.

At the artist's apartment, Harriet takes one look around and announces, "I'm done." I'm done too, but I lack Harriet's chutzpah. As we enter the kitchen to watch a short video about the artist, Harriet makes a hara-kiri motion across her stomach. "Kill me now," she says under her breath. Thank God for Harriet. Janet, the architect, married to Bert the radiologist, is too polite, like me. When the artist shows us photos of a couple of temples she's done murals for, Janet says, "I would love to be able to see your murals."

Sonya translates for Janet and the woman, whose eyes light up.

"She says she will go to the temple with you," Sonya reports to a horrified Janet, who backpedals to our laughter.

"Were I a member of the congregation," Janet says, "I'd love to study your mural." She looks at Bert and says, "I'm getting into something!"

"It was rhetorical," I say.

"Figurative," says Roger.

In this moment we bond, and somehow that exchange transforms us from a tired group into a tired group with some life left in it. Don't ask me how it happens, but before long Janet and Harriet have urged the boys to sing the Sigma Alpha Mu song for me, and they do. They serenade us all with a song I don't know and couldn't honestly sing if I did. But still, this moment almost feels like acceptance.

↶

On our second-to-last day in Argentina, we drag ourselves as a group to Martinez, a suburb of Buenos Aires about forty-five minutes distant by train. We're going to visit Steve, an alum expat who's lived in Argentina the better part of the decade. The train is a rickety old thing, crammed with commuters, and we're all standing in the center of the car, holding on to whatever we can, hot and breathing through our mouths to avoid the smell of body odor.

"Do you need the Purell?" Owen asks Harriet.

"Head to toe," she says.

"How about a hazmat suit?" he asks, handing her the small bottle of hand sanitizer. "This is why we wouldn't make a good couple on *The Amazing Race*," he tells me. "We did the jungle canopy ride in Costa Rica. She broke a fingernail, and it was all over."

"I would be fine," she insists. "The jungle canopy didn't like me." She explains to me her ordeal, and Owen stands by with a sad face, letting go of the bar above his head long enough to play an invisible violin to accompany her tale.

At the train station, we're met by Steve, a man in his early fifties who has a kind of manic, talkative energy. So unlike most Jews.

He grabs my hand, and I feel him trying to maneuver my fingers around in some strange way. It's like some alien probe. What's going on?

"No!" David yells. "He's not a Sammy yet."

Ah, the secret handshake. Don't worry, boys. Your secret is safe. I've forgotten how to do it, and I have no idea what Steve was trying to make my hand do. Yes, I'm not a Sammy yet. Roger and David are friendly but noncommittal. Roger has told me that he'll bring up a possible nomination for me in a few weeks when they meet next, and I'll hear from him then. Feeling the strange tingle in my hand from Steve's handshake, I have no idea what it presages, if anything; what is and isn't *bashert*; to what group I belong. If my nomination goes through, I'll most likely be initiated at the Sammies' annual convention in August. But there's a lot that can happen between now and August, other do-overs to complete, a baby to be born, and who knows what else.

I have no way of knowing while standing at the train station in Martinez, but perhaps at that very moment, on another continent, in my front yard, a group of frat boys is vandalizing my property. When I return home from Argentina, I'll find the crab apple tree I planted in the fall stripped of all its leaves, its branches torn off.

Who would do such a thing? When I get home, I walk in disbelief to the little tree and see the ring of beer cans around its sorry trunk. Picking them up and emptying the old beer on my lawn, what can I do but shake my head?

But my faith in fraternity is restored when, a couple of months later, Owen makes the front page of the *Los Angeles Times* for the charity work he's been doing for years, raising money for breast cancer research. I still won't know by then whether I'm approved for membership, but I pledge a donation, not because I want his vote, but because it's nothing really, it's the least I can do, it's *sedukah,* a Jewish obligation to give. And besides, I can just imagine him on a street corner when he was in college, welcoming some strange kid who comes out of nowhere and asks if he can help.

CHAPTER SIX

A REAL COOL GUY

Eighth Grade Do-Over

> ORIGINAL AGE: 13
> DO-OVER AGE: 48
> ORIGINAL LOCATION: JEFFERSON JUNIOR HIGH SCHOOL, COLUMBIA, MISSOURI
> DO-OVER LOCATION: JEFFERSON JUNIOR HIGH SCHOOL, COLUMBIA, MISSOURI

Although eighth grade was probably the worst year of my life, I still have my yearbook: *J Cycle Cyclones 71–72*, with a maroon cover and pop-art letters. I don't know why I've kept it because there's not even a photo of me inside, not even in the late pictures, because I was undoubtedly in Psych Ward School when the photos were taken, and there's no Psych Ward Yearbook, no football team, no dances.

The previous year, seventh grade, had been golden. My mother had found a job far from dreaded Slippery Rock, Pennsylvania, at Stephens College, a small private college for girls in Columbia, Missouri. Stephens had its own lake where I frequently fished, and I was as popular at school as I'd ever been, because I was able to make a clean start in this new town. I won two awards that year at Jefferson Junior, one for the biggest mouth, the other for the second-biggest feet. I wore these honors proudly. The class clown, I remade myself into the confident and funny boy I wanted to be. I even changed my name unofficially from Robin to Peter to complete this transformation. I had two girls competing for me, Susan Fitzpatrick and Susan Steinholz. Susan Fitzpatrick, the daughter of a doctor in my neighborhood, towered over me and had straight brown hair. Susan Steinholz had curly blond hair and a face full of zits. I chose Susan Fitzpatrick, who provided me with a full program of benchmarks we would accomplish within the first two weeks of going steady. I only lasted that long before proving an utter disappointment to her. Still, it was a great year overall.

Everything changed in eighth grade. My older sister Nola was diagnosed with schizophrenia that year, and my mother and I had to drive out to Massachusetts to retrieve her from grad school. Back in Missouri, she was hallucinating, talking to invisible beings, and attempting suicide. She spent the next year in and out of Mid-Missouri Mental Health Center. Unhinged by seeing my older sister in this state, I deteriorated too. I stopped going to school. I retreated into comic books, saw a psychiatrist weekly, and finally became a day patient and a student at the school run by the hospital's children's ward.

When I returned to Jeff Junior High in the spring of 1972, my name was Robin again, and I was no longer the class clown. Word had spread that I was "a nutcase," and kids who had previously been my friends saw me now as a pariah. When I asked Susan Fitzpatrick to sign my yearbook, she flipped to a page and signed rapidly. But when I returned home and looked through the pages, I couldn't find it. She had only pretended to sign the book. Susan Steinholz, the girl I had rejected, wasn't so stuck up. "To a real cool guy," she wrote. "I like you a whole lot."

Marcel Proust's great project in his three-thousand-page auto-biographical novel, *Remembrance of Things Past,* was to live in a multilayered world that combined the present and the past into a dimension that was neither. Proust wrote that the sound of a spoon against a plate or the taste of a madeleine was enough sometimes to transport him back into the past or to make him feel as though he were alive outside of time. I can't say the same for my junior high yearbook, which fails to transport me — and, in any case, my goal wasn't to turn it into Proust's madeleine. My goal was to create a different story, a past modified from the past clamped inside my yearbook. Maybe it was too late for Susan Fitzpatrick's signature, but I needed to go back to Jeff Junior with my yearbook for a second round of autographs. I wasn't sure, but it seemed that the right signatures might help undo all the terrible inscriptions I still carried from that time.

In December I called Jeff Junior and spoke with the principal of the school, Nyle Klinginsmith, who had a soft measured voice, tinged with an accent that Missourians would probably say is southern, but southerners wouldn't. Nyle was friendly from the start, and he seemed agreeable to the project. He simply said he needed to clear it with *his* boss first, the superintendent of schools.

Nyle told me that he had started teaching at Jefferson Junior High the year I first attended, a coincidence that pleased me in light of my project. He was a homegrown principal, working his way up from social studies teacher. He said he didn't remember me, which didn't surprise me at all, but he explained that he remembered almost every kid from his class those first two important years of his teaching career. He hadn't been my social studies teacher, and I didn't remember him either. But after we hung up, I went to my yearbook and found him there, wearing a tie but no jacket, his dark hair combed neatly, the kind of smile that a kid can trust, friendly but not overly friendly. You could just tell from the faculty photos who was nice and who wasn't, like balding Mr. Mayhew, my math teacher, who looked like a peanut and who appears nowhere in my yearbook without a Hitler mustache I had drawn on him.

↶

A do-over is like facing a real-life dream monster and attacking it instead of running away. But I suspect that the monster of eighth grade won't be slain so easily, so I enlist the help of Margie and Shoshie to make the drive and spend the week with me in Columbia while I relive the dark days of eighth grade. As it turns out, they're all too happy to be my companions on this trip, as they are faithfully my companions in my everyday life.

On the morning of our drive from Iowa City to Columbia, I pad down the hall to Shoshie's room, which is full of the cushions of childhood: a fully deployed battalion of stuffed animals, glow-in-the-dark stars on her ceiling, a rocking-horse lamp, and a bed laden with pillows. Shoshie, herself slightly larger than a pillow, sleeps the sleep of children and the Just, her expression so worry-free I can't bring myself to disturb her for a moment. Then, sitting down beside her, I touch her arm softly, and she awakens with a smile for me. She passed her fourth birthday in January, and she's completely turned the corner now from toddler to young girl — for the first three years, her hair was thin and wispy, but now she has dark curls to spare. She's the only one of my daughters who's inherited my curls, though she has her mother's large dark eyes, and olive skin in between my complexion and Margie's.

"Shoshie, do you know we're going to Missouri today?" I say.

"Yes," she says. "This morning I thought about it on my bed, and my brain said, 'Yes, it's time to go to junior high!'"

Although I'm a frequent traveler, I'm a nervous one, and I spend the better part of the morning frantically making sure I have everything I need for the weeklong trip. On the way out the door, I almost forget my yearbook, and so I run back in the house, and retrieve it from my bedside table. Back in the car I show the yearbook to Margie, who's looking at a map in the front seat.

"At the end of the week, I'm going to get the principal to sign my yearbook," I tell her.

"Exciting," she says, glancing up momentarily.

All the way to Missouri — that is, for the better part of a four-hour drive — Shoshie keeps a running commentary from the backseat. Another thing she's inherited from me is my big mouth. She simply does not stop talking while she's awake, and it's hard for all of us, including her older sisters, to keep patience with her sometimes. But most of the time I enjoy our absurd conversations as she pieces together the world the way all of us do (though some more silently than others), by floating an armada of theories and seeing which ones sail.

"After moms and dads, everyone are kids," she says.

"What about old people?" I ask.

"They're bigger kids; right, Dad?"

"Right."

"Shoshie, what would you do with three wishes?" I ask her.

"Who will give me three wishes?"

"A genie."

"What's a genie?"

"It's a kind of spirit."

"Oh, it's like a bush?" she asks.

A bush. How did she ever come up with that? I should know better than to tussle with her when it comes to the imagination. She trumps me every time.

"Bushes aren't spirits," I tell her. "Unless they're burning bushes."

"Okay, Dad," she says. "On the way to Missouri, let's look out for some fire bushes so we can get some wishes." I suppose I should be arrested or given a time-out at the very least for not answering her serious questions seriously. But I like to play as much as any kid, and Shoshie's a great playmate. Besides, I think of our conversations as verbal judo. No one gets hurt, and she learns important lessons about the world: It's bendable. It has moving parts.

All the way to Missouri, we entertain each other and Margie, who indulges both of us most of the time or closes her eyes and sleeps when we're too much for her.

I suppose all this playful bravado on my part simply masks terror. Despite having Shoshie and Margie along for support, I have to take a sleeping pill that night, and I *still* sleep fitfully. Filled with the trepidation of a kid transferring schools, I awaken an hour before the alarm goes off and seriously consider skipping school as I did frequently during my first time at Jeff Junior. There are plenty of reasons why this experience shouldn't matter to me, but none of them carries any weight with my subconscious. Of course, all this matters terribly because I'm not simply going to any junior high.

I'm going back to mine, and it won't be 2007 all the time this week. Sometimes it will be 1971. Unfortunately, we did not see even one burning bush on the way from Iowa City to Columbia, and so my wish to simply wake when the week is over goes unanswered.

Jefferson Junior High is only a few blocks from downtown Columbia — it was built as a high school in 1911 and became Jeff Junior in 1927. Expanded a number of times over the years, it still looks essentially the same as it did when I left it in 1972. As usual, Margie and Shoshie drive me to school, and Margie has to maneuver around the bustle of activity that surrounds any public school in the morning: the school buses lined up and the parents dropping off their kids, students adjusting their backpacks or yelling to friends as they dash across the street without heed under the protection of the safety patrol. Is there a more quintessentially American image than this? I could close my eyes and describe Jeff Junior today and thirty-five years ago and get only one or two details wrong. The flagpole seems to have been moved from one side of the small square in front of the building to the other, and a sign has been added:

ONE OF THE NATION'S OUTSTANDING SCHOOLS
JEFFERSON JUNIOR HIGH SCHOOL
NATIONAL SCHOOL RECOGNITION AWARD WINNER

But then I notice that there are two flagpoles, one on either side of the small courtyard, and that the old flagpole has been swallowed up by a gum tree and isn't flying anything. Now, and in my day too, a lower addition extends from one side of the original building, ruining its symmetry so that the eye might easily overlook the twin copper cupolas on the roof (the building's most distinctive features and what date it) in favor of the steps below the entrance. In my mind, this has always been a grand entrance with many steps, enough for Rocky Balboa to climb and raise his gloves in triumph, or for a baby carriage to bounce down terrifyingly as in *The Battleship Potemkin*, or for a pyramid, atop which a victim could be sacrificed to the sun god. But there are only four steps, and on the top stands not Quetzalcoatl in his raiment but Nyle Klinginsmith in a blue shirt and a gray tie that matches his hair, looking, if not immortal, at least recognizably the same as his 1972 picture, wearing a friendly, slightly lopsided smile that would relax just about any new kid.

Despite my misgivings, I consider myself fortunate that the school is even allowing me to return, considering the world we live in. A month before my return to Jeff Junior, there's news that in a creepy alternate version of my project, a twenty-nine-year-old pedophile has been caught in Arizona masquerading as a twelve-year-old boy. For four months he attended school in the town of Surprise, covering his stubble with makeup, getting kicked out finally for poor attendance. He lived with two older pedophiles who posed as his uncle and grandfather, and who even attended parent-teacher conferences for him. For months I've been joking about all my background checks, unable to imagine a pedophile going to all the trouble of pretending to write a book about childhood in order to find his victims. Now I can imagine it, and it's not funny.

Nyle leads me to his office, which is dominated not by a paddle as it was in his predecessor's office in my day (and I might add, a paddle I was threatened with) but by a Hokusai print, one of the artist's *Thirty-six Views of Mount Fuji,* and by family photos. Briefly, we reminisce. He brings out my seventh-grade yearbook and flips through it a few seconds. "There you are!" he says, and I look at a photo of me gazing downright angelically, the boy in the picture unaware that his life is about to fall apart for a while and that it will continue and come together again in ways he cannot imagine. Even so, this twelve-year-old is me, who I am internally. I'm not saying I'm this twelve-year-old in all respects, but I still see myself as the class clown with big feet and a big mouth.

"We do not grow absolutely, chronologically," Anaïs Nin wrote in her diary. "We grow sometimes in one dimension, and not in another; unevenly. We grow partially. We are relative. We are mature in one realm, childish in another. The past, present, and future mingle and pull us backward, forward, or fix us in the present. We are made up of layers, cells, constellations." Amen to that.

Nyle types up my schedule and locker number and combination. (This is a full-service principal! But it comes naturally to him. He was a guidance counselor before becoming principal nine years ago.) Then he takes me to the guidance office, the first stop for any eighth-grade transfer student. I'm introduced to Mike Hogan, a current guidance counselor, who shakes my hand and says, "I see you've been drinking your milk," then brings me to his office, where he gives me a planner and a supply of hall passes. "Eighth-grade boys struggle most with organization," he tells me. Oh, *that's* why I'm still so poorly organized. I never received a planner the first time around.

Back then, the only time you received the attention of an adult was if you'd done something wrong. Once in assembly, a teacher grabbed me roughly and shook me, accusing me of running in the halls *and* shooting spit wads. I wasn't *always* innocent, but I was innocent this time. She dragged me to the principal's office, and he gave me a choice of being paddled ten times or of missing assembly for the rest of the year. His paddle was legendary, so I chose to miss assembly and spent the rest of the year sitting on a bench by the entrance whenever we were told to go to the auditorium. That bench was the first thing I noticed when I walked into school this morning, that same bench where I had spent so many afternoons. I passed it by like it was someone I was purposefully ignoring. *I don't even have to acknowledge you, bench,* I thought.

But ignoring ghosts doesn't make them go away. In one hall I'd been threatened after school by a bully I'd carelessly insulted in shop. This kid shook me down for money after school every day, and I'd finally told him he was a stupid pig. He didn't appreciate that, and he told me he was going to tear me limb from limb, but I thought I could wait him out. In shop I was safe and full of bravado, but for the rest of the day, his emissaries whispered to me that I was dead meat. After school that day, I went across the street to Garrett's, the little store behind the school, and waited until I was sure I was safe. But when I went back into the building, he was still there waiting for me. He grabbed me by the collar and told me he was going to kill me. He probably could have killed me too. I had to think fast, so I used my only defense against the kid: my words. I started talking to him about Gandhi and passive resistance. I told him that I was simply teaching him about passive resistance in shop, that I had nothing against him personally, merely colonialism, and that he would break his own shackles of predetermined slavery to violence if this one time he turned his back on it and let me live. "Be like Gandhi," I urged him. "Join me in passive resistance." I talked to him for about fifteen minutes, and by the end of it he was too exhausted and confused to do anything. To this day, this remains my most impressive argumentative essay, an essay written aloud in fear and inspiration.

↶

By the time I've been properly advised, guided, and informed, my first class, math, is almost over. Greg, a serious eighth grader with a buzz cut, a member of the Cyclone Host Club, brings me to math (not only is this the Bible Belt, but it's also Tornado Alley, so that's why it's the home of the Cyclones). My teacher, Mrs. Holbein, is a woman eight to ten years younger than me with shoulder length blond hair and an engaging smile. I like her immensely because of that smile and because she is not my old math teacher, Mr. Mayhew. If given a yearbook, I would not deface her with a Hitler mustache. She guides me to an empty desk beside an eighth-grade boy who regards me suspiciously and scoots away. The students in front of me turn around and do double takes. "What are you?" one of them asks. "A parent?"

I'm used to this by now. "A student," I say without further explanation, and let them gawk.

One thing I notice immediately is that all the students have calculators that they use to help them with, in this case, quadratic equations. When I was in school, calculators were the size of a booster rocket and cost nearly as much. Daily planners. Calculators. I feel like Rip Van Winkle.

Wednesday is International Pi Day, the teacher informs me before the end of class, and we're all going to do special activities associated with Pi, and I'm going to be a Pi Day Singer, whatever that means. "Is that okay?" she asks.

"Sure, just treat me like any eighth grader," I say, and the class erupts in a spontaneous cheer. This response terrifies me. Can I take it back? Treat me like the principal. Treat me like a Cyclone, a real cyclone. Run from me in terror. Keep your distance. Get behind me, Foul Spawn of Junior High. Just don't treat me like one of you.

The bell rings, and we gather up our books. The suspicious boy regards me the way someone who's had his eyes dilated regards the full sun. "What's your next class?" he asks, despite the discomfort I cause him.

"Mr. Rasmussen."

He makes a little snort. "Have fun with *him.*"

My Cyclone Host, Greg, meets me at the door and leads me to Mr. Rasmussen's class on the second floor. Mr. Rasmussen stands in front of his door. He's forty-two years old, but he looks thirty. In every sense of the word, he's a veteran. Not only did he attend Jeff Junior, but many members of his family attended the school, back to his grandmother. For eight years he's been a teacher at Jeff. Before that, he was a sergeant in the military, but he hardly needs to tell me that. He's wearing a blue shirt and khaki pants and stands with a military bearing, his blond hair cut short. He regards me as though sighting me through a gun turret — his face doesn't move a muscle as he shakes hands and gets down to business. "Tell you what," he tells me. "So you won't have to sit in a little seat, there's a big one over there," and he exiles me to a long table by the window where he keeps some of his papers and handouts. I'd rather sit among the students in one of the little desks, but the request dies a coward's death somewhere midthroat, and I sit down as he clears away some of his papers.

Mr. Rasmussen's subject is social studies. He hands me a hernia-inducing textbook titled *Call to Freedom!* As the class slowly fills until it's crowded with about thirty students, he goes over the week's schedule with the students while simultaneously pacing and keeping the peace:

"Samuel. You need to stay after class. We can't have that coat in class. We'll need to talk about that so we can resolve this issue. We don't want to see that coat again."

"Marty, is that appropriate?"

"Sylvan, stay focused, please!"

"Mr. Rasmussen, I turned in my summary."

"What did I say about the summary? I said, talk to me later."

The technology might be different now, but thankfully the films that are shown in eighth-grade social studies are just as stultifying as they were in my day. I'm fully behind the idea of making the little imps suffer as much as I did. In this case, Mr. Rasmussen shows us a film on the Alamo that's not quite as inspiring as a commercial for Alamo Rent A Car. "The funeral pyre of the defenders ignited the fires of freedom!" the announcer intones, as though he's the Voice of God. "Even today we might still feel the heat of that flame!"

By the end of the film, the students look as though they've been staring into a fireplace for the past ten minutes, but, other than that, the makers of this particular little documentary haven't generated much heat in this room. If social studies films don't trip your trigger, try *Call to Freedom!* which like *History Alive!* — my history text for the sixth grade — makes the Mexican-American War read like the proceedings of a zoning commission hearing in San Antonio.

Here I am complaining, and it's only my second class of my first day. Might I have a few issues that need resolving that have something to do with my own history, my own social studies? I decide to be careful and not make snap judgments about my old school. After all, I've parachuted in here in the middle of the term, and I want to be fair.

The highlights of my first day are art class and lunch. In art I'm sandwiched between my Cyclone Host, Greg, and Samantha, a smart, talkative girl with dark blond hair pulled back in a rubber band. She wears glasses right out of the 1970s and looks like a latter-day sister from *The Brady Bunch*. Also in the class is a kid who must be six feet at age thirteen. His name is Will, and he has that goofy Frankensteinish quality that only giant thirteen-year-olds possess, simultaneously puppy dog–like and capable of crushing you like an empty can of Dr Pepper. "Finally, I'm not the oldest-looking student in the room," he tells me.

"He's not a student. He's a teacher," one girl insists, but Miss Know-It-All soon gets in trouble for yakking, and the art teacher, Mrs. Prell, banishes the killjoy out into the hall.

We're doing papier-mâché sculptures of sports figures. Hello, papier-mâché, my old friend! How I've missed you all these years since junior high. There's nothing that says junior high quite like papier-mâché.

First we mold wire into a skeletal figure, then attach it to a wood

base, then wrap masking tape around the form. Then we dip thin strips of newspaper in paste and cover the tape with this gooey flesh. My only problem is that the other students have been working on this project for more than a week, and I'm just beginning mine, so Mrs. Prell hands me a wire figure whose relation to any sport is ambiguous. Actually, he looks as though he's falling off a cliff, arms flailing.

"We've had this figure left over from the seventies, I think," she tells me.

"Did you do it?" Greg asks me.

"Yeah, I left it here in 1971."

"Really?"

"No, I'm just kidding," I say, and Mrs. Prell gives me a look — I had better keep quiet, or she's going to send me out in the hall too.

"It was probably started when you were a student here," she says.

I'm honored to take over, of course.

Beside me, Greg doesn't seem overly humiliated by my eighth grade–like dig, but there's something so earnest about him, it's hard to resist picking on him just a little. I guess I'm not alone in this feeling. I think his figure is supposed to be a diver, though it looks impaled by the wire in its back, and Big Will dubs it "Shish kebab Jesus." Indeed, that's exactly what the figure looks like, some postmodern piece of Christian iconography. Samantha, meanwhile, on my other side, is working on a golfer.

"Awesome arm," she says of my wire guy, and I smile. Hey, hey. Impressing the eighth-grade ladies, just like the old days.

I decide that my flailing wire guy should show his age a bit, especially if he's been gathering dust since the seventies, so I spend a lot of time filling in his belly with masking tape.

"Do you want him to be pregnant?" Samantha asks.

"I want him to have a gut to work off," I say.

"Cool," she says and gives me a high five. "What's he supposed to be doing?"

"I think the flamenco or the tango," I say.

"Cool."

After art, it's lunch. Greg's going to be in class when lunch is over, so he wants to show me now how to get to my business management class in room 137. I follow him downstairs through the lunchroom, then through another door outside where we cross some blacktop and enter the new wing of the building. He leads me through more halls until, miraculously, we wind up a few feet from where we started. "That's room 137," he tells me, about twenty feet from the lunchroom stairs.

"I hope I don't have to take that same route," I tell him. What was that the guidance counselor told me about eighth-grade boys and organization? I guess he was taking me on the Emergency Cyclone Evacuation Route to room 137.

"No, you can just come up the stairs," he tells me, never breaking his Cyclone Host Cloak of Earnestness.

At lunch, I'm sitting alone at a table when a boy with unruly hair, broad shoulders, and a slight smirk, comes over and introduces himself to me as Seamus. He's a big guy, much bigger than me, probably a football player. I'd say he weighs 220 pounds, and there's nothing puppy doggish about him. He asks me if I want to sit with a group of ninth graders. So I squeeze myself between them on the narrow bench — it *does* necessitate some yogalike moves to figure out how to get my legs and body onto the bench between the ninth graders. The big guy is surrounded by a bevy of five pretty ninth-grade girls. One who wears a cheerleading T-shirt seems to be his girlfriend. She leans her head on his shoulder and gives him hugs and squeezes from time to time that he all but ignores. "You can sit here all week," he tells me and smiles beatifically. His girlfriends all beam at me.

"So how do you like ninth grade?" I ask them.

The girl on his shoulder yawns. "Not much," she says. "We don't like being with eighth graders. We should be in high school."

No one likes eighth graders, not even other eighth graders. But someone has to deal with them.

Next is business management in the computer lab, where I'm teamed with a group of three boys to buy stocks and track them. One of the boys sleeps through the entire class while the other two make decisions on which stocks to buy simply by looking at their ticker symbols. Our group is ranked fourteenth out of nineteen groups competing in the stock-buying game.

"Last week, we were eighteenth," says one of the boys, a skinny kid named Matt who's wearing a T-shirt that reads, CHUCK NORRIS DOESN'T THROW UP. HE THROWS DOWN. "We're moving up," he tells me. Still, they're not doing so well. They're panicky investors. "Cooper Tires is tanking big time," Matt's partner Allen says, ignoring the other kid who's literally asleep in the corner. They decide to sell all their shares of Cooper Tires, against my advice, and sink it all into Rite Aid because they like the symbol. "Dude, with a symbol like RAD, how can you go wrong?" Matt tells me.

After business, Resolute Greg guides me to my next class, Spanish, with all the intensity of a Sherpa climbing Mount Everest, past throngs of junior high kids opening and slamming their lockers. I risk breaking his concentration (after all, we might fall into a crevasse) long enough to ask him about Garrett's, the store where I used to go for candy after school, located directly behind Jeff Junior.

"Garrett's was gone before I got here," he says. "But my dad told me about it," he says.

"Your dad went here?"

"And so did my grandma. Both my grandmas."

I suppose it's not all that remarkable, but I've moved around so much in my life that I can't imagine what it would feel like to attend the same school as my grandparents. Much of Jeff Junior looks exactly as I remember it: the rows of lockers, the bench in front of the principal's office, the hall where I was nearly beat up. But I attended this school so long ago that my time here seems almost like someone else's life, like an elder brother's or father's. I'm not the same person I was then, but we're closely related.

My Sherpa guide delivers me safely to Spanish class, a group of boisterous boys and girls who seem mostly concerned with what my name should be in this class. One kid suggests "Dog." I like it, but the teacher thinks we can do better. "How about *Jesus?*" one girl suggests. No. Next. "Diablo," a boy shouts out. Not that either. Finally, I settle on Roberto. Not too imaginative, I admit, but not as much baggage as the other three, and besides, it's not taken. Then we play *Chispa,* a Spanish spelling bee, and, remarkably, I win.

"Does he have to do homework?" the boy who wanted to call me dog asks the teacher.

"Yes," she says. "Judging from how he beat you at *Chispa,* it won't be an issue."

As I'm getting stuff out of my locker at the end of the day, a girl named Bethany, who has the locker beside mine, glances my way. "I heard you sat at lunch with the popular kids," she says.

I did? That never would have happened when I was really in eighth grade. This seems like the triumph of the day. I sat with the popular kids. I'm a popular kid.

"I thought you were someone's dad," she tells me. "I'd never let my dad near my locker."

Nope, no dad in sight. Just a popular kid. Put on your sunglasses as you behold me, all you unpopular kids.

Margie and Shoshie are waiting for me after school, parked on a side street. "Guess what?" I tell Margie almost immediately as I climb in. "I sat with the popular kids at lunch today."

"Then tomorrow you sit with the unpopular ones," she tells me.

"What?! That's no fair," I tell her. "I've never sat with the popular kids before." This, I can see, will go nowhere with Margie, and so I suggest we head to the mall for pizza. What eighth grader doesn't like pizza? Shoshie, at least, doesn't seem to mind how old I act. If she's lost a dad, at least she's gained a playmate. At the pizza place, she grabs a napkin and puts it on my back. "Here's a cape for Horsie Boy!" she yells.

"Neigh," I say.

At the hotel, I give Margie my parent/guardian worksheet to fill out. She takes it, but she's feeling some morning sickness. She looks at it and clucks her tongue. "I don't want to do it," she says. "It's making me nauseated."

"Please," I beg.

She takes the pen and lies on the bed. " 'What is the last book your student read and got really excited about?' " she asks in a really unexcited voice.

"*Fun Home* by Alison Bechdel," I say.

" 'What are your student's strengths, talents, preferences, likes, and dislikes?' You're pretty good at writing," she says, and I peevishly tap her hand with my pen. "You have a pretty good voice. You have a good memory . . . oh, no, I take that back."

Her eyes widen, and she grabs her stomach — she really *is* nauseated I see, and so I wave my hands and say, "Okay, never mind. Bad idea."

Anyway, it's too Freudian having my pregnant wife fill out my parent/guardian worksheet. It seemed like a good idea for a millisecond.

The following day in social studies, Mr. Rasmussen once again reviews the troops, but I detect a difference. An eighth-grade teacher in the public schools is always trying to wrest order from chaos, and for this reason, in junior high perhaps we should employ only martial arts experts and military men and women who can mete out love like K rations. It's there, the love, I mean. It's just not sticky-bun love. More like beef-jerky love in Mr. Rasmussen's case. As he takes attendance, he ticks off questions.

"Looks as though Thulani's still not here," he says. "Anyone know what's wrong with Thulani, because I'm hoping she's sick. But not too sick."

"How's your dad doing, Scott?"

"Good."

"Excellent. Tell him I said hello."

Meanwhile, a slideshow projects on a screen in the front of the room, domestic scenes presumably from Mr. Rasmussen's home life. A young girl reaches for a cookie. In another shot, she picks her nose. Then there's a shot of an infant. Then there's a painting of a big spirit woman carrying a Bible over a frontier landscape, with the banner MANIFEST DESTINY. Not the mother of Mr. Rasmussen's children, I gather, but the beginning of today's lesson.

If the painting of Manifest Destiny is packed with allegory, aren't Mr. Rasmussen's family photos allegorical too? The painting of Manifest Destiny shows a stagecoach below the great white spirit, a wagon pulled by horses, settlers walking a trail. There are people on horseback, a train cutting through the land, oxen herded along. Besides her Bible, Manifest Destiny carries a telegraph wire. A group of Native Americans run ahead of this wave of "civilization," looking over their shoulders. Mr. Rasmussen's family pictures are humbler allegories, not obnoxious or painful in the way a twenty-first century American would find the painting. Now the toddler picking her nose is Manifest Destiny reincarnated. These projected children are the promise to his students: work hard, apply yourself, and you might find your way across the hostile fields of childhood to the land of Adults, where domestic bliss reigns.

"What does *manifest* mean?" Mr. Rasmussen asks the class.

"Clear," a student says.

"And *destiny?*" Mr. Rasmussen reaches into the projected painting, and it tattoos his forearm.

"Sure to happen."

Yes, sure to happen. Am I ready for another child? I wonder as I stare at Ms. Destiny. I'm forty-eight. The child will be born when I'm forty-nine and won't finish college until I'm seventy-one. My father died at fifty-one. What are the odds I'll live to see my child graduate? And I know what it's like to grow up without a father. Maybe I wouldn't have to revisit my childhood if he had lived. I've always thought there were secrets that only a father could tell his son that I'll never know.

The screen changes, and Mr. Rasmussen tells us about the election of 1844. "The Democrats won the election partly on the promise of the slogan 'Fifty-four Forty or Fight.' What do you think *fifty-four forty* means?" he asks a girl in the front row who's bobbing her head sleepily.

"I don't know," she says, which really means "I don't care."

"Good," he says with the force of enthusiasm you've got to admire. "You're going to learn something."

Probably not, but some of these kids will. Me too. I'm all ears.

"Last hour, someone asked, 'Is it an area code?'" he says, and just about everyone in the room of thirty laughs, even the sleepyheads. What eighth grader would pass up the opportunity to laugh derisively at someone else's foolishness?

"Don't laugh," he says. "She was closest to the correct answer. Does that give you a clue?"

A pensive, curly-headed boy named Adam, sitting at a desk beside me, startles as though pinched. "Oh! Longitude and latitude," he says.

"Correct!" says Mr. Rasmussen with a smile.

There's a lot to remember here: fifty-four forty or fight, the Treaty of Guadalupe Hidalgo, the Alamo, Manifest Destiny, the Northwest Ordinance of 1787. I can't keep it all straight. While Mr. Rasmussen is showing us a slide about the end of the Battle of the Alamo, labeled "March 2, 1836," one astute lad named John says, "I thought you said it ended March sixth?"

"You're right," says Mr. Rasmussen. "You're absolutely right. March sixth. I was preparing this in a hurry this morning. You know, I make mistakes too. I'm not mistake free. I wish I were."

Mr. Rasmussen makes mistakes too? That's a relief. If his mistakes are limited to getting the end of the Battle of the Alamo wrong by four days, I don't think anyone but the Daughters of the Republic of Texas are going to demand his hide (and they will, you know!). Mr. Rasmussen could probably take on the Daughters of the Republic of Texas in a fair fight. He's from Missouri after all, a state with almost as much pride and spunk as Texas. Actually, I wouldn't mind staying in his class for another two periods and learning about some more wars and treaties rather than attending my next two classes. But the bell rings and off I go, to battle my old implacable enemies: shop and PE.

When I attended Jeff Junior, all boys had to take shop and all girls had to take home ec. I hated anything to do with routers and safety goggles and wooden desk organizers and would have preferred home ec. They've put me in shop again. Now it's called space and aero, but they can't fool me. It's still shop. The instructor, Mr. Starkey, is a friendly guy, a few years younger than me — he has a bit of a surfer dude look to him. Light hair, straight teeth, the hint of a mustache and stubbly beard. The boys and girls are making motorized planes and are well into the project, so he brings me to the next room, filled with computer stations, and tells me he's going to have me build a Lego robot, a project the other students have already completed. We decide together which robot I'm going to build (there are several models to choose from). The easiest. He hands me a little plastic bin and shows me drawers that are full of various Lego components. I spend the next forty-five minutes puttering about like a demented old man, muttering to myself. By the end of the period, I have, if not a deep sense of accomplishment, a deep bucket of Legos. I should be in a bathrobe and slippers: *Poor Mr. Hemley. He's been that way for years. Thinks he's in eighth-grade shop. Humor him, and admire his shiny Legos.*

Next comes PE. Thankfully, Coach Nordeen puts me at ease right away. He's been here since 1978 and even worked for my PE teacher, Coach Adams, who always looked and acted like he could bench-press the Loch Ness Monster and bounce a meteor off his abs. Nordeen, on the other hand, has, like me, a bit of a gut. I'm not going to define the word *bit* in this instance. For this reason alone, I like him immensely. Coach Adams thought I was a wimp for nearly fainting on the track one day when I was hypoglycemic. Skeptical of my condition, he considered it akin to hypochondria.

The locker room is the same as I remember it, a subterranean grotto near the lunchroom. This time I don't have to worry about getting wet towels snapped at my genitals by ninth graders. Or do I? No, the administration has banned showers at school, a great innovation. You never outgrow the trauma of eighth-grade showers.

I change into my sweat pants and T-shirt in the coach's office while the boys change by their lockers. Unfettered testosterone reigns in the locker room just like the old days, minus the snapping towels.

Kids are yelling, throwing punches, using the F-word (*faggot*) liberally with one another. I cause a bit of a stir among them. "How old are you?" "Did you fail eighth grade a thousand times?" I'm not quite Methuselah, but any one of these kids could take me. A former student of mine says that's what all guys think when they meet another guy. "Can I take him?" I never thought this way until he mentioned it because it's too depressing. Every guy can take me. As Woody Allen once said, "In the event of war, I'm a hostage." Ever since my student told me about guys thinking about taking one another, it's been hard to get out of my mind. When another of my students told me about having an audience with the pope, I asked, "Did you wonder if you could take him?" Now that I'm back in an eighth-grade locker room, I see this is where such thoughts must originate.

Coach Nordeen gathers us — in all we number about fifty — in a semicircle outside his office and asks us what "food source" causes more choking than any other.

"Hard-boiled eggs," one boy shouts.

"Yolk tacos," another boy says. Yolk tacos. Only an eighth grader could come up with that.

"Gum," says the coach. "Tell you what. A girl choked on her gum when she collided with a boy going the other way on the track. We had to do the Heimlich maneuver on her." This makes little impression on the boys, except for one who demonstrates with his own lewd version of the Heimlich.

"That's an extra lap," the coach tells him.

Another gets in trouble for wearing a sleeveless T-shirt. "Why can't we wear shirts like that?" another kid asks.

"Beaters?" another boy answers. "We'd get the girls too excited," and this cracks up the boys, who let out whoops and hollers. *No*, I think. *It's because* you'd *get too excited thinking you were getting the girls excited, and you wouldn't look where you were going, and you'd run into them on the track and then would want to perform lewd Heimlich maneuvers on them.*

"Why do we have to tuck in our shirts?" says the boy who asked about the "beaters."

"Well, we have a problem with sagging britches," Coach tells us.

At least, it's only their britches that are sagging, unlike the coach and me. "If you don't tuck in your shirt, we don't know where your waistline is until your britches are about an inch from the ground."

The coach tells us we're going to play flag football today. This is the worst news, like a death sentence for me. What good could possibly come of a forty-eight-year-old playing flag football with thirteen- and fourteen-year-olds? I don't have time to ponder this because we head out of the locker room and cross the street to the track and playing fields. Unfortunately, it's a beautiful spring day, sunny and warm and no chance of rain.

But I rally as the coach tells us to do four laps, and I forget my age. I am Robin the Fleet Footed as I run my laps, hardly getting winded at all, passing eighth graders right and left. I'm not the fastest, but I'm not the slowest by a long shot, something I couldn't say my first time on this track when Coach Adams timed me as the slowest of all eighth graders in the hundred-yard dash. Today I even have the hope that PE might not be a complete disaster.

As we're doing warm-up stretches, a breeze catches a loose page from my notebook and sends it skittering across the field. I run after it and wind up on the edge of the playing field, on a slight rise above the sidewalk, where four girls and their teacher, all dressed in gym clothes, are walking toward the school.

"Oooh, what's that?" one of the girls says, pointing at me.

"Dude, who *are* you?" says another.

I just wave. I don't have time to explain I'm some fool in gym clothes. They can see that for themselves.

The coach has us stand in a line and count off in teams of six. When I see my team and the opposing team, I realize that Ms. Destiny, Manifest or one of her siblings, doesn't want me to have a good day in gym class. Two of the opposing players are actually first-string players on the Jefferson Junior High football team, burly guys who look older than me and are bigger than I am.

My team is a casting call for *Winnie the Pooh*. There's a pot-bellied, big-butted boy named Stanley who is Eeyore personified. He wears a red Columbia Fire Department T-shirt, but other than that he is invisible. He is the Kid to Whom No One Will Ever Pass the Ball. The coach has told us that everyone should get his hands on the ball, but we know that's a remark with an asterisk. "Except for that kid" is unstated but floats an inch above awareness. We *would* give him the ball. *I* would. But he will become invisible as soon as the game starts.

There's also a tall kid named Roger, a gazelle of a boy, which in itself would bode well for us, except that he looks as odd as I was at his age. He stands completely straight, rigid in fact, even as he runs, his arms at his sides. If he does not lift his arms, it's unlikely he's going to pass or catch a football. Another boy looks fit enough but has the nickname "Banana," which doesn't strike me as promising. Then there's redheaded Harry, who wears glasses and has an ironic detachment that is likewise not well suited for football. There's only one possible player among us, a small, swift boy from Sri Lanka named Baba. It's like some classic Hollywood moment, the team from the Hundred Acre Wood facing the Chicago Bears. What's a Pooh bear to do?

Within the first thirty seconds, the opposing team scores a touchdown, and most of our team slackens. Still, Baba, our quarterback, can run and pass, and I tell him he should pass to me. The next play he does just that. I leap to catch the ball and . . . it's intercepted. The player who scored the first touchdown scores another. Baba doesn't show any emotion, but I feel pretty bad, letting everyone down like that. A few plays later, Baba runs the ball for a touchdown. When Baba throws me another pass, I catch it this time and manage to make some yardage. Several plays later, I stop one of the opposing players (who at six-two stands an inch taller than me) from scoring on the third down. A miracle happens. The Boy Who Will Not Lift His Arms suddenly does so, and into his arms the football flies. He scores a touchdown easily, just to show that it can be done, I assume, then he resumes his stance of geeky boredom. The other team wipes the field with us, but I've managed to redeem myself a little. The final score is 28–14.

On our way back to the locker room, Stanley suddenly materializes beside us. "I seem to recall everyone gets the ball," he states in a tone both bitter and apathetic. "I didn't get it once."

No one bothers to reply, as he's simply stating the obvious. Welcome to eighth grade, Stanley.

"Make any touchdowns?" Coach asks me back in the locker room.

"No, as a matter of fact, I had the ball intercepted," I tell him, still stinging with that old feeling of athletic failure. Stanley and I are brethren, really.

"Tell you what," he says. "I admire you for getting in there. You don't see me out on the field."

This small remark from Coach Nordeen completely undoes me, and I leave the locker room beaming. I can't remember a coach ever saying he admired me, not that there *was* anything to admire. Unfortunately, as soon as he says this, I start sweating and I can't stop. Now I long for the old showers. Halfway up the stairs, my shirt is soaked. Olivia and Isabel's mother used to say, "Horses sweat, men perspire, women glow." But I sweat more than a horse, and Olivia often acts as though I do it on purpose. "That's gross, Dad," she says, when she sees my shirt dripping wet. And I suppose it is. Now as I walk through the halls, my shirt a dark shade of wet blue, a hundred Olivias turn their heads to look at the old wet guy smiling like an idiot as he makes his way to his locker.

↶

The next day, International Pi Day, our math class meets in the library under a banner proclaiming HAPPY PI DAY. Mrs. Holbein wears a white blouse with a sparkly pi on it today, and she cheerily cracks pi jokes after we complete several practice measurements of pi.

"What do you get when you divide a Native Alaskan by his circumference?

"Eskimo pi."

"What do you get when you divide a jack-o'-lantern by its circumference?

"Pumpkin pi."

Speaking of which, we're supposed to eat some pie, but one of the students, in typical eighth-grade fashion, forgot he was supposed to bring in forks and plates (a nice touch, those daily planners for eighth graders, but a losing battle against an eighth-grade boy's natural catatonia). What do you get when you divide an eighth-grade boy by his circumference?

"Pie? Did someone say pie?"

Luckily, eighth-grade girls are the solution to eighth-grade boys, at least in this instance. My art partner, Samantha, volunteers to run to the cafeteria for forks and plates while Mrs. Holbein projects a computer screen on the wall with various illustrations of pi. I doubt Mr. Mayhew would have used a computer even if they'd been around when I was here. He definitely wouldn't have given us pie. And he would have thought singing songs about pi an abomination. In that last instance, I would agree wholeheartedly with Mr. Mayhew, at least when eighth-grade boys are involved. Apparently, I'm supposed to stand in front of the group with three other eighth-grade boys who might as well be in leg irons for all their enthusiasm, and mumble some Pi Day songs along with them. They've probably practiced once more than I have (zero), so I join in a song sung to the tune of "O Christmas Tree":

O number pi, O number pi
Your digits are unending!

When Samantha returns with forks and plates, we break briefly for some pie, in groups of five to avoid a stampede, and then Mrs. Holbein attempts to show us an online birthday pi calculator. Unfortunately, it's blocked by the Jeff Junior firewall, and she can't get to it. "I checked it," Mrs. Holbein says, "but I made the mistake of checking it from home."

One of the boys from my unfortunate football team, the boy with the nickname "Banana," raises his hand. "I can probably hack my way in," he says. She considers this for a moment and then invites him to take a look but turns the projector off so no one can see how he's hacking. Quicker than you can say "security breach," Banana has successfully hacked his way around the firewall and is into the birthday pi page.

"I will thank you from my jail cell," Mrs. Holbein says.

But Banana's victory is premature as the site fails to load past its home page. "Your hacking sucks," another boy tells Banana as he takes his seat again. Implied here is the notion that the other boy could probably do a better job, if he were a Total Suck-Up like Banana.

I'm actually enjoying math as taught by Mrs. Holbein, and I'm not sure what to do with this alien feeling. It must be like suddenly discovering a different sexual preference (after living a lie!).

I'm afraid that social studies is a different matter. I've turned into something of a slacker in here. I haven't done my homework. Today we're reviewing the material thus far. With his forceful manner and his intense blue eyes, Mr. Rasmussen is as good as a cup of coffee for me and most of his students. "Let's start here," he says. "Manifest Destiny. We defined *manifest*. We defined *destiny*." *Now do fifty push-ups!*

Instead of push-ups, he asks the students to get out their pens and take notes. There *will* be a test, but happily I won't be here for it.

"Ariel, are you without a writing utensil?" he asks a girl in the front row leaning on an elbow.

"I'm lost," she says.

"We're at Texas Annexation." The rest of the class is furiously taking notes. This in itself seems a minor miracle, an entire eighth-grade class taking notes with the fear and anxiety of a group of Harvard Law students, with the exception of Ariel. I respect tough teachers. They're usually the best in the long run. But tough doesn't necessarily imply meanness, a distinction we don't always understand as students. Mr. Rasmussen bends toward Ariel now, and his tone and his manner change. "You look tired," he tells her. "You look like you're having a rough day. I'm tired too. I had two hours' sleep last night. My baby wasn't crying, just going, 'Oooh, aaaah.' So I sat up and stared at her. Then she smiled." He stands again and talks to the class as they're finishing their notes. "Children are fantastic. If I could afford it, I'd have twenty. If my wife would allow it."

The class laughs, and one boy says, "That's crazy."

Mr. Rasmussen simply smiles and goes back to Texas Annexation. "If you're the president of the United States," Mr. Rasmussen says, "and you want to go to war, but you don't want to start the war, what can you do?"

"C'mon," he prods. "You're all veterans of the hallway wars. You're experts. I could write a book on the hallway wars." So could I. When I was here, the fights were frequent and ugly, often interracial, and sometimes the cops had to be called in. A little less than a fifth of the school is African American now, but when I went to Jefferson, integration was still relatively new. While it's by no means perfect now, there's more intermingling, and the hallway wars are almost all between kids of the same race. Yesterday two African American girls went at it. I arrived on the scene a minute too late, but the air felt charged as though a clap of thunder had just connected. I have never witnessed more fights than in junior high. In junior high, every kid is an Alamo of one, overwhelmed by superior forces but ready to die for independence from oppressors seen and unseen.

"President Polk is tired of bickering with Mexico over the border," Mr. Rasmussen continues. "He wants to provoke Mexico into firing shots. So he sends a U.S. force under the leadership of Zachary Taylor to the disputed territory, the Rio Grande, 'to protect the U.S. from invasion.' Mexico responds by sending troops across the Rio Grande to remove Zachary Taylor's troops."

Mr. Rasmussen suddenly pauses and casts a gloomy eye in the direction of the projection screen. Following his gaze, I notice the object of his consternation. "Darn," says Mr. Rasmussen, smiling ruefully. "Made another mistake. Don't you hate it when you make mistakes? This is my week for mistakes."

In response to his question, I'd have to agree. I hate it when I make mistakes. And they haunt me. Who's to say what's trivial to one person when it might be the world to another? Mexico made a mistake in sending troops to meet Zachary Taylor. In my case, I've made some big mistakes — my first marriage, I suppose, might qualify. No treaty will change the results of that one, no do-over will revise the outcome. Still, it's the little patches we use to cover our mistakes that define us for the good, I think. I'm full of patches.

And on the screen, Mr. Rasmussen has inadvertently given us our first Korean commander-in-chief, "President Pok."

"Is it possible for there to be more than fifty states?" a boy asks Mr. Rasmussen, moving class along.

"It's very possible," he says. "Puerto Rico has voted three times on the issue of statehood, and it's been defeated three times."

"What about the Bahamas?" the tousle-headed boy named Adam, seated next to me, asks.

Yes, what about the Bahamas? What about France? Wouldn't the French really like to be Americans instead of having to worry about being French all the time? France would make a lovely state.

"The Bahamas is just territory," Mr. Rasmussen says distractedly, his lack of sleep obviously catching up with him. "The issue has not come up." I have an image of some blot on a map: Just Territory. The issue has not come up because the Commonwealth of the Bahamas is a sovereign nation, never ruled by the United States.

He gives us our assignment to trace U.S. land acquisitions and says we can work in small groups if we want. Like Ariel, I'm a little lost, so I scooch over to the boy who wanted to know about the Bahamas and ask if he'd like to work together. He glowers at me. "I like to work alone," he says.

"Um, okay," I say and scooch my chair back. But it's nothing personal, I learn. Adam is a smart but temperamental boy. The next day, when Adam puts his head down on his desk, Mr. Rasmussen says, "Adam, you're supposed to be studying."

"I'm reading!" Adam whines.

"Adam, you had your head down on your desk," Mr. Rasmussen says. "You can see why I thought that."

The next day, he's got his head on the desk again. "Yesterday I came by, and you had your head on your desk but you were reading. Today you have your head on your desk, and I know you're not reading."

"I'm tired," Adam nearly shouts.

"I'm tired too. I have a little baby keeping me awake at night."

"You're killing me!"

"You've got to work through that," Mr. Rasmussen says softly. "It makes us a better person."

I love that exchange, both Adam's drama and Mr. Rasmussen's patience and gentle guidance. I don't think Mr. Rasmussen cares finally so much for dates and treaties, but he teaches them because this is what he needs to do to shepherd his students through the hoops of the educational system. What I think he cares about, besides his family, his friends, and the Indianapolis Colts (as he tells us one day) is this community of fragile kids trying to survive the hallway wars just as I did thirty-five years ago. I love the way he quietly works the room, talking to them about everything from trout fishing to fatherhood to the bullet trains of Japan. His comments aren't really digressions because he keeps the class on task admirably. They're more like sidebars, reminders that the world is larger than this class-room. As we're working, I hear Mr. Rasmussen's voice, a soft mur-mur above the sighs and clicks of pens and seat adjustments. "Feeling better, Thulani? Were you sick?" I look up to see a girl with fish ear-rings nodding her head, smiling wanly at Mr. Rasmussen.

But Mr. Rasmussen, like Santa, knows who's naughty and who's nice. To another student who claims not to be feeling well, he eyes him like the sergeant he is. "Are you not feeling well? Oh, I'm sorry. Well, maybe a correct answer will make you feel better."

The phone rings, and Mr. Rasmussen answers. "*Ohayo gozai-masu!*" he says cheerily. "Good morning" in Japanese.

"Yes, I sent Samuel Pridell down to you," he says. "Maybe he needs to speak with Nyle." Samuel, the boy who got in trouble on Monday for his coat, is in trouble again today for not having his books and for having a bandana, "unauthorized clothing," hanging from his pants. I remember what Liz Monroe told me in sixth grade, that the gap between the slow learners and the fast learners widens with every year. In eighth grade that gap becomes the Sahara, and kids like Samuel see their classmates far away, on some sand dune, and wave their bandanas in salute, then turn and jog defiantly in the other direction, their heels kicking up sand. In math class too, there's one polite girl who shows up every day but refuses to do any work. "She's pleasant. She smiles," Mrs. Holbein told me, "but says she's not going to do any of the work. We've got a lot of kids like her, not all as polite. It's a dilemma across the nation, how to deal with these students at risk." Here, nothing beats the conventional wisdom: as any teacher knows, the problems start at home. A math test is the least of this girl's problems, in the same way that my eighth-grade life fell apart, not because of bullies or bad teachers, but because my sister had supernovaed, and my galaxy had turned to a crisp in a flash.

This is my day for Hard Realities, I suppose. At lunch I sit at the Popular Table, and they ignore me. I'm not sure why I'm suddenly uncool or why they've just now noticed I'm uncool. Maybe it has something to do with the fact that I sat at a table of unpopular kids yesterday, acquiescing to Margie's wishes. I rejected the popular kids, in effect, and there's no reentering the magic circle once you've left.

Seamus's girlfriend is hurriedly finishing her social studies homework today, but he tells her not to bother. "She gives you the answers in class, and she doesn't collect them."

Banana walks by wearing a birthday hat.

"Is that gay or what?" Seamus shouts, passing a hand over his red buzz cut as though he's removing his own "gay" hat.

"It's for Pi Day," Banana says. "And Einstein's birthday."

"You know what?" Seamus says. "You're gay without the hat." He wiggles his fingers and says in imitation of the Lucky Charms elf, "Hooo-hooo! They're magically delicious."

I don't say anything, but I squeeze out of the table, shaking my head, not at Seamus, but at myself. And then I walk across the room to where Banana sits with his friends and join them.

Eighth grade is eighth grade is eighth grade. I take my victories when and where I find them. On the way to shop, I run into Banana again.

"You still here?" he asks. He's going to cooking class, "Creative Cuisine," what I once knew as home ec and where I was forbidden to tread.

"Darn," I tell him. "I'd prefer that."

"Maybe you can be our judge," he says. "We're having a chili cook-off."

So I go into shop and break the news to my teacher that I'm defecting to cooking class where I will be treated well and fed and not made to gather Legos in a bucket (which I think violates the Geneva Convention). He takes it well. He's heard all the excuses in his nineteen years at Jeff Junior. Nineteen years! By choice. "When I first got here," he tells me, "I didn't plan on staying. But I liked it, and if there are no hitches in the road, next year will be my twentieth." Like Mr. Rasmussen, he looks about nineteen. As we're chatting, I notice a piece of paper stuck to the bulletin board. It's a contract with Seamus. In it Seamus promises to work hard and not be a behavior problem or he'll go straight to the office. The Treaty of Space and Aero.

While I can't say I liked shop any better than the first time around, I'm fine with PE this time. Coach Nordeen makes us take a fitness test in the gym after running twenty-five laps, stretching, and doing sit-ups. We're being tested on push-ups, the hard kind, where you pause before raising yourself up again. Push-ups. Normally, this would terrify me, but by the end of the week, I'm on an eighth-grade high, and I'm in love with everything about Jeff Junior, even new opportunities for humiliation. What makes it even more humiliating is that we have to do our push-ups in squads of five while the class watches and Coach records the results. We're supposed to do the push-ups, then tell Coach our name, age, and number of push-ups completed. "The school record is by Taylor Crane," says Coach. "Wrestler, isn't he?" he says. "One hundred twenty-eight. If you want a shot at the school record, come by after school. We're going to limit it here to twenty. Once you hit twenty, you've gone beyond the Missouri Health standard. It's your age plus two."

That's not good news. That means fifty for me. Poor Stanley the Potbellied and Robin the Potbellied are doomed. While Stanley is invisible in football, his big butt might as well be dipped candy apple red while doing push-ups. A neon sign might as well appear above him and flash the pathetic number of push-ups he completes. Three. When he's done, he goes up to Coach and says, "Stanley Hake, fifteen, three," betraying no emotion, the name, rank, and serial number equivalent of PE. When I'm done, I go up to Coach and proclaim a little more enthusiastically: "Robin Hemley, forty-eight, eleven."

"Got you," says the coach.

"At least you did some," says Banana, trying to make me feel better. But I feel great. I did better than I thought. I even feel like bragging. "Not too bad for someone who never does them."

"Right," says the coach. "You don't see me out there."

While Susan Fitzpatrick is long gone from these halls, I bring my old yearbook with me to school on Friday, my last day. In art class, both Samantha and Cyclone Host Greg ask me if they can sign it, and, of course, I'm delighted. Samantha is my surrogate Susan Fitzpatrick, and Greg is my surrogate locker buddy and best friend, Glenn. Naturally, I bypass Seamus, and though I'd like Banana's signature, I don't see him all day. Actually, I'm skipping out on half the school day today, not for old times' sake, but because Margie and Shoshie plan to pick me up early so we can make the long drive from Missouri to Milwaukee, where Izzy will join us for the weekend to spend her thirteenth birthday. Of course, I can't leave without saying good-bye and thanks to Nyle — he's easy to find. He's usually in the front of the building, chatting with teachers and benevolently watching over the students as they change classes.

On the way to the office, a teacher stops me and asks me for my hall pass. I'm easy to fluster, but not this time. I keep walking. "You know, if you really want to relive eighth grade," she calls after me, "you should fake a stomachache." Little does she know. Today I woke up with a sore throat and didn't want to go to school at all. Thirty-five years ago, I didn't even need that much of an excuse to skip.

Nyle and I sit in his office and chat about my first and second experiences at Jeff Junior, and I tell him a couple of the stories I've been carrying around inside me all these years, about almost getting beat up by a student and about almost getting beat by the principal, Mr. Fritz. He loves the Gandhi story, but a look of concern crosses his face when I tell him about being given the choice to miss assembly or get whacked by Mr. Fritz. "You didn't want John Fritz swatting you," he says. "He was a football player. That's why I didn't want to be a principal for a long time, not until corporal punishment was phased out. I couldn't imagine myself swatting kids."

I can't imagine him swatting kids either. I ask him to sign my yearbook and thank him for not micromanaging my visit. "We are what we are," he tells me, before taking me on my last tour of this building he knows by heart, including the gym, where the sign from the old store behind the school, Garrett's, hangs on a wall. I didn't notice it there before, so intent was I on my push-ups.

"A lot of the old coaches think it's funny that we have the Garrett's sign. The players used to be threatened to be kicked off the team if they went to Garrett's."

"Why's that?" I ask.

"I guess you don't remember. That's where kids used to smoke and get into fights. But we went over there too. They used to have sinfully good sticky buns." Nyle and I shake hands, I thank him again, and I skip eighth grade for the last time, passing by the bench outside the office.

For me the halls are no longer haunted. The bench in front of the principal's office is just a bench, and the hall where I was almost beat up is just a hall. Just territory. A sign on the wall beams brotherhood in sign language: "Good things happen to people who try." Maybe. Maybe not. But for today, let's take it for gospel. Let's say we have our whole lives left to try.

Outside by the flagpole, I wait for Margie and Shoshie on another bench. Alone again while the rest of the school goes about its business, but not sad. Waiting not in exile this time but in anticipation. I open the yearbook to the page with Nyle's signature on it and run my finger across, sure it's not an illusion.

The next day, I'm reunited with Izzy, who will be, if not where I've just been, in her own version of it next year. Olivia can't be with us again because she has to practice for her choir group. In the hotel room in Milwaukee, I tell Izzy about my experience with the popular kids at lunch. "Wait," I say. "Where do you sit?"

"With the popular kids, I guess," she says.

"You've got to sit with the unpopular kids from now on," I tell her.

"Why?" she says. But I don't bother explaining. I know she has no intention of sitting with the kids like her dad at lunch. Somehow, when Margie says to sit with the unpopular kids, it carries more weight.

"Anything you want to know about eighth grade?" I ask her.

"No, Dad," she says. "I think I'm good."

CHAPTER SEVEN

MYSTERY DATE
Prom Do-Over

ORIGINAL AGE: 16
DO-OVER AGE: 48
ORIGINAL LOCATION: ST. ANDREW'S SCHOOL, SEWANEE, TENNESSEE
DO-OVER LOCATION: ST. ANDREW'S-SEWANEE SCHOOL, SEWANEE,
TENNESSEE

After only two years in Columbia, Missouri, we moved again when my mother found a new teaching position in South Bend, Indiana. Columbia had started out promising, but eighth grade had ruined that, and so I didn't mind starting fresh yet again. The Geographical Cure, alcoholics call it. Make a mess of your life. Move somewhere else.

I wasn't keen on returning to a public school following my experience at Jeff Junior. As odd as going to school in a psych ward felt during the few months I'd been at Mid-Missouri Mental Health Center, it had its benefits. Small student-teacher ratio. Quirky student body. No one could make fun of you for acting strange. Strange was the norm. So when we moved to South Bend, I asked my mother to send me to a school smaller than John Adams, the mammoth public high school. She got wind of a school called Magdalene, run by Bruce Fingerhut, a rotund man with a booming voice and an approach to education that was both visionary and classical. At its height, Magdalene had twenty-six students and perhaps eight teachers. Its first year, we met in a church that we sometimes shared with funerals — I remember coming across an open casket on my lunch break more than once. The second year our classes met in the basement of another church — and no more funerals. Bruce wanted us to learn the classics, and he was proud of the fact that nearly all our textbooks were meant for college students. For two years I took Latin, French, philosophy (in which we read Plato's dialogues), rhetoric (in which we read Aristotle), ancient history, logic, math, science, and English. As always, I did terribly in math, actually flunking algebra my first year, and performing not much better in science. But I loved the school, and the student-to-teacher ratio couldn't be beat.

A couple of the students had millionaire parents who offered to fund Bruce's project indefinitely, but the student body was evenly divided between Kickback Kids (the kids who were kicked from one school to another) and smart but lost kids like me, and Bruce decided to fold up shop. The student body wasn't living up to his vision of a coterie of bookish boys and girls who would disdain Harvard in favor of Oxford. As it stood, I hadn't noticed much difference between Magdalene and Psych Ward School, so I was comfortable enough there and soundly disappointed when Bruce called it quits. That left me with the grim certainty of going into my junior year at John Adams High School, which had a student population of more than fifteen hundred.

That summer, a friend my age named Chris told me in passing about the school in Tennessee that he was attending. Chris seemed like a nice guy, and he liked the school, which was located in the middle of the mountains between Nashville and Chattanooga and, best of all, had only 180 or so students. The school was Episcopalian, but that didn't seem like a problem. My brother had gone to an Episcopalian school in Connecticut, and he'd hardly noticed its religious affiliation.

And so I entered St. Andrew's in Sewanee, Tennessee, in 1974, when I was sixteen. The kid in the room next door to mine also turned out to be a boy named Robin — a senior who seemed like a pretty nice guy, except that he was expelled within a day. Caught smoking pot the very next day, my friend Chris was expelled too. Now I knew no one at the school. My biggest surprise was mandatory chapel twice a week, Thursday evenings and Sunday mornings. There had to be some mistake. Before my first chapel, I found the headmaster, Father Martin, on the tennis court in shorts and a T-shirt.

"I don't have to go to chapel, do I?" I asked. "No hard feelings, but I'm Jewish."

He took a ball out of his pocket and looked at me like I had just said something ridiculous. For a second I thought maybe he didn't know what a Jew was. "Everyone has to go to chapel, or you get demerits and you'll wind up on work crew Saturday morning."

"But that's unfair," I said.

"This is an Episcopalian school," he said. "Didn't you read the literature?" He raised his eyebrows and gave me an indulgent smile, then excused himself and served.

I hadn't read the literature. I suppose I should have read it when it arrived, but I was too excited and lazy, and my mother was too busy or lazy to closely read the literature too.

But my classes turned out to be every bit as good as if not better than my classes at Magdalene. My roommate was an exchange student from Japan named Hiroshi Oshiro, and we became fast friends. Mandatory chapel wasn't so bad either. I hung out with the exchange students mostly, the two Alis from Iran (whom we differentiated as Good Ali and Bad Ali); Antouman Seka, who claimed to be a prince in his native country of Gambia; Hiroshi and Kyoichi from Japan; and a guy from Laos whose name I don't remember. Shintoists, Muslims, a Jew, and at least one animist — there wasn't a Christian among us. They all went up for Communion — it was a weekly contest to see how big a gulp they could get before Father Martin snatched away the chalice. At first I resisted, but eventually I gave in and got pretty good at sucking in the wine.

At St. Andrew's my grades were so good that I won all the awards for the best student in each class, except math, including Mr. Norton's southern literature class in which we read four Faulkner books: *As I Lay Dying; The Sound and the Fury; Absalom, Absalom!;* and, my favorite, *Light in August.* Mr. Norton was the kind of irascible, tough teacher under whom I excelled. Tough love. The tougher the better. He constantly urged us to "get your heads out of your duffle bags" and referred fondly to "your small but perfect minds." Mr. Norton either had two horses shot from under a great-grandfather at the Battle of Gettysburg or two great-grandfathers shot from under their horses. The point was that he came to southern literature honestly, while I, a Yankee Jew from New York City, did not. "You'll never know how much it pains me to give you this award, Mr. Hemley," he whispered when I took the stage. He couldn't have said anything that would have pleased me more.

I also landed the lead role of Creon in our school production of *Antigone,* opposite Lizzie Clark, who played Antigone. Lizzie was a smart and funny girl my age, a day student, on whom I had an enormous, though never verbalized, crush. Did I mention that of 186 students, only about thirty-five were girls? I didn't stand a chance with Lizzie or any of the other girls, boarders or day students. Lizzie and I also were responsible for most of the content of our student newspaper as well as the student literary magazine.

St. Andrew's was a wonderful place for a fledgling writer like myself. James Agee, who'd written *A Death in the Family* and *Let Us Now Praise Famous Men,* had been a student at St. Andrew's, and the school library was named after him. The venerable literary magazine *Sewanee Review* was published just down the road at the University of the South, and another one of my English teachers, Claire Reishman, took a personal interest in my literary desires. When the university held a seventy-fifth birthday celebration for the poet Allen Tate, most famous for "Ode to the Confederate Dead," Mrs. Reishman brought me along, and in a small auditorium on campus I was awed by celebratory readings by such literary giants as Eudora

Welty and Robert Penn Warren. Mrs. Reishman also taught me how to write a term paper, something I silently thanked her for many times during my college career.

So what could I possibly have to do over at St. Andrew's?

Mainly, there was the prom. I remember standing outside the dining hall where the dance was held, peering in the window while the couples danced, wishing I could be one of them. But I was too shy and too skinny, and even though I'd won a letter on the soccer team, it was a junior varsity letter. I was a bench warmer, and no one wants to go out with a bench warmer. Plus I looked about twelve.

I didn't know exactly how I'd go about doing over the prom, but I figured I'd call St. Andrew's and see if they could help me out. I didn't imagine myself simply showing up at a dance and leaving after it was finished. Ideally, I wanted to spend a week or so back at my old school, taking classes. Although I had left St. Andrew's as a junior, I had intended to return for my senior year but hadn't. I'd gotten on so well with my roommate, Hiroshi, that I asked if I could be an exchange student at his high school in Osaka, Japan. And that's what I did. I went to Osaka the next year, and Hiroshi's family was my host family. I was supposed to return to St. Andrew's for a makeup year, but instead I dropped out of the exchange program early, too homesick and bratty to last the full year, and went directly to college, starting midyear. One day in the summer of 1976, I mysteriously received in the mail a diploma from St. Andrew's, signed by Father Martin himself. No note accompanied the diploma, and my mother and I were perplexed as to why I was receiving this when I hadn't fulfilled the requirements. I never found out because Father Martin passed away a number of years ago, and I hadn't had contact with the school since I left in 1975. Maybe if I returned now to St. Andrew's, I could see what I had missed by not coming back for my senior year.

But who would I bring to the dance? I couldn't bring a sixteen- or seventeen-year-old. Much too creepy a thought.

Trusting in luck if not kismet, I called St. Andrew's, which was now St. Andrew's-Sewanee, having merged with nearby Sewanee Academy twenty-five years earlier to ensure the survival of both schools.

The person who answered the phone was a secretary, and although I knew she didn't have the authority to grant my wish one way or the other, I went through my normal tortured spiel. After about ten minutes of prattling, there was silence on the other end, the kind of silence that usually means that the person has hung up or self-immolated.

"Well," she said finally. "You'll have to speak to our alumni director about that, Lizzie Clark Duncan. I'll connect you."

This confused me. I hadn't heard anyone speak the name Lizzie Clark for more than thirty years. I had expected to be connected to a complete stranger, and I had been prepared for that, but I wasn't prepared at all to reach the woman I'd had a crush on in 1975. Not only was it disconcerting but bizarre. Out of twenty-six students in my graduating class of 1976, what were the chances that one of them, and one central to my year at St. Andrew's, would be the gatekeeper for this do-over? My skin started blotching. Hearing her name gave me an instant case of hives. I reached her answering machine. I definitely recognized her voice after all these years. I could hear her as Antigone with a slight Tennessee accent.

I started uncertainly. "Hi, Lizzie. This is Robin Hemley. I think we were classmates . . ." Then I explained my project. I called her again an hour later, and this time she answered.

"Robin Hemley," she said cheerily. "How are you?"

We spoke for about twenty minutes, not only about my project, but catching up on the intervening thirty-two years since the last time we'd spoken. She told me that in her twenties she had gone to L.A. to become an actress, and after scrambling for roles for eleven years, she had had enough and decided she didn't want to run around L.A. auditioning for commercials into her fifties. So she returned to her hometown of Sewanee and, after being "missing in action," found her way back to St. Andrew's-Sewanee, where she became alumni director of the school. She had also married and had a son who was now eight years old.

She liked the project idea a lot, but she said of course she'd have to check with the other powers that be: the headmaster, Father Wade, and a couple of the assistant headmasters, including Claire Reishman.

Once again, I was dumbstruck. Not only was the object of my teenage affections still at St. Andrew's, but so was my former English teacher. Like Mr. Norton, Claire Reishman had been a formidable teacher. She handed out demerits like stickers at a dentist's office, and when she taught us the fire and brimstone religious tracts of Jonathan Edwards, she made even me, a heathen (at least in Edwards's eyes), sit up and envision perdition. I was thrilled at the thought of seeing her again, but I dreaded one thing: calling her Claire. In my mind she was still Mrs. Reishman. I couldn't imagine being forced as an adult to call her by her first name.

Of course, I would also have to undergo another background check, Lizzie told me, but as long as I passed that, she supported the idea.

I told her too about the prom and standing outside wishing I could be inside dancing. I didn't say, "wishing I was in there dancing with you." That seemed a little stalkerish, and I imagined the entire conversation taking a turn south to Antarctica if I mentioned I'd once had a crush on her.

"Well, it wasn't exactly a prom," she said. "We don't have anything we call a prom, but we do have senior dances. I suppose I could suggest to the seniors that they organize a winter dance, and I could throw some money their way to help out."

I had no notion of the difference between a prom and a senior dance — never having been to either. My idea of a prom conjured loneliness, alienation, and terror. Around the same time as my sad little school dance memory, Stephen King published *Carrie,* with its memorable prom scene. And the movie *Grease* came out not long after. These are the two poles of high school dance experiences, and even those of us who never got in the front door of a prom still have a prom experience, even if it's only known as longing. On the prom spectrum, more people I know tip toward the *Carrie* side of things, humiliated and isolated, than dancing up a storm with Olivia Newton-John and John Travolta. I needed to do something about that. I needed to be John Travolta once in my life (though without the Scientology, and I don't need to fly my own jet either).

"So, Lizzie, will you go to the dance with me?"

"Sure," she said, laughing. "That would be fun. I'll just need to clear it with my husband."

If it had only been that easy thirty-two years ago. "Great," I said. "And I'll clear it with my wife."

Happily, her husband approved. My wife approved, though begrudgingly, threatening to come down to Tennessee as my chaperone. The difference here was that Margie knew I'd once had a crush on Lizzie, so she had at least a little reason to be suspicious, though I told her that the operative word was *once*. I'd kept Lizzie and her husband Rick in the dark about this, and I meant to keep it that way — I meant, in fact, not to mention it to anyone ever. But I did mention it — to the drama critic for the *Atlanta Journal-Constitution,* who put the fact that I'd had a crush on Lizzie in an article he wrote about me during my *Littlest Angel* do-over. The article appeared on the front page, and so I figured I'd better come clean to Lizzie. Her reply to my e-mail about the article was gracious. She said she was surprised that anyone would have had a crush on her during her awkward teenage years. Well, who better than another awkward teen?

Other than that glitch, the planning proceeded well. Everyone who needed to approve my weeklong visit approved, though there were some reservations. There was always the creep factor — one faculty member felt the idea was a little perverse, but Father Wade supported my visit, and Claire Reishman was downright enthusiastic about it. Thankfully, the fun of the idea outweighed its creepiness, though they were not going to allow me to have a roommate. That would be too much. Such precautions were fine with me, but if I remembered dorm life accurately, teenage kids could be a lot creepier than any adults I knew.

〜

Arriving in Nashville on a sunny day in mid-February, I rent my car and then sit in the parking lot trying to figure out the route to Sewanee — it's not difficult at all, but I'm a nervous traveler. I own one of those GPS units in which you can program any address. (I received it as a giveaway from my credit card company, which should give an idea of how much my credit card company loves me. It's great to be loved by people, but it's a very bad sign when credit card companies send you gifts.) Out of the box, the GPS unit could be programmed to have a variety of accents. I would have chosen Filipino, but that wasn't an option. On a whim, I chose a British accent. Ever since, my family has known our GPS unit as the British Lady. I'm the only one who loves her. Margie doesn't like the British Lady at all. The British Lady often gets small things wrong. She'll announce in her clipped tone, "Arriving at destination on left!" and you'll look left and see an empty lot. Look right, and there's the address you wanted. Or she'll tell you to turn into a fence. Or the address you want will be a block away. It's not a matter of her needing updating. Although she's a machine and a British-sounding one at that, she was still made by humans, and so I forgive her. But Margie doesn't. I especially like it when I disobey the British Lady and she scolds me. "Recalculating!" she says with the British frisson in her voice that just makes a lad tingle all over.

Unfortunately, I've misplaced the British Lady. I thought she was in my backpack, but she's not. So I pop the trunk and find her in the luggage. Thank the Lord. Of course I understand that my personification of her could be the sign of a serious disorder, that it might also say something negative (Lies! Lies!) about my relationship with women, or at the very least cast me with the unholy glow of the Creep Factor, but many people, and men in particular, historically speaking, have intimate relationships with their cars, and their cars don't even talk to them, so I think I can be forgiven my slight separation issues with my GPS unit. Does that make most men creeps? Rhetorical question.

Reunited, we drive leisurely down Highway 24 this Sunday morning, passing signs for the Jack Daniel's distillery, George Dickel billboards, and other familiar indicators that I'm happily back in the South; that Elvis has returned to the building; that I can, if I so choose, see Rock City, as the painted roofs of barns urge; that it is my God-given right to visit Ruby Falls. I can tune in only one rock station on the radio. The rest are split between country and fire-and-brimstone preachers, which of course is only natural for a Sunday morning in the mountains of southern Tennessee.

At the Monteagle exit, I head toward Sewanee, past barbecue restaurants, the Piggly Wiggly, and Hallelujah Pottery. After several miles of winding two-lane road, I find myself once again at the gates of St. Andrew's-Sewanee, its pine-studded campus looking much as it did when I last saw it in 1975. The school owns 550 acres on top of a "mountain" in the southern Cumberland Plateau, about 2,100 feet above sea level. Although I haven't been here in more than thirty years, I've visited countless times in my dreams. It's always a variation of the same dream. I'm in my old dorm, a two-story concrete block rectangle. I look out my window at an enormous field, the kind Holden Caulfield describes in *The Catcher in the Rye,* with "thousands of little kids" near the edge of a cliff. It's that kind of landscape, the crazy field of nightmares. I meet a group of students and teachers in that field, and they ask me what I'm doing back. "I'm back to graduate," I say. In another version, I'm stuck in Monteagle, on foot, and I need to walk back ten miles for graduation. Holden Caulfield ran away from his stifling boarding school "full of phonies." I, on the other hand, want to run back to my school. Despite its rigor, I've never thought of St. Andrew's as stifling, nor any more or less populated with phonies than any other institution in the world.

When I finally arrive at St. Andrew's in the dream, the ceremony has already begun, and the room is packed. I catch Father Martin's eye. He looks at me disapprovingly as if to say, "You'll be late for your own funeral, won't you, Robin?"

It's sunny now, but it rained heavily this morning, and my car splashes through puddles, the only car on the little campus road, past the gym and the spot where a new million-dollar performing arts center has recently been dedicated. The center of campus is lined with wooded walks surrounded by dorms and other buildings, some familiar and some not. The chapel looks the same except for its wooden doors, which seem more worn than I remember. Everything else is where I remember it: just up the road from the chapel are the administration building, the cafeteria, another set of dorms. And in front of the administration building stands Lizzie, looking not all that different from the last time I saw her. "Recalculating!" the British Lady snaps, and I pull her plug from the cigarette lighter. In a bit of a snit, are we?

Dressed in a red beret and glasses, a colorful scarf, a winter vest, and jeans and boots, Lizzie still cuts a youthful figure, though her dark hair is shorter and flecked with gray. But I'd recognize her anywhere. I pull up beside her.

"Hey, Robin Hemley," she says.

There's no one around, so I cut the engine and step out of the car, and we shake hands, then I turn to get my luggage from the trunk.

"You need a hand?"

"No, I'm fine," I say, grabbing the handle and yanking it out of the trunk. The suitcase flies open, and my towel, shirts, and underwear land in an enormous puddle. I forgot to zip the suitcase after retrieving the British Lady at the airport. The British Lady's revenge.

"I'm not looking!" Lizzie shouts, turning around in a way that means she definitely was looking. Yes, it's underwear, but it's clean, and at least I didn't bring my SpongeBob jammies.

Smooth, Robin, I think. I couldn't have made a more awkward move if I were sixteen.

I gather my soggy clothes and stuff them back into my suitcase, then follow Lizzie to my digs for the next week. I can't stay in my old room because it's now in a girls' dorm, so I've been assigned an empty room in the dorm beside the cafeteria. In my day the dorm was called St. Patrick's, but it was renamed Harvey House after an alum who was killed in the first Gulf War in Kuwait. It's a two-story stucco building, with trim and roof in a shade you might call Episcopal red. Three cloisterlike arches line the front of the building. A number of the buildings on campus have this same color scheme, the tasteful arches sparking subliminal thoughts of tradition and continuity.

The campus is eerily quiet. Most of the students, Lizzie informs me, are in the gym watching a performance of *Footloose.* Normally, I'd be up for seeing the musical. If I were a student, I would have probably been in it. But I'm a little tired from traveling, and I'd like to get reacclimated to campus, so Lizzie shows me to my room. The first difference I notice is the two common rooms, one on each floor, with TVs and video game consoles. Let's not even talk about video games. I don't mean to do one of those, "When I was here, we hunted one another with crossbows for fun," but, really, this was pre-Pac-Man. And we had one TV on the whole campus, located in the sorry excuse for a student lounge that also housed a Coke machine, a pay phone, and a Ping-Pong table. And our crossbows.

"Woman on the floor!" Lizzie yells, as she opens the door to the mine-shaft-dark hallway on the second floor where my room, number 207, is. Truly, I have to feel my way along the hall to find my room. The darkness isn't a result of frugality or energy-saving measures on the part of St. Andrew's-Sewanee. This is the Lair of the Mole People, junior and senior boys. The message is clear: humans, enter at your own peril.

I don't know how to describe my room except to say it's my room. And it's your room too, if you ever lived in a dorm of the Mole People variety. A bunk bed, two desks, both sturdy and durable, blue carpet that could double as sandpaper, an overhead light, and two closets, a knocky old heater underneath the window. But I'm not complaining. I feel right at home. I wouldn't expect anything more or less, and Lizzie has kindly supplied me with sheets and a blanket and towels from her own apartment.

After I've settled a bit, Lizzie gives me the grand tour. The layout and feel of the campus haven't changed much in thirty years. The old monastery (which I have no memory of) burned down in the 1990s, Lizzie tells me, and Father Flye's house was moved to a different location. Father Flye, who lived to a ripe old age, had a famous correspondence with James Agee collected into a book and was an institution as tied to St. Andrew's as Agee himself.

In some ways, the student body has changed since my day. When I was here, the school was struggling a bit with 186 students. Now it has upwards of 250, and the demographics reflect the realities of boarding school life. A third of the students come from other countries where well-heeled parents want their kids to have the benefits of an American education. South Korea could practically staff a consulate in Sewanee, there are so many students from that country, twenty-five or more, as well as students from Taiwan and China. The full tuition of nearly $34,000 for boarding students is well beyond my means if I wanted to send my kids here. I couldn't even afford that much a year to send my kids to college.

The old building that housed our student Ping-Pong closet was torn down long ago, replaced in a different location with a new student union with its own radio station(!). That old building also housed the infamous smoking lounge, where I unfortunately picked up the habit that took me nearly nineteen years to break. I'm flabbergasted that my mother gave me permission, especially since my father died because of smoking, but I was a stubborn and independent kid, and she was a permissive mom — not always a winning combination. I started smoking when one of the Japanese students, Kyoichi, a senior, received a box full of exotically packaged Japanese cigarettes. Hiroshi and I both raided Kyoichi's stash, and that's how it began. Now smoking is completely banned on campus, with or without parents' permission.

Lizzie leads me to Simmons Hall, the classroom building that was the classroom building in my day too. Simmons looks different from most of the other buildings, more of a low-lying sixties design. It's not ugly, but it's nice that it's quarantined so none of the other more traditional buildings catch what it's got. The path to Simmons used to be merely a gravel walk, along which we'd sometimes find a stray copperhead sunning itself. Now there's a paved walk with fancy street lamps and blue Adirondack chairs clustered at various points along the way. A new wing has been added to Simmons, and the Agee library in Simmons has been moved, classrooms rearranged. Although the building is virtually empty on a Sunday afternoon, I see my Gambian friend, Antouman, standing fearfully in the doorway on a snowy day. Someone has told him snow is poisonous, and he's afraid to leave the building. I see Julian, a boy from Georgia, telling Mrs. Gooch, the librarian, that he's so angry at her he's not going to tell his daddy to send her a box of peaches from their orchard this summer. I see my roommate Hiroshi getting in a lot of trouble on the first day of class with Mrs. Reishman. A ne'er-do-well, a hooligan, a *thug* named Arnold has told Hiroshi that a common sign of respect is to address a female teacher by calling her a bitch. Later in the hour, Mrs. Reishman asks if anyone has any questions. Hiroshi's hand pops up. "I do, bitch!" The temperature in the room drops. We bow our heads in prayer. Mrs. Reishman stands up slowly from her desk and smiles at my roommate. "Hiroshi," she says. "May I see you in the hall a moment?"

A few minutes later, Hiroshi returns, and Mrs. Reishman goes on with her lesson on Jonathan Edwards as though nothing extraordinary has occurred. He has refused to rat out Arnold, and so he's given six demerits, enough to earn him Saturday morning work crew. This was no small punishment. I spent my year at St. Andrew's in dread of work crew. They were out at 6:00 a.m. every Saturday under the supervision of the assistant headmaster, Mr. Simmonds, who showed no mercy. Work crew built the two-acre pond by the track.

I suppose I feel a kind of nostalgia as I'm walking through Simmons. That old saying comes to mind, "If these walls could talk . . ." They do. They talk and I listen, and as I listen, I shed layers of something like clothing, though I'm not embarrassed by this nakedness.

Lizzie and I run into Martha Keeble, a visual arts teacher who's doing a workshop for students and faculty on light therapy. This is something new. No one did light therapy at St. Andrew's in 1975. But she's credentialed. She attended a special workshop on it in New York. "One person asked me what the school would think if they knew I had attended the workshop. 'They paid for it!' I said. Here's the thing. The Egyptians did it!"

I'm not sure that's an ironclad recommendation. The Egyptians also thought the brain was a useless organ (in the case of some people — David Duke comes to mind — I'd agree), pulverized it after death with a hook through the nose, then removed it with a spatula, while preserving more-vital organs, such as the appendix, in jars.

Still, I'm up for anything the Egyptians did short of brain pulverization. Light therapy sounds noninvasive in any case. She holds up a green scarf. "Think of your skin as a sponge and this vibrating seven hundred million times a second. Hey, if my lights are in my car, I'll give you a quick immune boost." First she gives us a bunch of colored glasses to try on. For the first time in my life, I literally put on a pair of rose-colored glasses. Martha tells us to switch to a different colored pair after our eyes adjust. Then she does a "brain balance" on us, with colored lights next to our temples and under the nose, followed by rejuvenating oil rubbed on our hands. Although I hide it well, I'm more open to suggestion than most people on the planet. If I were Caesar, I would certainly beware the Ides of March. I do not believe in fortune cookies, but I pay attention to them. Same with horoscopes. Anyone with a confident voice and an air of authority can make me do nearly anything. Martha is no exception. I take my brain balances where I find them. She tells me to stop wearing my watch on my left hand because it sends the wrong electric signals to my heart, and to prove it she tells me to take off my watch. She presses on my left arm with all her might and tells me to resist. My arm doesn't budge. When I replace my watch and she presses again, she's able to push my arm down to my side with no difficulty at all. I immediately switch my watch to my right wrist (next to the friendship bracelet Snoopy gave me at Camp Echo — I'm still wearing it). Lizzie and I both make appointments with Martha for follow-up sessions.

If Martha Keeble is any indication, St. Andrew's-Sewanee has changed a great deal since my time here.

I take my leave from Lizzie and rest a bit in my room. Before dinner, three boys stop by, curious about the new kid.

There's a frizzy-haired boy named Frank, a senior; Oliver, a friendly kid about twice my size; and a skinny fifteen-year-old. Although his name is Rob, I can only think of him as the Fifteen-Year-Old because he seems quintessentially that: all arms and legs and an aura of certainty that masks a soup of confusion. They're here to give me the lowdown on what happens at St. Andrew's-Sewanee. Lizzie told them all to be on their best behavior, but we'll see how long that lasts. It all depends, of course, on how comfortable they feel with me, whose side they think I'm on. Naturally, it's not *all* about sides, and most of the time you don't get a choice whose side you're on. We compare notes on school disasters and mishaps. It's a bonding moment. I tell them about the kid who broke into the Communion wine when I was a student.

"Oh yeah," says Oliver, waving a hand dismissively. "That's happened in our day too." Of the three, Oliver is dressed most preppy, in a blue sweater vest and gray slacks, his hair combed neatly. He could have come from my class, but he wears a backwards baseball cap, and that's a fashion that's relatively new.

"What's the worst thing that happened in your day?" the Fifteen-Year-Old asks.

"Well, one of the students fell off Piney Point." Piney Point is a cliff on the edge of campus, a hundred-and-fifty-foot drop below and a view of the mountains and woods for miles. At least that's what it looked out on thirty-two years ago. I definitely want to go there again, but I'm afraid when I look down I'll see a Wal-Mart, a Taco Bell, a strip mall, and a new housing development. Students used to have to sign out in a log to go to Piney Point, where they'd most often smoke pot, euphemistically recorded in the log as a "nature hike." I was never a big pot smoker, but I tried it from time to time, most memorably sitting atop Piney Point with the exchange students and a local kid named Bill who always had plenty of pot and a bong. Once the Gambian prince, Antouman, blew into the bong instead of inhaling and soaked Bill's weed, but that was our only mishap. We never fell off, though a bratty kid named Mike did. Reportedly, he was spitting on dogs below and lost his grip on the sandy ledge, dropped fifty feet, bounced off a ledge, and fell the rest of the way. You could hear his screams all over campus. Miraculously, he didn't die, though he broke just about everything and spent nearly a month in the hospital, after which he ran or hobbled away a week later, and we never saw him again.

I tell my new friends this story, though I leave out the part about the pot.

This is nothing to them. "Yeah, we heard about that," says Oliver.

The Fifteen-Year-Old tells me his dad went here. "In my dad's day, one of the monks hung himself."

"Someone," says the frizzy-haired boy, and he gives the others a look like they know exactly who that someone is, "came into my room and trashed my roommate's side of the room. He urinated in the refrigerator."

"Oooh," says Oliver, and we all laugh.

"Yeah, well, this one girl crapped in the clothing of her rival," says the Fifteen-Year-Old. That's the word he uses, *rival.*

"Oliver here got suspended for throwing firecrackers at a teacher's window," says Frank.

Oliver shrugs and smiles.

"That'll do it," I say. "Sounds like the good old days."

"One word of warning," Oliver tells me. "The guy next door, Ivan, keeps his music on all hours of the night."

"Are you going to use real names?" the Fifteen-Year-Old asks.

"No, not for anyone under eighteen," I say.

"And you're going to be a student?"

"Yes, for a week."

"And you won't tell on us if you see something bad?"

"Nope," I say slowly, and I'm about to add the caveat, "unless I see something that endangers someone." But I don't get a chance because there's a commotion in the hall, a lot of yelling — someone's threatening to cut off another kid's hair, and I hear scuffling and muffled cries. Does this count as someone endangering someone else? Hard to tell, and I'm late meeting Lizzie on the quad for dinner off campus. Two of the boys I've been talking to have already bolted to the hallway to find out what's going on. I can see shapes moving in the darkness but nothing specific. Oliver slowly gets off my bed and claps me on the back.

"You're just like Billy Madison," he says.

At dinner that evening with Lizzie, I order a glass of wine, my last legal drink of the week, and she fills me in on my class schedule and we, of course, reminisce. Whatever happens in a boarding school, from drugs to sex, happens in every other sector of society too. At a boarding school, people are less spread out, scandals more noticeable. Of the various scandals we remember, foremost in our mind is the wife of the math teacher who slept with a number of students (she must have been all of twenty-three, but to us she was a hoary-headed adult), including the lanky, effeminate boy who played blind Tiresias the prophet in our production of *Antigone*.

The mention of *Antigone* makes us both thoughtful. For Lizzie, this play had been a kind of turning point. Our drama teacher, Scott Feaster, was ambitious in even staging the play. Lizzie remembered a performance we did for Parents' Weekend.

"It was the first time I ever connected emotionally with a character. I didn't know what hit me. You threw me down on the stage. All that crying and emotion felt real for the first time." Earlier, while Lizzie was giving me my tour of campus, we ran into a group of four seniors, three girls and a boy. She proudly told me to what colleges they'd been accepted and the scholarships they'd been awarded. "Sometimes I forget that my whole life isn't in front of me the way theirs is," she confided. "Sometimes I forget that I'm not as young as they are because I feel their age still." I knew exactly what she meant. Sometimes I forget too that my whole life isn't before me. That moment I threw Lizzie down on stage thirty years earlier was a watershed of some sort, when all kinds of choices lay before us. Who knew that it would lead to this moment? When I ask Lizzie what she remembers of me from that time, she says, "I remember your big wave of hair, and I was kind of awed by your acting ability."

Damn. Lizzie was in awe of my acting ability? I should have become an actor.

We all have regrets. She talks now about possibly wanting to go for a doctorate in psychology. She mentions a play she should have done. Some of us even have pregrets. Recently, Olivia has been backing off her stated ambition to be an opera singer. Right on schedule, she's started doubting herself the way so many adolescent girls do. Our whole lives we struggle with our personal sense of failure. To the outside world, our failures are strangers, but to us, they're our closest intimates, closer than friends, children, spouses, parents; nourished from an early age, they may become so strong that they overcome us. I see Olivia already struggling. Not getting a part in an audition in Milwaukee. Not getting the part she wanted in the school play. Each failure is tucked away, emerging again thirty years from now as a line on the face, a stutter, an inability to look someone in the eye. Like any parent, all I want is her happiness. Izzy still seems strong, and she hasn't given in yet to that terrible insecurity that suddenly comes upon so many formerly confident adolescent girls. Olivia says she might major in psychology in college as a backup. Only fifteen and she's talking about a backup already. "Psychology majors are a dime a dozen," I tell her. "It's only worth it if you go on for a doctorate, and getting into graduate school in psychology is just about as hard as being an opera singer, maybe harder. Why don't you at least give yourself until your midtwenties to pursue your dreams? You'll still have plenty of time to do something else if it doesn't pan out."

I'm afraid that opera will be her backup, not psychology, and that it will back up until it disappears. I only want her to try. Battles are lost in the same spirit in which they are won.

It is here at St. Andrew's that I first read Walt Whitman's "Song of Myself" in Claire Reishman's English class:

With music strong I come, with my cornets and my drums,
I play not marches for accepted victors only, I play marches for
conquered and slain persons.
Have you heard that it was good to gain the day?
I also say it is good to fall, battles are lost in the same spirit in
which they are won.
I beat and pound for the dead,
I blow through my embouchures my loudest and gayest for them.
Vivas to those who have failed!
And to those whose war vessels sank in the sea!
And to those themselves who sank in the sea!
And to all generals that lost engagements, and all overcome
heroes!
And the numberless unknown heroes equal to the greatest heroes
known!

We arrive back on campus with five minutes to spare before Compline. I don't remember having to go to Compline when I was a student here. We went to chapel on Thursday nights and Sundays, but the main service has been changed to Monday morning at 8:00 a.m. because the policy didn't seem fair to the boarding students. When chapel was on Sunday, only boarding students needed to attend. Now that it's on Monday morning, everyone suffers. Okay, *suffer* is a bad word choice. Christ suffered on the cross. We merely fidget. We fidget in the pews for our sins.

Back at Harvey House, the students seem unconcerned that they have to be in chapel in less than five minutes. A group of five boys clusters around a TV in the first-floor common area playing a video game. Jerry, a senior who wears a bandana around his face, is playing *God of War*. He's just upgraded his powers and feels reluctant to give up on death and mayhem in favor of peace and charity right now. "It's kind of a story," he tells me through his bandana. "Well, no, you just kill things."

"I don't think lower house has to go to Compline," says one of the boys around Jerry's chair.

"Yes, we all have to go or we get demerits," another says.

It's odd, but I actually feel nervous about getting in trouble.

"Why do we have to do this every Sunday?" the first boy asks.

"So God will forgive us for all the bad stuff we did over the weekend," Jerry says, pulling his bandana around his neck and reluctantly loosening his death grip on the controls. We make it to chapel with about fifteen seconds to spare. Of course, I should have known that these kids would have it timed.

Apparently, while I was watching Jerry play *God of War* downstairs, the dorm parent, a teacher in his early thirties, was upstairs knocking on my door. After Compline, he approaches me in the hallway and says sweetly, "You missed Compline."

Uh-oh. "No, I was there," I say, trying to keep my voice from whining, weirdly afraid of being given demerits, even though work crew doesn't exist anymore. He believes me, I think, but tells me in any case that I shouldn't be standing in the hall. Between eight and ten, I need to be in my room studying.

I don't have anything to study yet, so I give Olivia and Isabel a call. They're both in good moods. Isabel has found a friend to bring to Iowa City for spring break. Last year, Olivia brought a "friend" for spring break. Now Izzy has found a "friend" to bring. I ask if this girl is a real friend. I'm not really keen on bringing any available friend-like kid to feed and house for a week. The last kid seemed more like a pet than a friend, the kind that your child promises she'll feed and clean the litter box of and then forgets all about. She spent more time with Izzy than Olivia and wouldn't eat. I found out later that she and Olivia barely knew each other. I suppose they imagine some Disney Channel movie titled *Best Time Ever: Spring Break at Dad's*. I don't think bringing a friend means that the girls are bored stiff with me and would rather have a complete stranger their age around than endure a week alone with me. Or does it? "Why do you want to bring a friend?" I ask Izzy.

"I don't know," she says. "I think it'll be fun." See. Just as I thought.

Olivia is happy for another reason. She's going to Washington, DC, for spring break with her choir, and they're going to sing at the National Cathedral. I haven't seen her for six weeks, since January, and I chafe at the thought of losing more time with her, but I also know how important this is to her. Still, I consider for a moment being a complete hypocrite and forbidding her, as though that would do any good. "That's wonderful," I tell her instead. "I'm so proud of you." But I imagine I could be proud of a psychologist too.

At breakfast the next day, the boy with the bandana, Jerry, introduces me as a new kid to the other students sitting groggily beside us at one of the dining hall tables. The dining hall is a classic, one of the places I most associate with St. Andrew's, with long wooden tables and benches and a high ceiling where class banners normally hang, though they've been removed for cleaning. Lizzie says our class banner is embarrassing: the bicentennial logo on one side and on the other the words "Let It Be!"

Among the students I've joined is Cody, a boy with spiky dyed black hair. Despite the air of Goth about him, he has a sweet face and looks more lost than I am. That's because he's only been here a week. He's "transferred" from a school in Indiana. I know what that means. For some, St. Andrew's-Sewanee is a Second Chance school. Kids who have been kicked out of one school for drugs or acting out in other ways sometimes find their way to St. Andrew's-Sewanee. It's a role the school embraces and that I admire. Even though I chose to come to St. Andrew's, I could easily have been Cody.

Jerry also introduces me to Emily Jean, a senior who's been up all night preparing her notecards for the Big Hamlet Research Paper due in Susan Core's English class. Susan Core started teaching part time the year I arrived at St. Andrew's, but she's been assigning that dreaded research paper just about ever since. This research paper is a multileveled thing that takes weeks to complete, and it's coupled with Mrs. Core's requirement that the students memorize half of Hamlet's "To be or not to be" soliloquy and recite it to her without a mistake.

This morning the chapel is packed with day students, faculty, and boarding students alike. I'm seated in the back by Father William Wade, to whom Lizzie introduces me. Father Wade is a soft-spoken man with thinning gray hair and glasses, who's been headmaster since 1982 when St. Andrew's merged with Sewanee Academy. He has an intelligent and open face, and there's something about him that makes him not only immediately likeable but the kind of person you'd put your confidence in. It's a first impression but a lasting one.

Sitting in the chapel through the service, I do what I always do during services. I look around. I space out. I admire the tongue-and-groove ceiling of the old chapel. And I resist going up for Communion and trying to guzzle wine the way I used to. After the service comes the announcements, and after that, two German exchange students, a boy and a girl, give a PowerPoint presentation on their home country. Then it's my turn. Lizzie asked me to introduce myself and my project at chapel by way of introduction to the St. Andrew's-Sewanee community. Although it's a little terrifying standing in front of 250 or so people and asking them to accept me as a student for a week, I can't say no. Not only would it be rude, but I'd get detention. By and large, the students and faculty seem enthusiastic about my project. I look out into the audience and see Claire Reishman and Susan Core smiling at me. The sense of community in this chapel is almost overwhelming. I feel just like one of those exchange students. Where have I landed, on what shore of memory? Perhaps I should have brought a map, a description of the place I live, of the country in which I've lived apart for thirty years. Lizzie says she was missing in action from St. Andrew's for twenty-five years, but now it's an integral part of her life again. As I'm standing up there, I wonder at the strangeness of this return, the first time I've ever felt the meaning of the phrase "the return of the prodigal son."

By 9:00 a.m. I've already misplaced my schedule and have to take the walk of shame to the office in Simmons to ask for a replacement from Miss Hargus, the avenging angel of absences and detention who has drill bits for eyes and can tell with a glance whether you're lying or not. After a skeptical look and a remark about my organizational skills, she prints out my schedule again, after which I hurry to my first class, religion with Father Wade. This is a class all seniors had to take in my day too, but I'm sure the contents have changed a lot since then. In 1975, religion meant one thing, one view, but before my arrival the class has already studied Buddhism, Taoism, Judaism, Hinduism, and now they're on Islam. "In this world, we need to do a better job teaching about Islam," Father Wade tells me.

There's nothing patronizing or judgmental in Father Wade's assessment of Islam as he relates the Biblical account of the split between the Jews and the Muslims, the story of Abraham and Sarah and Isaac, of Hagar and Ishmael, a story of resentment and misunderstanding that seems even now to define the relationship between the two groups.

"Why can't Christians, Jews, and Muslims get along in this crazy world?" Father Wade asks the class, a rhetorical question perhaps, but his students are idealistic enough to attempt an answer.

"Because we misinterpret our own religions," one student says.

"Literalism," says another.

I can't say I disagree. If religion used to be the opiate of the masses, in its fundamentalist and intolerant form at least, it's now the crack of the masses. This doesn't apply to the Episcopalians, as far as I can tell. Father Wade mentions in passing to the class that the bishop of New Hampshire is openly gay, and proudly adds that he's a Sewanee grad. Although I didn't appreciate it at the time, Father Martin was tolerant in his own manner too. After I wrote a series of scathing editorials in the student newspaper about mandatory chapel, I wore poor Father Martin down and he capitulated, making a separate peace with me, at least containing if not converting me. If I could find alternative services on Sunday, I could go. It wasn't easy finding alternative services in the Tennessee mountains, but one of my teachers, Doug Cameron, went to Quaker meetings run by an eighty-five-year-old firebrand named Dorothy Hutchinson. He offered to bring me and Hiroshi along, so every Sunday morning we went to Dorothy's home, meditated, talked about the evils of the B-1 bomber, and drank tea and ate cookies.

⌒

In every one of my do-overs, even kindergarten, I've learned something I didn't know or had something reinforced I should have known. I've wanted to learn Hamlet's soliloquy since sixth grade when I tried to learn it on my own after school. And I would have learned it at St. Andrew's if I'd returned for my senior year. Better late, as they say. Now's my chance, and Mrs. Core, taking pity on me, gives me an extension. I'm also put in advanced Spanish, a class taught by a lively, unflappable woman the students simply call Señora, who's teaching Laura Esquivel's *Like Water for Chocolate* and who will be leading the class on a trip to Mexico in the coming weeks. In biology, we're studying DNA and reading James Watson's memoir about the discovery, *The Double Helix*. In Greek literature, Bill Seavey teaches a rapt group of seniors Plato's *Apologia*. Emily Jean, the red-haired senior who stayed up all night with her Hamlet paper, is also in this class and pronounces Mr. Seavey "a genius," and surely he is, to get a class of seniors impassioned about Plato. By the end of the day, instead of washing away my regrets, I've instead found a new one. I regret that I was in such a hurry, that I didn't finish my exchange program in Japan and return to St. Andrew's for another year.

Back in my dorm room before dinner, big Oliver knocks and asks if I want to hang out with him and a few others at Ivan's, the guy next door who has his music on all day and night. Of course, I say yes. Ivan is eighteen, and his room is full of football posters — he almost looks as though he could be a football player too. Ivan has curly blond hair and the kind of earnest expression that I was always wary of when I was a teen. This is Perry from sixth grade grown up, the troublemaker center of attention, the power broker. I'm a little wary of him still.

Oliver closes the door, and I shake hands with Ivan and the Fifteen-Year-Old I met yesterday, who has his shirt off and perches on the bed as though he's about to pounce.

"What's the most fu . . . screwed-up thing you ever saw in your time at Saint Andrew's?" Ivan wants to know.

That's a hard one. Let's see, the most fu . . . screwed-up thing I ever saw at St. Andrew's . . . Before I can answer, the Fifteen-Year-Old says, "I saw someone do a line of cocaine."

I'm not surprised that the Fifteen-Year-Old saw another kid do a line of cocaine. Olivia and Isabel both know kids in their school in Grafton, Wisconsin, who do drugs, fifteen years old and younger, and they've lost friends over drugs. What surprises me is Oliver's response. He's visibly shaken. "Was it someone I know?" he asks. "If it was someone I know and care about," he says, "I'd like to help her." He tells me he has substance abuse in his family and that's why he's against drugs. "I've been drug-free my whole life," he says. "But I drink."

"I'll tell you later," the boy tells Oliver.

Ivan gets a call on his cell phone and steps into the hall.

"What do you think of underage drinking?" Oliver asks me, continuing the quiz.

"I think kids should be introduced to wine and such at an early age, like Europeans do," I say. "So they won't think it's such a big deal. A lot of students where I live go on binges because it's the first time they're away from home. And too often teenagers drink and drive," I say.

"That makes me so mad," says the Fifteen-Year-Old.

What I recognize and love about this age is how quickly the pendulum swings from moral outrage to complicity. We're all hypocrites to a certain extent, but teens are such earnest hypocrites, it's endearing. Oliver, previously so outraged about the student who did cocaine, admits to having cracked up his car while blind drunk. Oh well. Just another one of those I-fail-to-see-the-irony-here moments of adolescence.

While Ivan's out in the hall, we trade pranks we've played. They're a little more advanced than my day, like something out of *Fight Club*. I'm terrified of Oliver's description of "Night Frights," in which a group of boys pummel another boy while he's asleep. He recalls Night Frights fondly from his freshman days, and I get the feeling he was probably more often the victim than the perpetrator.

"God," I say, hoping they won't decide to do that to me some night.

"It wasn't so bad," he says. "We didn't do it hard. Later, we'd all laugh."

The Fifteen-Year-Old's favorite prank is putting shaving cream in someone's hand when they're asleep. "We made it even funner when we put their hand in a bowl of water and shaving cream on their face. But we made a bad decision when we did it with permanent ink once. The guy pushed the ink around his face, and it got all in his hair. He was pretty mad at us."

"Did you get suspended?" I ask.

"No, we don't tell on each other."

I love his use of the phrase "bad decision." It sounds like kindergartenspeak. It makes me nostalgic. I wonder if he remembers "Different is great" too?

I tell them about one of my bad decisions. Once, I put two full glasses of water on the back of the hands of a nice Japanese boy who wandered innocently into the exchange program lounge at my school in Osaka. After I placed the glasses on his hands, I walked out of the room. The only way for him to remove the glasses would be by letting them fall.

"Hey, that's a good one!" the Fifteen-Year-Old says.

"Oh no," I say. "I just taught you a new prank."

"We'll say we read it in a book," says Oliver, pausing for effect. "By Robin Hemley."

Ivan comes back in the room and smiles sadly at me, then takes a seat on a pillow by his bed. "I wish I could be here this week to hang out with you," he says. "You seem pretty cool. But I'm going away for three to six months."

"Why?" I ask. "Did you get suspended?"

"No," he says. "I'm going to jail. Probably. My court date is tomorrow in Florida." Ivan gets up and puts on some music, which he plays out his open window, not blasting it, not so loud that it can be heard in Chattanooga or Nashville. Just loud enough to be heard throughout the county. I can tell he views this as a public service he's performing. His taste is eclectic, everything from George Harrison to 50 Cent.

"I've made a lot of mistakes," he tells me. "But I feel myself growing."

The kids here obviously feel a bond. A lot of them have made mistakes. All of them. All of us. As a forty-eight-year-old, it would be easy for me to be cynical, to roll my mind's eye at the self-help language of his statement — that he feels himself growing. Remember what it was like to be his age, I tell myself, how everything meant so little and so much and how you tried on phrases, such as "I feel myself growing," like the newest version of the same old song lyrics, while now I wouldn't feel myself growing. I'd simply say, "I'm so screwed," and I'd kick everyone out of my room.

"This is going to be a positive experience for him," Oliver tells me, and the forty-eight-year-old in me bites his lip and nods. Mmm hmm. Positive for his cell mate maybe.

But Ivan is the original Carpe Diem Boy. He's not in jail yet, and he doesn't believe in moping, so he turns the attention to me again. Or maybe he doesn't want me to ask him about what his violation was. If so, he needn't worry. I'm not going to pry.

"When did you graduate?" he asks me.

"Nineteen seventy-six."

"Nineteen seventy-six," he says. "You're young."

"I'm old," I say.

"My dad graduated in nineteen seventy-one," the Fifteen-Year-Old says.

"No, you're still young," Ivan says. "But we're younger," and he and Oliver high-five. Perfect high fives. I envy their technique if not their callow youth.

"You're reliving it," the Fifteen-Year-Old says. "But we're living it." I might be cut by those words, if not for what he says next: "I hope I can do what you're doing someday." For me, it's a remarkable moment. I've had plenty of adults tell me that they'd like to do a few things over, but, now that I think of it, the kids have been supportive too. The kids, at least the ones who understand what it means to make a mistake, a bad decision, or whatever you want to call it, would like to think they might get a second chance too, someday. Even the kindergartners knew that I wanted to take a bad time and make it a "great time." I suppose this is what most religions are founded on, the principle of remaking yourself, of refashioning the soul. Correcting bad decisions. No wonder they're so darn popular.

Over the next several days, I meet a wide variety of the students at St. Andrew's-Sewanee. One of the exchange students from Germany, a small studious boy from Bonn, tells me St. Andrew's-Sewanee is "fabulous." He tells me he feels so much more isolated in Bonn where he doesn't even know his neighbors. Here, he has many friends, and he's even taking a class at the University of the South.

He dreads returning to Germany. A blond pimply boy tells me at lunch one day that he transferred here from "a terrible public school in Georgia." In algebra, he sat in the back of the class, and the teacher didn't even notice him for half the term. "I didn't learn anything, and I told my mother if she wanted me to learn something I had to go somewhere else." Like the boy from Bonn, and every other student I meet, he tells me he loves St. Andrew's-Sewanee. When he arrived here, one of his teachers asked if she could see him after class. He thought he'd done something wrong. "That's the only time teachers ever wanted to speak with me at my old school.

"'I just want you to know,' the teacher told me, 'that if you need any help or have any questions, let me know.'"

The boy's eyes are misty when he tells me this. He's dyslexic and has ADD and struggles with writing, but he loves languages and hopes to learn a few and travel. "I'm paid attention here," he tells me.

Melissa, a junior from New Jersey, had "a shitty home life" and went from AP Honors to straight Fs. Her first year at St. Andrew's-Sewanee felt like a prison. She couldn't go home for Easter because she had so many detentions, and her father called to complain, but the administration held its ground, and her father was told the same rules apply to everyone. This year Melissa thinks of St. Andrew's-Sewanee as "her second home." Her grades are back up, and she even landed the lead in *Footloose*. Still, she falls asleep in class all the time and that's how she gets detention.

"You have to figure your way around Saint Andrew's," she tells me. "The things you can get away with and the things you can't get away with. I'm not talking about socially. You learn about the things that will piss off the administration, which teachers are cool, which want you to kiss their ass."

In my day, it was *only* "social" things that pissed off the administration, for which you'd get kicked out, no ifs ands or buts, on the first offense. Now, students get a second chance (unless they're selling drugs). In 1974, two of our overzealous male teachers spent Friday and Saturday nights on "Bush Patrol," scouting around campus for couples having sex. Even now, Bush Patrol strikes me as perverse. But we also had a couple of teachers both in their twenties, who allowed us to smoke cigarettes and pot in their apartment and drink. What can I say? It was 1974. Now, this behavior seems as perverse as Bush Patrol.

We didn't have locks on our doors as the students do today. I constantly wrote editorials in the student newspaper about the lack of privacy, after things were stolen from my room several times. I suppose *that* must have pissed off the administration, or at least I *wanted* to piss them off, but they probably liked the fact that I was writing weekly arguments in the paper.

Lesson number one I learned at boarding school: the world keeps spinning no matter what you think.

Lizzie was a bit shocked when I admitted at dinner that I had smoked pot out at Piney Point.

"You?" she said in a way that made me feel like a nerdy sixteen-year-old again.

But, like Melissa, I knew what I could get away with and what I couldn't. I once cheated on a math test at St. Andrew's. I got away with that.

Lesson number two: The things you think you got away with trail you and become some of your most persistent memories.

~

"I want to be part of the conversation, by god!" Ivan tells me two days later on a yellow school bus headed for Chattanooga. Breakout. That's what this is called. Yes, Ivan, the one previously headed for jail in Florida, and yes, Breakout. But it's not what you might think. I haven't completely flipped out and fled with Ivan to avoid prosecution, him for whatever he did in Florida and me for smoking pot on Piney Point thirty-two years ago.

After listening to his music next door all night, I wished he would go to prison already, for a long, long time. As so often happens with Our Delinquent Youth, the young thug has been given yet another chance by our Liberal Judicial System, and he doesn't need to go to jail at all. He doesn't need to go to Florida either. Not even for a couple of days. He's not even facing charges anymore. Was he really going to jail or was this just an elaborate prank they played on me? Ah, that's the beauty of boarding school.

I'm not even sure what conversation Ivan wants to be a part of. I think he means the social conversation. I think he means the conversation I'm having this week with the students and faculty of St. Andrew's-Sewanee. But around Ivan, there's not really any conversation. There's just listening. First and foremost, you have to listen to his music. We're seated across from each other in the back of the school bus headed for downtown Chattanooga with about eighty other students, and Ivan has his laptop open, playing tunes to serenade our breakout.

"Sweeeeeeeet emooootion!" Aerosmith belts out. Well, the music hasn't changed.

An annual event that I've lucked into, Breakout features the entire school traveling to Chattanooga for dinner and movies. We never had anything like this when I attended St. Andrew's. We were pretty much on twenty-four-hour lockdown and were allowed into Sewanee once a week — those of us who maintained good grades, that is. We had to wear a coat and tie into town, and there wasn't anything to do once we got there except go to the student union where I'd order a tuna fish sandwich every week. I'm not sure why I bothered, except that it tasted better than the mystery meat served at the cafeteria. Now, every night a bus takes the kids on a "pig run" to the Piggly Wiggly or one of several other stores in Monteagle.

I don't know what qualifies as rare form for Ivan because I don't know him well enough, but somehow I suspect his behavior on the bus is typical. Halfway to Chattanooga, he wants to pee in a bottle. Perhaps he's nostalgic for drug tests. Then he yells out the window at a state trooper. An old acquaintance? For this, he gets in trouble with the teacher driving the bus (a guy wearing a fool's cap, always a sure sign of authority).

"What name is on the side of this bus?" the teacher asks, eyeing Ivan in the rearview.

"Saint Andrew's," says Ivan.

"That's right. How does that make us look?"

How does a fool's cap make you *look?* I want to say, but Ivan surprises me. "I'm sorry," says Ivan. "I just said hello."

If I were betting, I'd lay my money down that he was telling the truth about having to go to jail. Ivan can't seem to help himself. He has to do the wrong thing, and for that, he earns my admiration, the way you admire the dumb lug who's the first out of the foxhole.

"Follow me, lads!" And then he's blown up. And you're still in your foxhole, bits of dirt and Ivan raining down on you, and you're thinking quite sensibly, *I'm not going out there.* But someone's got to be the guy who takes one for the boys. And girls. The designated cannon fodder for boundary-testing teens everywhere.

In writing about his own all-boys boarding school, W. H. Auden got it exactly right in "Honour" when he wrote, "The first truth a schoolmaster has to learn is that if the fool would persist in his folly he would become wise; in other words, to leave well enough alone and not to give advice until it is asked for, remembering that nearly all his education is done by the boy himself with the help of other boys his own age. There is far too much talk of ideals at all schools. Ideals are the conclusions drawn from a man of experience, not the data: they are essentially for the mature."

As soon as we find a place to park downtown, Ivan, his girl-friend, Melissa, and a girl named Diana split off from the chaperone, walking in the opposite direction. I start following the chaperone, but Diana comes over to me and invites me along with them. I don't have a good feeling about this. The chaperone has told everyone where to meet and has warned them not to cross the river. Of course, Ivan and Diana and Melissa decide to cross the river. Although I'm feeling odd about this, I follow them a ways. As soon as we're out of sight of the rest of the group, Melissa takes out a cigarette.

"Will this get you in trouble?" she asks.

"Maybe," I say. "Maybe I should go off on my own."

"No, I just won't smoke," she says.

This is where I run smack into a conflict between my project and my adulthood. I don't want to smoke cigarettes with teens. I certainly don't want to drink with them. For the first time, I actually *do* feel a little creepy. Who knows? Maybe I *do* want to smoke with them. Maybe I *do* want to drink with them! With all the background checks I've been through, you'd think only angelic thoughts ever crossed my mind. But there's no background check for desire, just warning bells. All I know for sure is that I have to flee. Now. I'm too old to follow Ivan out of the foxhole.

"You know, I think I'm going to get a beer anyway," I say.

"Because you can," says Ivan, ambiguously. Contempt, disdain, misplaced admiration? It's hard to tell.

"Yeah, I guess."

Perhaps I shouldn't have said I was going to get a beer. It seems a little cruel. But I don't want them to feel guilty about ditching me. Let them think I'm an ass, that I'm ditching them. It's probably safer for all of us that way.

They head across a public garden toward the river, and I walk in the opposite direction, so briskly that I catch up with the chaperone after only a few minutes. Suddenly, I'm a bit confused. I'm not on campus anymore, and so what rules apply to me and what rules don't?

"Is it okay if I stop for a beer?" I ask him.

He looks at me as though I'm wearing the fool's cap now. "I don't think I'm in the position to give that permission," he says.

What am I doing? What *am* I doing? I've just asked a man at least fifteen years younger than me if it's okay if I get a beer. Notice he doesn't invite me along wherever he's going with his friends. Notice that I don't blame him. I'm on my own recognizance, by god! Isn't this what you get when you grow up: your own recognizance? I am not part of the conversation, at least not the one Ivan and his friends are having. Still, it would be ironic if I got kicked out of St. Andrew's-Sewanee on a liquor violation. I leave the poor guy alone and have a beer, consoling myself that at least they give students two chances these days.

⌒

The next morning, I'm sitting in the packed chapel again, when Lizzie walks past and smiles, "I heard you had a little knee crawl in Chattanooga."

Knee crawl? Since when does one beer qualify as a knee crawl? It's true I *was* the last one back on my bus and made the others wait forty-five minutes for me, but that had nothing to do with beer or bars. I swear. The movie I saw was *Perfume,* with a few kids from one of the other buses. The ticket taker was only going to let one of them into the R-rated movie, Jerry, the boy with the red bandana, who's eighteen. The three others with us were sixteen and seventeen, and they could only gain entrance if accompanied by someone over twenty-one. I knew I was that, so, fully aware that I was corrupting their small but perfect minds, I bought their tickets, or, rather, Jerry gave me the money to buy them. By the time we got out of the movie, it was almost an hour past the time we were supposed to return to the bus. My movie companions were all on another bus, so I had to endure the hoots and applause alone when I clambered back on my bus with the guy wearing the fool's cap who probably thought, when I told him that I'd been in a movie theater all that time, *What do you take me for? A fool?* And now Lizzie thinks I went on a bender.

But I don't have time to explain because there's a procession of students carrying a cross and a banner followed by Father Wade and the school chaplain, Robert Van Dyke, known as "Buddy" (though spelled "Bude"), who take their places in the seats in front of the choir, a diverse bunch of white and Asian students. Bude is not someone you'd pass on campus and automatically think of as the school chaplain. His hair is curly and unkempt, and he has a kind of unguarded ease about him — maybe it's humility — that makes him seem more like a camp counselor than a priest. Adding to that impression is his penchant for cooking up kid-friendly food for anyone who wants to drop by and eat nachos and chili and play something called Mexican dominoes.

"We are treated as impostors and yet are known," Bude says in the beginning of the service. Boy, do I ever know *that!*

This is my third service in three days, but that's unusual even for St. Andrew's-Sewanee. My visit happens to coincide with the beginning of the season of Lent, a time of introspection and evaluation, and today is Ash Wednesday.

Father Wade, wearing his clerical collar, delivers a sermon in which he exhorts us to become "more authentically who you are." He tells the story of Alfred Nobel, who read his own obituary when it was erroneously published in a newspaper that was supposed to have published an obit for Nobel's brother. He saw himself described as a "merchant of death" for having invented dynamite, and the shock of his legacy made him into one of the greatest advocates for peace afterward. While I'm no Alfred Nobel, nor am I Scrooge, another person (albeit fictional) given a chance to revisit his life, the notion of becoming more authentically who I am resonates deeply. "This is a time to slow down and take stock of who you are," Father Wade tells us.

Then it's time to receive the Lenten mark, which Lizzie receives as well as Claire Reishman and Susan Core, Ivan, the German exchange students, and about 60 percent of the congregants. Although I don't join them, the call and response of the litany, asking for forgiveness of both communal and individual sins, reminds me of Yom Kippur when the Jewish community asks for forgiveness. In a way, I've stepped out of time in this service. Mircea Eliade, the Romanian philosopher, posited famously that all ritual is a return to the original event on which the ritual is based, not merely a replication. But, in another way, simply sitting in this chapel is a return too. The author Jorge Luis Borges writes of stepping out of time several times in his life. In one story, the old Borges runs into his youthful self, and the two argue. In my case, there's no argument. My younger self asks if it's okay if he takes the Eucharist. It's not my permission to give, I say. Go up there if you want. Have a knee crawl. I'm content to just sit here and absorb.

↶

This might be the season of Lent, but because of Susan Core and her Hamlet paper, for the seniors, it's hell week. "She tries to kill us all," Emily Jean tells me. In class one day, Mrs. Core's teaching assistant, DiAnthony, places a student paper on an overhead projector to explain the proper format.

"What shall we call this paper?" DiAnthony asks.

"This sucks!" someone yells.

"The theme of death," another yells.

"Hamlet sucks," says one of the Korean students.

"And then he dies," the first student suggests.

But they do the work. This is all part of being a senior, one of the perks. You get to blow off steam. You get to be irreverent and talk back as long as you do the work, you don't lose control, and no one gets hurt. It alleviates the anxiety they all feel about running toward the edge of the cliff with no one there to catch them.

Plenty of things at St. Andrew's-Sewanee cause me anxiety: Hamlet's soliloquy, for instance, though I don't see this task as one of hell's torments. On the contrary, I become obsessed with the soliloquy during the course of the week, staying up late each evening in my room trying to memorize the speech. In Spanish class, I do my best to remember my decades-rusty vocabulary from college, and I manage to write garbled sentences that are nonetheless oddly comprehensible, such as this gem: *"En la madrugada cuerdo estoy triste a veces mi vida en toda regresa de un solo golpe,"* which means, "At dawn sane I am sad sometimes my life in everything returns of a single blow." In Mr. Seavey's Greek lit class, I find an ally in Plato, who reminds me once again that "The unexamined life is not worth living." This time around, I'm homesick again, but a little less so than my first stint at St. Andrew's. I only have to last a week. One day, I run into Cody, the new Goth kid from Indiana, and I ask him how he's doing. He's just returned from a run to Piney Point and says it's beautiful. "But I'm having a homesick moment," he tells me.

I'm touched by his honesty. "I used to feel that way all the time," I tell him. "Don't worry. It will get a lot better."

I want to make it to Piney Point too, so I make a date with my senior friends Oliver and Theo to hike out there after class. Theo is the son of two lawyers and lives off campus in his own house in Monteagle that his parents bought him. He drives an Infiniti sports car, but other than these obvious accoutrements, you couldn't tell by his attitude that he's any richer or poorer than our other companion, Emily Jean, whom I invited along via a note passed in Mr. Seavey's class. Yes, by the end of the week I'm passing notes in Greek literature. But she started the note passing, not me! She asked me if I'd seen the horses in the pasture. I told her I hadn't, but I was heading out that way to Piney Point with Oliver and Theo and she was welcome to join us.

So we all meet after class by Oliver's dorm and hike past the pond built in my day by work crew, past the track and soccer fields and into the woods. I tell them why we used to go to Piney Point, and they laugh. "Kids don't get high on Piney Point anymore," Oliver says. "It's too obvious."

Obvious? Not when you're high. It's a wonder anyone can find it sober. It's deep in the woods, a good ten-minute hike complete with forking paths and switchbacks. The air is cool and a little musty with the scent of old leaves and mud puddles left from melted snow. The path narrows eventually, and we clamber down a steep descent to a point where the vegetation closes in and then suddenly parts to reveal a large boulder in front of us and, beyond that, miles of hills and forest. To get to the lookout we have to jump a small crevasse, and then we're on Piney Point proper, a hundred and fifty feet above the forest floor, and, gloriously, a view that seems unaltered since 1975. We scamper around the rocks taking photos of one another bracing against the wind and inching as close to the edge as we feel comfortable with. In my case, not so close. In Emily Jean's case, she hops down to another boulder as Theo makes the observation that not much is holding Piney Point up and that it will eventually collapse. But odds are, not today. Emily Jean is a slight girl who wears camouflage pants and a thin orange hoodie a shade lighter than her red hair, which is parted in the middle and tied in back, wisps of it flickering in the breeze. A dog tag with her name on it hangs from her neck. I'm wearing a gray St. Andrew's-Sewanee hoodie, and Oliver wears a blue Ralph Lauren sweater that's snug despite the fact that it's probably a triple X. Of all the kids at St. Andrew's-Sewanee, Oliver has probably taken to me most. Oliver gives me high fives whenever he sees me, slaps me on the back, tells me to call when I'm in Atlanta next time.

"So how many times have you been back here since you graduated?" Theo asks me. Theo has wavy brown hair and the kind of languorous good looks of a young Peter Lawford. He wears simple clothes: jeans, a plain brown sweater, and a matching Eddie Bauer canvas jacket. In some superficial ways, he fits the stereotype of the boarding school kid.

"None," I say.

"None? When was the last time you were here?"

"Nineteen seventy-five. And it hasn't changed."

"It must have changed," says Oliver.

"No, this place won't change," says Theo. "Unless they put a Wal-Mart down there."

"Yeah, in thirty years maybe you'll come back and it won't have changed," I say.

"That would be cool," Emily Jean says. "I've moved around a lot in my life. And everywhere I go, when I return it's not the same."

She says this as though she's an army brat or a professor's brat, like me. I ask her how she came to St. Andrew's-Sewanee.

"Well, that's kind of a long story," she says and laughs. I expect to hear a typical story of haywire hormones, bad decisions, of misunderstood and misdirected youth, but none of the other stories I've heard this week approach Emily Jean's.

Two years ago, Emily Jean was living in Chattanooga where she attended Tyner Academy, a public high school with low student morale and high teacher burnout. She'd been given a break when a teacher, recognizing Emily Jean's talent, secured a scholarship for her to a summer program in creative writing and philosophy at Williams College. Emily Jean spent a month there, and when she returned, she found her house boarded up and her father arrested and in prison. So she moved in with her boyfriend at age sixteen, took on three jobs at minimum wage, and still didn't have enough to get by. Figuring this would be her life for the next fifty years, hopelessness was her copilot. But the teacher who had helped her with the scholarship tracked her down and asked her what she was going to do. Her mother, who didn't have custody of her, had "three types of cancer" and lived in Arizona. So the teacher brought her one day to St. Andrew's-Sewanee. "Why did you bring me here?" she asked the teacher bitterly. "I can't afford to go here." A group of donors, organized by this teacher, pooled their money and gave her a full scholarship. Once Emily Jean was at St. Andrew's-Sewanee, Claire Reishman was able to file power of attorney over the sixteen-year-old.

Mrs. Reishman made sure Emily Jean had a checking account ("I'm the type of person who would put it under a mattress") and made her apply to good colleges when the time came.

"I've never had much authority in my life," Emily Jean says, "even when my parents were around. So it's not something I'm used to. I don't respond well to it, but Mrs. Reishman gives me this look and I can't resist. She wants me to learn how to drive, but I'm too scared. I know she'll win in the end. You can't make me do anything I don't want. If you give me advice or tell me what to do, I squirm, but when Mrs. Reishman gives me that look and says, 'You're learning,' I know I'm going to do it."

Now Emily Jean takes horseback riding and is learning dressage. She's also studying Chinese at SAS, wants to be a Chinese translator, and will travel to China with a group from St. Andrew's-Sewanee this summer. Several excellent liberal arts colleges have offered her full rides. "I didn't even think I was going to college, but when I got here they said 'Of course, you're going to college,' and they were so encouraging I felt like an idiot for thinking I wouldn't go."

On Monday, she turns eighteen, becomes an adult, but, of course, she's one of those people who has been forced by circumstance to grow up much faster than she would have liked. At one point, she hadn't seen her mother in five years and wanted to visit. "I only have enough money to visit you once," she told her, "and I think it's better for me to see you while you're alive than go to your funeral."

"I'm glad I went," she says, simply, telling me that her mother died four months ago, in October. If you look at Emily Jean, none of these troubles shows on her face. She talks a blue streak and smiles and laughs more often than not.

I'm so glad I went too, if thirty-two years late, for a taste of my senior year. I can still look out at the unspoiled land off Piney Point and marvel that anyone here would even remember me after all the remarkable people who have been here since.

But they do remember me: Susan Core, Claire Reishman, Lizzie. One night, Claire invites me over for a drink. We've had a little difficulty getting together this week: she's in the middle of an on-campus interview to search for a new headmaster, and she's got a fox hunt on Saturday morning. A fox hunt! This is so out of my realm. I can hardly imagine my English teacher in hunting tack. But can any student imagine his teacher engaged in any human activity outside of the classroom?

Mrs. Reishman looks exactly as she did in 1975. This and the fact that I've been invited to have a *drink* with my English teacher (and the fact that she hunts foxes, who probably just roll over and die when she fixes them with her look) have me almost as freaked out as reciting Hamlet for Susan Core. She has some serious Dorian Gray issues. She wears her light hair at the same length she did when I was a student, short and swept, and she has an unmistakably patrician look, the face of European nobility cum Sewanee, Tennessee. It would be easier for me to call her "Duchess" than Claire.

I feel very grown-up sitting in Mrs. Reishman's living room, chatting about the past, and nursing a glass of scotch, only one — I'm driving and I wouldn't want Lizzie to accuse me of going on a knee crawl with Claire Reishman. This is one of those milestones that make you realize you've grown up. Of course, you might act like a grown-up 99 percent of the time, but who are you fooling? No matter how old we are, I think adulthood shocks us from time to time all the way to the grave: buying matching furniture for your living room for the first time, for instance, or using a phrase on your child that your parents once used on you (my personal favorite: if you don't stop, your face might freeze like that!), or that somber moment when you become the guardian of an aged parent who once was your guardian. These are all benchmarks of adulthood. Add to that listening to your high school English teacher reminisce about her memories of your interpretation of Faulkner's *The Unvanquished* thirty years ago.

"I have very definite memories of you in class," she tells me. "Maybe I'd pass you on the street now and not recognize you, but I have vivid memories of you in class. I think we were talking about *The Unvanquished,* and you understood it in a way that no one else in that class did. You understood language and metaphor, and you were so creative."

The only thing that would make the moment more perfect would be if I'd ever read *The Unvanquished.* Perhaps that accounts for me understanding it in a way no one else did. More likely, she's talking about another book or story, or even, God forbid, another star student.

After that, it's on to Susan Core's house for my recitation. She seats me in her living room opposite her and her husband, the formidable George Core, longtime editor of the venerable literary magazine the *Sewanee Review.* George Core is not the type of person you want to recite Hamlet's soliloquy in front of: well-dressed

and formal and in his late sixties, he trails with him, like Marley trailing his chains, the South's literary legacy. He asks me the title of the book I'm working on, and I tell him. "I don't like it," he sniffs and takes a sip of his drink. Then Susan takes out her grading notebook and tells me to look away so I won't get nervous and to begin whenever I'm ready.

I start reciting, not in an overly dramatic fashion, but not in a monotone either. Although Hamlet is a young man's role, I think it's middle-aged men and women who must understand him best. When he wrote the play, Shakespeare was thirty-five, tipping from youth to middle age. The older you become, the more secure you're supposed to be in your identity, but the opposite is true for many of us. Why do you think old men drive so slowly and don't turn off their left turn signals? Why do you think T. S. Eliot's J. Alfred Prufrock lamented, "In a minute there is time / For decisions and revisions which a minute will reverse"? (Actually, Eliot was only twenty-three when he wrote this middle-aged man's lament, proving, of course, that it's the imagination that counts, not the age of the author). Still, I'd say Hamlet is a man growing old in a young man's body. I'm the opposite, at least for the duration of this year of do-overs, a man growing young in an older man's body.

Finally, I reach the end with hardly a stumble. Well, one stumble. Susan informs me that I missed a word near the beginning of the speech, but she says she always gives students a second chance and asks me to recite it again, but only until the words, "There's the respect / That makes calamity of so long life."

Again, I go through the speech and stop where she tells me. "Perfect," she says. "I'm giving you an A plus."

"Very impressive," George Core says. "Very impressive," and I don't think I've ever felt more relieved after a test. "It must be nice," one of the students said at dinner the other night, "knowing that your whole life isn't riding on what you do this week." I suppose it seemed to him that way, but I feel my whole life *is* riding on this week. It has to be right. I don't want to have to do over a do-over. "As long as there are final exams," reads a sign in the classroom shared by Father Wade and Susan Core, " there will be prayer in the schools." I might say the same of tough teachers.

⌒

The day of the prom, Father Wade takes me to lunch in Sewanee at Shenanigans, a sandwich place that opened in 1975, and the first place I ever ate sprouts on a sandwich. There were a lot of firsts at St. Andrew's for me in 1975: the first place I ate grits; the first and only time I ate squirrel; the first and only time I tried moonshine, just a capful (at the time, there were rumored to be 150 stills within ten miles of campus); the first time I smoked a cigarette; the first time I rock climbed and played soccer; the first time I lived away from home; the first time I knotted a tie (Hiroshi taught me); the first time I kept a journal. And more than thirty years later, the first place I had a brain balance. If only it would last. At lunch, I eat a Shennaniwich, the same sprout-covered sandwich I ate when I was a student, and I admit to Father Wade that Father Martin sent me my diploma even though I didn't complete my senior year. He gives me an appraising look. "I wouldn't have done it."

"I wouldn't have done it either," I say, and laugh. I don't feel guilty about it. I'm grateful to be an alum, a graduate of St. Andrew's, and I wonder if I would have been welcomed as warmly if I hadn't been a graduate. Even without the prom, the week has been, I want to say, almost a religious experience. But no, it's been a dream. Memory and dreams and imaginings — they all blend together over a lifetime. I call up my old school, and I'm transferred to the woman I had a crush on. My old English teacher, the person as responsible as anyone for my love of writing and books, is still here, still helping the students who need her help. *Antigone* is playing all week in Sewanee at the University of the South during my visit. Last night, I asked Lizzie if she'd let me see my old room, now in a girls' dorm. I didn't remember the number, but I found it easily once she led me there and yelled, "Man on the floor!" Room 207, the same number as the room I'm in at Harvey House this week. This is all dream logic. That's the only way any of this makes sense to me, but I don't question the coincidences so much as relish them. "What dreams may come," Hamlet asks, himself the dream of a mysterious middle-aged author some people think was himself dreamed up. I've always believed in dreams. Blame it on the Egyptians. Blame it on that toddler anthem "Row, Row, Row Your Boat," which seems as true a statement about life as any. In Room 207, I once dreamed a poem, and I wrote it in my journal when I was sixteen:

> *I sleep like a man who can't stop laughing.*
> *In a dream of apples, I eat pears.*

I'm still that man. Perhaps I'm also the culmination of some strange dream of Father Martin's, thirty years ago, in which he gave me a diploma, as a kind of passport to a future dream.

When Father Wade drops me off on campus, I venture into the dining hall, where Lizzie, Susan Core, and several seniors are decorating the ceilings and walls with streamers and balloons. Lizzie admits to me she's a little nervous about tonight, and, actually, I feel a little nervous too. We're both happily married, but it's still a prom. My first. Of course, a boy's going to be a tad nervous. At least I don't have to worry about things I would have worried about when I was seventeen. I don't have to buy a corsage for Lizzie because the seniors decided against flowers. I don't even have to wear a tux. Most important, I know I'm not going to kiss Lizzie. That's about 90 percent of the pressure off right there. God, how I always dreaded that moment. I was the most awkward first kisser in the world, usually choosing the most inappropriate, most unromantic moment to strike. Not that it was predatory, but it *did* feel more like a strike than a kiss. Something birdlike and quick, like the time I tried to kiss Dana Isacoff while crossing the street from my grandmother's house to hers. Midstride. I grabbed her and pecked. She covered her lips and looked at me as though I had just tried to steal food from her mouth.

It suddenly occurs to me the right thing to do. "I was thinking of taking you all out to dinner tonight before the prom, you and Rick and Elliot," I say. This is undoubtedly a first in the annals of prom history, treating your date as well as her husband and son to dinner before the dance. She says she'll check with Rick but that it sounds like a good idea, and we agree that I'll pick them up at six.

A storm seems to be blowing in, and as six o'clock approaches, the wind picks up, and the tops of the pine trees that dot the campus shake and bend as I wait outside the dorm where I used to live and where Lizzie, Rick, and Elliot now live in a faculty apartment. I'm one of these people who's perpetually early, and so I just stand under a pine tree, glancing at my watch (now on my right wrist thanks to Martha Keeble), and wonder whether maybe it would be prudent to stand somewhere other than under a violently shaking tree.

At thirty seconds after six (fashionably late in my mind), I knock on their door. They're still getting ready, so I chat with their son, Elliot, a cherubic eight-year-old with the high forehead and light curly hair of his father. Elliot is engrossed in his Spiderman book, and we have a good talk about Spiderman's foes, which for the most part have not changed since I was his age: Doc Oc, Hammerhead, and the Green Goblin. Spiderman was always my favorite too, the Hamlet of comic book heroes: conflicted, insecure, and obsessive. The family will be moving soon to a home they're building, but for now the living room is crammed with keepsakes: a piano, an heirloom mantel clock, and photos everywhere. The room is dominated by a tinted photograph of a uniformed man with a long beard and mustache, a receding hairline, and a look at once gentle, earnest, and brave. This is Lizzie's great-great-grandfather, General Edmund Kirby Smith, wounded in a number of battles and one of the last Confederate generals to surrender, a founder of the University of the South. If I were Elliot, this knowledge would only add to my appreciation of superheroes, knowing I had an ancestor who could take on the Green Goblin and have a sporting chance.

We eat dinner at a restaurant not far from campus, full of students and their dates, smiling and laughing at us from their tables. The lights go out briefly, and there are small shrieks of laughter and delight throughout the restaurant at this unexpected departure from the ordinary and orderly. The four of us have a lively and friendly conversation, punctuated by a phone call to Lizzie from one of the teachers. A tree, the tree I was standing under I learn later, has fallen and smashed the fence in front of Lizzie and Rick's place. But we're concerned about more important things than windstorms and life and limb. After all, this is serious business, this prom stuff.

"I have to go back and do my hair before the dance," Lizzie says.

Back on campus, after briefly surveying the fallen tree, we retreat to our respective abodes to get ready. The universe, or at least the campus, is singing in anticipation of the big night. The clackety old heater in my room, set on "stun," is doing a little metallic rap while I secure my tie with the same knot I learned here in 1975. The wind is making the trees sing, and one of the Korean boys coming from the shower belts a Korean song in the hallway while Enya bleeds through the wall that separates my room from Ivan's, wondering as she always does, "Who can say where the road goes, where the day flows, only time?"

As soon as I show up again at Lizzie and Rick's apartment, the breaker blows in the dining hall, so Rick goes to check on it while

Lizzie gets ready. I've been waiting thirty-two years for this dance, so I don't mind waiting a little longer. It doesn't occur to me that the dance might never happen, but when Rick returns at 8:40 (the dance is supposed to begin at 9:00) and informs us that he can't get the power back on, the thought crosses my mind. Lizzie emerges from the hallway unfazed, putting on an earring, and asks him about the possibility of running in an extension cord. She's wearing a black dress and a kind of jungle-patterned scarf, the perfect combination to attend a prom thirty-two years late, fashionable yet not overly concerned with propriety. I'm already enjoying the evening, bizarre as it is.

But can I really trust Rick to keep the lights on? Maybe he sabotaged them in the first place, physically or spiritually, prayed for a storm, enlisted Martha Keeble to shine black lights at some cumulus clouds, or Father Martin had second thoughts about me in heaven, put in a word with God, and the Old Guy delivered. Well no, not likely. Rick seems earnest, honest, and brave, just like General Kirby Smith, not underhanded at all. You have to be these things to agree to the idea of your wife going to a dance to which you're not invited with a guy from her past you don't know. Rick did seem a little tense about me at first, but now that he sees my intentions are honorable (if they weren't, I'd fully expect him to join forces with Spiderman and General Kirby Smith, who'd come howling back from the grave to hog-tie my little Yankee Jewish tush), we're buds. He sees I'm no Doc Oc, no Hammerhead, no Green Goblin. I don't want to do wrong by him and Lizzie. I just want to dance.

Finally, the lights go on at 9:05, and Lizzie and I dash across the wildly agitated campus, the wind making music fit for a Shakespeare play; *The Tempest* comes to mind. We've somehow defied the universe, told it that for one night we weren't going to play by its rules of loss and mortality, and now it's answering back. As we enter the dining hall, Shakira bursts over the loudspeaker telling us that her hips don't lie, and a hundred kids erupt in a cheer, and we take to the already crowded dance floor.

This night, I don't only dance with Lizzie but with my English teachers too. I dance with Susan Core to Sean Paul's "Give It Up to Me." She tells me she smells liquor on my breath — uh-oh. My second violation? And I dance with Claire Reishman to the B-52s' "Love Shack." Doing her own version of a fox-trot or bunny hop, she resembles something animal-like in any case, based I think on the sight of some furry little animal bounding in front of her horse.

"Could you imagine any of this thirty years ago?" I ask Lizzie as I'm dancing with her to "Staying Alive," which she's dedicated to me.

"Never," she says. "I never imagined I'd be back." Some of the students are doing moves that would have done the Bee Gees and John Travolta proud, but others have cleared the floor in confusion and disgust.

"I wouldn't want to be sixteen or seventeen again," I say.

"I wouldn't mind being sixteen or seventeen," she says, "if I knew then what I know now."

I request some Black Eyed Peas and the DJ, a woman with an amazing machine that can grab any song anywhere in the world, says, "How about 'My Humps'?"

"Sure," I say, but I think I should have asked for the most obscure song I could think of, maybe some old commercial jingle from the sixties, like the theme for the Mystery Date board game. The song has been looping through my head for the last day for some reason.

Mystery Date, are you ready for your mystery date?
Don't be late for your . . . mystery date.

I guess it's not exactly danceable. When "My Humps" comes on, the students crowd close and writhe against one another.

"What do you think of this?" one boy asks me.

"I requested it," I say.

He looks at me with the shock he expected my face to register. I remember watching Warren Beatty's movie *Reds* when I was in graduate school — part of the movie included real interviews with old Lefties and intellectuals. When Henry Miller was interviewed, he used the F-word, and a college student behind me gasped. "Did you hear what that old guy said?" he asked his date. Every generation believes that dirty words and sex began with them.

When the song gets to the part about mixing "your milk with my cocoa puff" (yes, my generation had Cocoa Puffs too!), Lizzie stands up on a table and gets on a mic and the music cuts off abruptly. "Y'all dance as good as you look," she says. The students cheer in response. "You can keep dancing, but there's a major storm about to blow through, and everyone must stay away from the windows. A gigantic thunderstorm is due to hit around midnight or before. You can stay here, but you can't go outside."

The students heed Lizzie's warning, bumping and grinding the night away under strobe lights, a few of them smooching discreetly, some aiming cameras at themselves and their friends. Some of the boys have untucked their shirts as the music gets progressively undanceable and unrecognizable for Lizzie and me.

"The Fall Frolic was four hours of stuff like this," Lizzie tells me as she and I and Claire and Susan start cleaning up, throwing cups of Coke and water into the trash can. "We didn't have a professional DJ. Just students."

A chubby boy from my Spanish class, a constant heckler of the unflappable Señora, shakes hands with me and wishes me well as a dewy girl at his side looks up at him beatifically. The three older women at my side shake their heads collectively like . . . (I *would* say like the Three Fates, but the Fates are timeless old hags, and Susan, Claire, and Lizzie are anything but that — however timeless they seem to me; did I get myself out of that one?), well, like themselves, as the boy and girl head off into the night.

"That poor girl," Susan says. "This *proves* love is blind."

"What, he's a ne'er-do-well?" I ask.

"That about sums it up," she says. "Yes, I'd say that," her eyes still following them. "Poor little girl from Kentucky. He's got her starstruck somehow."

Thirty years ago, we would have sent the Bush Patrol after them, but now we know better. Vigilance is overrated. So is permission. At any rate, as an adult, permission is not something one can really give to a child. One of the great delusions of adults everywhere is that their children can be protected. Kids regulate themselves finally. The fool persisting in his folly will sometimes become wise, sometimes stay a fool. But not everything risky is foolhardy. I wish, if anything, I had been a less timid student. I was, like Auden in his school days, "mentally precocious, physically backward, short-sighted, a rabbit at all games, very untidy and grubby, a nail-biter, a physical coward, dishonest, sentimental, with no community sense whatever." People like us should be much more worrisome to any administrator or parent than the kid who wears his faults like a varsity letter. I've spent the better part of my adulthood trying to coax that cowardly, nail-biting, dishonest sixteen-year-old I was (longingly staring after the ne'er-do-wells and their dates) out of his untidy and grubby little foxhole.

Some salsa starts up, and I take Lizzie out on the dance floor. Margie loves salsa, and I love Margie, so I dance with her sometimes, even going so far as to take samba lessons with her once, a class that completely undid any sense of dignity I might have regarding what my body can and can't do. Our instructor actually went into a teary fit of laughter when she saw me lumbering toward her in a samba line, shaking as though I were about to fall on the floor and burst into tongues. Samba I can't do. Salsa I at least look like I know what I'm doing.

The lights go out abruptly, and people do what they do when the lights go out. They cheer. Lizzie and I head for the kitchen, where there's emergency lighting, to find a flashlight. The dance is over. We head back to the dining hall, and Lizzie stands on the table again, flashlight in hand, and tries to coordinate an orderly retreat, while the kids look for their shoes, purses, and cell phones. As the students begin to trickle out, Lizzie waves her flashlight and sings, "We are the champions." Outside, the rain has started, though it's not the downpour predicted, and we dash for our dorms, students illuminating the dark with their cell phones.

All night long, I hear people running and screaming around campus. There's a knock on my door in the middle of the night, but I'm too tired to answer. Prank or promise. Trick or treat. The dreaded "Night Frights"? It doesn't matter. Tomorrow, I'm going home, getting on a plane and leaving the sixteen-year-old me here where he belongs. He'll get used to it eventually. The homesickness will seem like a bad dream, and he'll learn how to get along, how to make his way in the world, just as I did. He's somewhere out there now, stumbling, laughing in the rain, looking for trouble.

CHAPTER EIGHT

OUTCOMES ASSESSMENT
Standardized Test Do-Over

ORIGINAL AGE: 16
DO-OVER AGE: 48
ORIGINAL LOCATION: ST. ANDREW'S SCHOOL, SEWANEE, TENNESSEE
DO-OVER LOCATION: LYONS TOWNSHIP HIGH SCHOOL, LA GRANGE,
ILLINOIS

Nothing seemed more horrifying or masochistic to my friends and family than the idea of my again willfully subjecting myself to a standardized test. I hate such tests too and have never been good at them. That's why I wanted to do over the ACT. Actually, I wasn't doing *over* the ACT, strictly speaking, as I'd never taken the ACT in the first place. Or the SAT. I transferred directly from my high school exchange program in Japan to Indiana University South Bend, where I was accepted provisionally when I came home mid-year from Japan. I was able to skip the SAT solely due to my mother pulling strings at IUSB, where she taught. But that first semester, I made three As and a B and never looked back.

At St. Andrew's, I *had* taken the PSAT when I was sixteen, and I'd also taken a different kind of aptitude test that supposedly predicted the career for which you'd be most suited. This test pegged me for a gas station attendant, a bookstore owner, or a fingerprint technologist. Bookstore owner was fine, but I wanted to write books, not sell them. And gas station attendant! If I'd followed the test's advice and pursued my subliminal lifelong dream of pumping gas, my career would have been shattered a few short years later when self-service stations became the norm.

At the time, I'd gone into the office of my guidance counselor to complain. He looked over the test predictions and shook his head. "These tests don't lie," he told me. "They're computerized!" And then he said I should buck up because being a fingerprint technologist sounded like fun.

True, it intrigued me, but I didn't know what a fingerprint technologist did exactly. The guidance counselor told me that fingerprint technologists sort through sets of fingerprints and try to match them.

Oh, great. My big career. And when you found a matching pair, did you shout "Bingo!"? And what if I'd decided to become a fingerprint technologist? This profession too would have soon become obsolete. If nothing else, computers are good at sorting, though maybe not so good at sorting people. The biggest thug on campus was told he had a career ahead as a marine biologist. Maybe, but I kind of doubt it. Even bookstore owner, alas, would have been a troubled profession, as it's hard to find an independent bookstore anywhere in contemporary corporate America. On the other hand, if I'd heeded the computer's advice, perhaps now I'd be CEO of Barnes and Noble or Borders? I'm sure.

After this test, I never really trusted tests again. I wondered what the purpose of such tests was, really, if they could be so obviously wrong.

One thing that has clearly changed for the worse since my day is the ubiquity of standardized testing from grade school on. A special-ed teacher from Des Moines whom I met on a plane ridiculed the tests because the government penalizes schools for results that are beyond the control of teachers. In the case of her school, she bemoaned her special needs students scoring in the fortieth percentile, bringing down the school's average and putting it on the government's "watch list."

"Statistically, No Child Left Behind can't do what it's supposed to do," she told me. "The goal is to get one hundred percent of the students reading at the one hundred percent level. That's impossible. It's asinine. It's going to have to be altered."

Clearly, it's not the kids who need to take these tests but the politicians who mandate them. Such tests have little to do with learning, unless learning only has to do with memorization and test-taking strategies. In my case at least, I've lived quite happily all these years without taking an SAT or an ACT. But the irony here is that I live in one of the bastions of standardized testing, Iowa City, headquarters of the ACT.

I suppose it's curiosity as much as anything that leads me down the standardized path again, the same curiosity that motivated me to apply to Brown University for graduate school in 1980. I wanted to see if I could get into an Ivy League school, as I hadn't even *applied* to undergraduate school. My mother had done it for me! How pathetic. Brown offered me a tuition scholarship. And that was that. I didn't need to go. Getting accepted was enough for me.

I decide *not* to contact ACT directly to take a test but to go under the radar, as it were. My feeling, right or wrong, is that they might not appreciate my outright hostility toward them. After all, they belong to the Axis of Standardized Evil (GRE, SAT, ACT), and I know full well the unspeakable horrors of their Weapons of Mass Instruction. Diplomacy would do no good.

Tom, a former student of mine, administers the ACT at Lyons Township High School in suburban Chicago. He's happy to let me take the test at his school, though he too is horrified by the idea. When I went to high school, there was no such thing as "online," but now there is, and Tom tells me how to sign up for the test from home. At first I'm a little baffled by the online questionnaire, as there isn't an "old man do-over" option to check and so most questions don't apply to me. But once I relax, I actually enjoy filling out the questionnaire. First, I have to decide to whom my scores will be sent — there's a list of hundreds of colleges and universities and organizations, even public figures. Wouldn't it be fun to send my ACT scores to a couple of politicians? I decide to send one set of scores to my congressman and also one to the vice president of the United States, simply because it's an option. I'm sure he'll pore over them intently. I also choose to have my scores sent to Caribbean Union College in Trinidad. College in Trinidad sounds fun. My last choice is the Air Force ROTC Scholarship. Me, a flyboy. Imagine.

Likewise, I prefer to attend a college that is All Female.

My first preference is to attend a school in Alabama, second Utah, third All Other, fourth Mississippi, and fifth Massachusetts. Admittedly, none of this makes sense, so I also indicate that I prefer to attend a college with "a maximum yearly tuition" of five hundred dollars. I decide that I want to major in creative writing but that my occupation of choice will be international business management (this time around, I want to be rich!), with a secondary occupation in animal sciences. The pièce de résistance is a list of ninety possible activities I might like or dislike, ranging from "learn about star formations" to "write reviews of Broadway plays" and "help people in emergencies." I indicate I would dislike all ninety of these activities except for "Discuss a misleading advertisement with a salesperson" and "Watch a technician repair a television." How could any college or university turn down an applicant with *these* preferences? I can just hear the admissions officer: "*Why, he's perfect for our new major in Spacing Out and Whining!*" If they only included "Think up utterly insipid personality questions for useless tests," I certainly would check that as well, but, alas, the closest corollary I can find is "Pack things into boxes," so I check that instead.

Obviously, I'm not as terror struck about the test as I should be. Or, more than likely, my cavalier attitude simply masks my terror. At Jefferson Junior High, I told a student in art class about wanting to take the ACT.

"I hear that if you score a fourteen, it means you're retarded," he said with typical eighth-grade aplomb and subtlety. "If you get a fifteen, it means you're not completely pathetic."

"I'm aiming for pathetic," I said. "Pathetic would be an accomplishment."

When I speak with Olivia next, she finally awakens me to the solemnity of the event. "People study for this, Dad," she reminds me. "They take classes for the ACT." Of course, she's reflecting her own anxiety. She's going to have to take the test next year.

So I go to my local bookstore and buy a thick ACT prep guide and start doing the math. I tell Olivia I'll give her the book after I finish the test or it finishes me.

Other tests loom as well: the fatherhood do-over, for instance. I'm not sure how Olivia and Isabel will take the news that they're going to have a new baby brother or sister. By April, Margie is five months pregnant and we've scheduled an ultrasound a few days after my ACT test. What worries me more than the ACT is the fact that while I'm not getting any younger, my daughters aren't either. I worry that Olivia and Isabel will feel I'm trying to replace them. I worry that this child will grow up not knowing them, just as I grew up a stranger to my half brother and half sister from my father's first marriage. I saw them at my father's funeral and a few other times in my life, and then one day I learned, around the time of my Camp Echo do-over, that my sister Betsy had died. A year earlier. How can you not be told that your own sister has died? I e-mailed this news to my "full" brother, who lives in Israel, and he never responded. What a tragic legacy this seemed, and not one I hope to pass on to my children.

I tell Izzy first, when I see her for her thirteenth birthday. No sooner have we picked her up at her house than I want to blurt out the news. But she's preoccupied with showing us her latest school photos.

"So we've got something to tell you," I say, looking at Izzy in the rearview. "Margie is expecting in August. You're going to have another brother or sister."

"Cool," she says, and hands Margie the envelope with her school photo.

"Doesn't that surprise you?" I ask.

"Not really. You dropped a pretty big hint the last time I saw you."

"Really? What did I say?"

"You said, 'How would you feel if you had a new brother or sister?'"

"That's a pretty big hint," Margie agrees, and then withdraws Izzy's photo from its envelope, admiring it.

"So much for my ability to keep secrets," I say.

I ask Izzy not to mention anything to Olivia. I want to tell her myself, but the opportunity doesn't arise until the girls' spring break in early April. At first, we thought Olivia wouldn't be able to join us for spring break at all because her choir is taking a trip to DC, but they're not leaving until a few days into the break. We all miss her, and Shoshie hasn't seen her for months, so I agree to pick her up and return her early, though it means making that grueling drive back and forth from Iowa City to Milwaukee an extra time.

Again, I blurt out the news in the car when I pick them up.

"Cool," she says, just as Izzy had.

"It doesn't surprise you?" I ask.

"I kind of knew," she says. "Last time I was there I saw the prenatal vitamins."

While I can't surprise Olivia, she surprises me. She wears mascara now, a pink pearl necklace, and mod clothes. She's taking driver's ed. I can't slow things down. I can't go back in time. I can barely keep up. At least I can help her out with driving.

On Easter Sunday, I take her to the empty parking lot of Kohl's department store and put her behind the wheel. "I don't like this," she keeps repeating. "I don't want to drive."

"It'll get easier, sweetheart," I tell her.

"I know, but I don't like it."

We make half a dozen wide turns around the parking lot, her sitting rigidly at the wheel, putting on her signal as though launching a torpedo. Despite the holiday and the obviously empty parking lot, we seem to serve as bait for other cars, their occupants crazed by their inability to shop for one day. They draw near. Maybe they think we can open one of the stores so they can get a fix. Maybe we look as though we're an advance team of shoppers who've caught wind of an Easter Sunday sale. Maybe they think we'll sell them something out of our minivan. Whatever the case, they're truly annoying. They're upsetting my little girl, flustering her. "There's a car, Dad!" she nearly screams, about a car a football field's length away. She decides to brake to give it plenty of leeway but steps on the gas instead, nearly sending us into a concrete planter. My coffee cup goes flying.

"I think I'm done," she says.

"You don't want to end with that," I tell her. "Let's go around the parking lot another time."

"My driving instructor is so stupid," she tells me. The word surprises me. If Shoshie were in the car with us, she'd certainly point out that "*stupid* is a bad word." It's unusual for Olivia to be harsh, and I know she's simply expressing how much stress she feels.

"How is she stupid?" I ask.

"She didn't seem to realize that I'd only been behind the wheel once before I went out with her on the road."

"Well, I once took flying lessons," I tell her. "And I had to fly by the second lesson."

"That's weird," she says.

"Your mom bought me the lessons," I say, thinking fondly of this time when my ex-wife, not normally a risk taker, embraced risk.

"That's weird," Olivia repeats.

I'm tempted to launch into some wise nugget of Truth about Life. This would be the place to insert it. I've seen it on this very page in other wiser books. *When one door closes, another opens. Follow your bliss. Grant me the serenity to accept the things I cannot change.* That sort of thing. Or even something semiwise. *Don't leave your dry cleaning at the store past thirty days. A 20 percent tip is the new 15 percent. Plastic surgery makes you look plastic, not young. Hair coloring is fine, though stay away from Just For Men and (yuck!) Grecian Formula.* But I don't have any wise nuggets. Sometimes the only satisfying response to your fears and disappointments, the overblown expectations of yourself and others, the daily injustices is "That's weird." It's not always you who are out of whack, but the world around you, and who knows this better than teens?

Isabel too feels the stress of great expectations. That evening, I say good night to her and Shoshie, who share a room when Izzy visits. "Dad?" she says with a look of concern as I sit on her bed. "If I don't get on Broadway, I think I want to be a doctor."

"You sound as though you're admitting a defect," I say. "Every

Jewish family wants a doctor. Actually, you can be both. After you're on Broadway, you can study medicine."

"You only want to be two or three things?" Shoshie asks incredulously from her bed. "That's not very many."

"I got an A plus in science," Izzy says. "But I hate my teacher."

"*Hate*'s a bad word," Shoshie warns, flipping through a princess book on her bed.

"She said that anyone who gets a ninety-five on their test can be in the advanced group, and I got a ninety-four point two, and she wouldn't put me in the group. The next day I got a ninety-five point eight."

"And she put you in?"

"No, she still wouldn't. The kids in that group do nothing. They don't have to take quizzes, and she told them they didn't have to take the test, and then when the test day came she changed her mind. They all basically bombed."

"And so . . . I should feel sorry for you? Only an A plus? You poor kid. You didn't get to be part of the smug group that bombed the test."

"Yeah," she says and shrugs. "Anyway, at Juilliard they don't even look at your transcripts."

"How do you do on standardized tests?" I ask against my better judgment.

"I'm always in the advanced groups," she says.

I'd like to say "I hate you," but I don't because Shoshie would scold me. "That's weird" doesn't quite seem appropriate either, though it *is* weird that my sense of how smart I am or how smart I'm not is wrapped up almost entirely in a test that I logically know has little bearing on my intelligence.

As the fourteenth of April draws nigh, my date with destiny, I have a series of nightmares about the ACT. My attitude toward the test changes almost daily. One day, I don't care. The next, I decide to take the test twice, once unprepared in the spring and then prepared in the fall. In my ACT study book, I'm mired in prealgebra. I boldly tell one of my colleagues that because taking the test doesn't mean anything in terms of my future, I feel liberated from it, but that's not true. I'm shackled in the deepest dungeon of standardized hell.

Finally I chicken out. No other word for it. I won't soft-pedal the truth. Listen to me cluck. I'm just going to have to wait until the fall. So I e-mail Tom and tell him the news, as though he's going to be disappointed in me, when really I'm the only one disappointed in me. Still, he'd like for me to give the writing workshop to his high school students that I'd previously agreed to do. That's fine with me. I'm so relieved that I don't have to take the test that I decide to turn the trip into a vacation instead, a little weekend trip to Chicago for the family.

So we get up early that Friday and head toward Chicago, Margie riding shotgun, Isabel and Shoshie in back (Olivia's already in DC with her choir). We're driving toward the I-80 entrance, a route I take every day when I bring Shoshie to her preschool. At one of the corners, there's some road construction, and traffic has been reduced to one lane.

I see the light turn yellow, so I speed up at about the same instant that a car turns right on red into my lane. I have made a bad decision. I'm going forty-five or so to make the light when I see the car directly in front of me. Braking hard, I swerve toward the construction barriers, then back, and slam into the car. As we come to a halt, my tires smoking, the front of my car bashed in, I look around to see if everyone is okay. Margie touches the back of my neck, giving it a little massage, as though my shattered nerves are her main concern. But she's pregnant, and two of my daughters are in the backseat, stunned but okay. What was I thinking? This is the only kind of test that really counts, and I've failed it. The car is a mess, but we're all right. The impact of the crash pushed the fender into Margie's door, which won't open anymore.

The man I hit is okay, though he's clearly not happy. "I saw you coming," he tells me repeatedly. "I tried to get out of the way." Another car has parked on the shoulder, and a guy gets out, lopes over to us like an Irish setter, and yells, "I'm a witness. I'm a witness." He looks like a slightly grown-up version of the boy in eighth grade to whom no one would pass the football. Perhaps this is his dream come true, his version of having the ball passed to him finally after all these years, being a witness at a fender bender. "Do you need any help?" he asks the man whom I hit. "I'll stick around until the police arrive. By law, I'm not allowed to leave the scene of an accident. Here's my name in case you need a witness," and he looks at me skeptically, as though I'm evil incarnate, scheming even now to shift the blame to my pregnant wife, my children, anyone but me. I would like to tackle him and break his glasses, but that would be another bad decision.

Instead, I get back in the car and wait for the police. Only then do I notice where I am. The sign on the lawn in front of me reads in big letters: ACT. Yes, I have managed to crash my car directly in front of the headquarters of ACT. I point this out to Margie. "I guess I've angered the ACT gods," I say.

After calling my insurance, after waiting for the police and watching the officer write an enormous ticket and give me a court summons, after I've endured the humiliation and retrospective terror of it all, the police officer sends me on my way with words that seem, if not soothing, at least sympathetic: "Have a better day," he says. "Friday the thirteenth, huh?"

Indeed. The car is drivable at least, and so we continue on our way to Chicago, me sullen most of the way, still stuck in the moment before I started through the yellow light, playing it over and over as we do with moments of trauma, trying to find some angle that will allow me to escape and pretend it never happened. Unfortunately, it always turns out the same way.

But my day does improve . . . by increments. I arrive at Lyons Township High School in time to have lunch with Tom and some of the writing teachers in a private teacher's lounge. Lyons Township is an enormous school of four thousand students and a campus that's spread between two buildings more than a mile apart. But that doesn't intimidate me as much as the knowledge that actor David Hasselhoff was a student here. It's like walking the halls where Galileo or Einstein once trod.

Over turkey sandwiches and chips, the teachers and I chat about ACTs and accidents and all agree they work the same on our psyches.

"I wouldn't take the test for anything," one of Tom's colleagues tells me, a teacher who holds workshops for students preparing for their ACTs. "I had a student," she tells me, "who in his junior year was the highest achiever in the school and the next year barely passed. We found out that his parents were going through a divorce. You can't test for that kind of thing. He bombed the ACT, and I thought, *Yes, he bombed his ACT. Of course he did.*"

Oddly, I've yet to meet *anyone* who thinks the tests are worthwhile. "I'd like to have everyone walk around for a day with their test scores pinned to them and see how much it matters now," Tom tells me.

After my talk, Tom shows me the testing center where his office is, and I meet his staff of secretaries and counselors who disdain the tests more than I do.

"They're all moneymakers," says one middle-aged woman, handing me a thick packet of ACT information. "The SATs are even worse."

Although I like Tom and his staff, I think the only way they manage their jobs must be through gallows humor and simple denial. It's madness really, all a part of the gigantic impersonal machine called "Outcomes Assessment." I doubt if even the people who work at ACT, SAT, or GRE are true believers, for the most part. They're probably nice people. I've most likely even shaken hands (yuck!) with several of them at an Iowa City party or two. Once a system is in place, it's nearly impossible to dismantle, even if it's useless and stupid (sorry, Shoshie). Anyway, I'm sure that these tests and versions of them probably aren't causing too much irreparable psychic damage to our children, despite the fact that third and fifth graders often wet themselves because they're so terrified of the tests they have to take now.

"That's terrible," I tell the cheerful middle-aged woman in Tom's office who has imparted this information to me, cheerful because she doesn't ever have to take one of these tests again.

"Let's hope you don't wet yourself," she tells me.

No, I've already done the grown-up equivalent of wetting myself. I've dropped out of the test and wrecked my car at ACT headquarters.

Finally, Tom shows me his school's "report card." Just like the woman from Des Moines I met on the plane, he says their special-ed classes have lowered the scores of the school and they've received a couple of failing grades. So the school has put a lot of money and time into bringing up the scores of the special-ed kids, and this year they passed by one kid. "But we're still on probation," Tom tells me, "because we have to do it two years in a row. At some point, we're supposed to have one hundred percent of the kids at a passing level, even though that's statistically impossible."

On our way out of the building, Tom shows me the Wall of Fame, displaying portraits of the school's many successful alumni, most of them business tycoons and the like. There in the middle is their most famous alum, David Hasselhoff, in some kind of Hawaiian shirt, smiling but somehow uneasy.

"For years, he tried to pretend he wasn't from the Midwest," Tom says. "When we told him we were inducting him into our Wall of Fame, he brought his *Entertainment Tonight* film crew and completely blew off the kids here and their interviews. He wouldn't have anything to do with them. This is the second David Hasselhoff plaque. The first was defaced."

Poor David Hasselhoff. I wonder what his ACT scores were. Not that it matters. Truly, there's no way to quickly or easily measure outcomes. They're measured slowly, infinitesimally, over a lifetime. Sometimes success isn't even a good measure of success. A video all over the Internet shows an inebriated Hasselhoff trying to eat a hamburger and making a mess of himself while his teenage daughter begs him to stop drinking. This seems more troubling to me than being from the Midwest, than even having a lousy ACT score. Maybe he could use a do-over too.

"See you in the fall," Tom says, but I know I'm not coming back. This *was* my do-over, I see now. The first time I didn't take a standardized test, it haunted me, but I'm over that now. I've escaped it a second time, even though escape was costly to my auto insurance.

It's taken me a long time to figure out that it doesn't matter what anyone else wants me to become. I'm free. Let loose for the weekend in the Windy City, wrecked car and all. If I knew how, I'd organize one giant protest march of TV technicians, gas station attendants, bookstore owners, box packers, and former fingerprint

232 technologists, all of us who have been observed and categorized our whole lives with no outlet for complaint or redress. I wish we could demand the skins of our assessors or at least have the satisfaction of killing *their* dreams. But, of course, I don't know how to accomplish this. I never received the proper training.

DO-OVER!DO-OVER!

CHAPTER NINE

MAMA'S BOY
House Do-Over

ORIGINAL AGE: 16
DO-OVER AGE: 48
ORIGINAL LOCATION: SOUTH BEND, INDIANA
DO-OVER LOCATION: SOUTH BEND, INDIANA

"I wouldn't let a stranger stay in my house," one of my friends told me when I mentioned my plan to stay for a few days in one of my childhood homes again. Until he said this, it hadn't occurred that anyone might have an objection. I suppose this is one of the effects of growing up with a permissive parent. You tend to think anything is possible. You wear your pajamas to school if you like. You attempt to build a time machine in art class. You go back in time, in a sense, and change the outcomes of things that didn't originally work out. Who could possibly have a problem with you inviting yourself to stay at their house? If your mother were alive, she'd approve. She'd laugh and pat you on the cheek. "Go right ahead, Bubeleh! You should do whatever you want to do."

Actually, I don't think my mother ever patted me on the cheek like that or called me Bubeleh. The Yiddish Mama wasn't her style, but the sentiment was the same. There's nothing to stop you but your own fears and assumptions about the world — that's one of my most lasting inheritances from her. I'm the first to admit that there are downsides to having a permissive parent, one who believes you can do no wrong, but there are positive benefits too. I'm sure I would never have conceived this project at all had my mother not instilled in me a powerful sense of "Why not?"

But others, friends, family, and acquaintances alike, generally expressed almost as much horror about the prospect of this do-over as that of my taking a standardized test. The Creep Factor seemed almost insurmountable. A stranger in my house! I suppose, when put that way, it does seem pretty creepy. But I knew my intentions were good — it was a matter of convincing others of this that might prove difficult. There wasn't anything *specific* I wanted to do over in my old home. It wasn't as though I'd forgotten to clean up my room or hadn't made my bed properly (though I rarely cleaned my room or made my bed properly).

But I needed to go back all the same. Part of the reason lay in the fact that I had little sense of home, nowhere to return, and no family to which I could return. I had lived in many houses, but I considered none of them home. I moved around a lot as a kid. I lived on Riverside Drive in Manhattan until I was five, then in two homes in Athens, Ohio; in a town house in Slippery Rock, Pennsylvania; in an apartment and a house in Columbia, Missouri; and in a house in South Bend, Indiana; and I also spent most of my summers until I was eighteen at my grandmother's house in Long Beach, Long Island.

This do-over, more than any of my others, required an act of faith, both on my part and on the part of the present-day home owner. I wasn't sure what I was looking for, but I'd know it when I saw it. I didn't even know which home I'd get to stay in, but I trusted that whichever one it turned out to be would somehow be just the right one.

Which houses should I write to? I had plenty of memories of all the places I lived in as a child, including our apartment on Riverside Drive in Manhattan. Still, I crossed *that* apartment off the list. It's now a multimillion dollar condo, and I doubted my chances of ever setting foot there again. A friend of mine in Athens snooped around one of the houses in which I lived, only to find that the name of the street as I had known it had changed as well as the street address. I decided to write to both houses in Athens, as well as my grandmother's house in Long Beach and my old house in South Bend. Around the time of my kindergarten do-over, I carefully drafted a letter on university stationery and bundled it with a business card, an explanation of my project, and a copy of my camp article as it appeared in *New York* magazine, and sent this package blindly to the various addresses. I explained my project and told the home owners that I would be as respectful and nonintrusive as they wanted me to be, if they granted my request. I didn't have the names of any of the inhabitants of my old haunts, and so I could only address the letters to Occupant. Who opens letters addressed to Occupant? They're never good. To counter this, I decide to FedEx the letters. That at least added an aura of importance.

After a couple of weeks, I received a tentative e-mail from one of the owners of a house I lived in in Athens. I'll call her Lois. It turned out she's my age and even, remarkably, knew a couple of the people I went to school with at Putnam Elementary. But, she said she had a lot of questions to be answered before she could ever imagine this working out. Delighted by her response and the fact that she knew two of my old classmates, I figured I was as good as in the front door. And I did what I always do: I came on like a ton of drywall.

I wrote to the two classmates Lois knew — I still had their e-mail addresses from the Putnam reunion of the previous summer — and I asked them to put in a good word for me with Lois. One of them wrote back, one of the friendly Donnas with whom I went to school, and said she'd be happy to help, and she wished me luck. The other, a man with whom I was never particularly close in school, never replied. That in itself didn't bother me, but Lois stopped responding to my e-mails as well. Maybe my old classmate put in a bad word instead of a good word for me. Maybe he was angry that I never invited him for a sleepover or to my birthday party! So the slights of childhood die that hard? I wondered. Or maybe I was just being paranoid. Regardless, Lois never wrote another word to me, and after a couple of attempts, I decided to let her be. It was my wish to stay in my old home again for a few days, not my right.

I heard nothing at all from the occupants of the other houses, and I was about to admit defeat when in January, four months after I sent my letters, I received an e-mail from the owner of the house in which I had lived with my mother and sister Nola in South Bend. She apologized for not getting in touch sooner but told me that my letter had found its way into a stack of unopened mail from the fall and she had just now read it. Sure, I'd be welcome to spend a few days with her, though she wanted to know a little more about my project. Like my mother, she too was an English professor, though at Notre Dame, not at Indiana University South Bend, and she taught literature, not creative writing as my mother had. But in every other respect, she was definitely not my mother — she was a good ten or fifteen years younger than me in any case.

We decided that, for the sake of privacy, I wouldn't reveal her name or the address of my old house. Not that I expected pilgrims to gather on her lawn ("Show us the shag carpet on which he trod in his youth!"), but I was grateful that she trusted a complete stranger to camp out in her house for a few days, and I wanted to do everything I could to make her comfortable about this.

It seemed right that this house in South Bend was the one I would get to live in again for a few days. It's the house in which we were living when Nola died, though she was staying with my grandmother at the time in Long Beach, New York. My sister had gone to my grandmother's to be closer to her guru, Sri Chinmoy, who had an ashram in Queens. She had left South Bend only a few weeks earlier, then one day I walked in the front door of our house and found one of my mother's students, Bev Demario, a loud and cheerful woman who always spoke frankly. "Your mother's gone," she told me. "Your sister tried to kill herself, and so your mom went back east to be with her." Actually, it's debatable whether my sister's death

was a suicide or an accidental overdose of the lithium she had been prescribed for schizophrenia. She had tried to kill herself in the past, and, in the end, it didn't matter exactly how it happened. Her kidneys failed, and she was dead within a day. Then it was a matter of returning to Athens, Ohio, and burying her at Alexander Cemetery next to my father. My mother's grief was enormous, but she was able to stay sane largely because of me, because I still needed her at age fifteen.

This was also the last house I had lived in with my mother before going off to Japan. I remembered my mother taking some pictures of me standing at the front railing of the little stoop in front of the house before I left for Japan and sailed off forever into my own life without her.

My mother passed away a couple of years before my do-over project began, and her passing had not been a peaceful one, for her or for me. For years after she retired at age seventy, I had urged her to move away from South Bend, either to California where my brother Jonathan lived or to North Carolina where I lived for a time, while she was still healthy. She always claimed to hate South Bend. A dyed-in-the-wool New Yorker, she had only reluctantly moved away from Manhattan when my father moved us all to Athens when she was in her late forties. She never blamed him, but she always wanted to return. She constantly complained that she didn't have any friends in South Bend, but she had plenty of friends who cared deeply for her despite the fact that she could be cantankerous and overly critical. She loved to throw parties for these friends (and for me when I visited) and go to movies and dine with them on a regular basis.

Finally, she decided to move to Bellingham, Washington, at the age of eighty, a decade after she should have made the move. I found her a lovely apartment in Bellingham, not far from where I lived with my first wife and Olivia and Isabel, but it soon became apparent that she couldn't live alone. She thought people were trying to break into her apartment. She thought people were living with her, camping out in her bedrooms. I started receiving phone calls from the police in the middle of the night after she had called 911. To this day, I don't know if the move from South Bend triggered the dementia or if she'd been suffering for some time, but numerous visits to the doctor confirmed that she had suffered a series of ministrokes and that she wasn't going to get better, only worse. One of the hardest and saddest things I ever had to do was to move this independence-loving woman into an assisted living residence in downtown Bellingham. She and my wife did not get along very well, and we were also worried about the safety of the children around her. But eventually, she grew to like the place, housed in a historic hotel on the bay, staffed by friendly and compassionate people who appreciated her sense of humor and quirks.

We lived in this way for five years, but after my divorce, after Olivia and Isabel moved to Wisconsin with their mother, and after I found a new job, it was my brother's turn, and so my mother went to live in L.A. And her condition grew steadily worse. Then I moved again, to Iowa, in large part to be closer to Olivia and Isabel, while my brother, whose aim it had long been to move to Israel, sold his house and decided to make good on his goal. I started to look into good nursing homes in the Iowa City area.

My mother's health started failing rapidly that June, just as my brother and I were moving. My brother, who at this point had power of attorney, was adamant in his conviction to sustain her life and put her on life support. From this moment on, a machine breathed for her, and there was no way to move her and no facility that would accept her until the breathing tube was removed. Margie and others told me that once the breathing tube is in place, it's almost impossible to remove from patients as old and frail as my mother after a certain point. And that point had passed. So had the point at which my brother and I could have reversed our decisions to move to different locales, our own versions of life support. I had no means or way of living in L.A., and my brother had sold his house and quit his job and had found a new life in Israel.

And so my mother was alone. That September, I flew back to L.A. with the intention of signing whatever forms I needed to sign to take her off life support, if possible, or at least to ensure that no extraordinary measures were taken to prolong her life. Of course, it wasn't about the cost of the nursing home. One thing about my mother: she had great insurance. But she was in a coma. She had not been awake since June. The doctors and nurses, with whom I maintained frequent contact, told me her bedsores were terrible. Margie, who was a nurse and had seen bedsores, expressed her horror at the thought. She told me that "bedsores" was a name that didn't properly express how terrible an affliction such things are. These pressure ulcers can be cavernous and putrid and terribly painful, even life threatening. Before the bedsores, my mother's skin seemed almost translucent, brittle as mica.

When I reached the hospital, with my cousin David there for moral support, I found there was nothing I could do. My brother called from Israel and told me he wouldn't agree to my wishes, that all measures, no matter how extraordinary, were to be used to keep her alive. We argued and argued, and finally I had nothing more to say but good-bye to my mother, as she lay prone in a hospital bed, the hush-hush of the breathing tube her only sound.

"I'll never forget that as long as I live," David said. "She's been dead since June."

Within a month, she was truly dead, and my brother and I made plans for her funeral, not in Athens where my father and sister are buried, but in our family plot in Brooklyn. My brother was calling the shots here, and although my mother was agnostic at best, he planned an Orthodox burial, which traditionally takes place within twenty-four hours of death.

But things were not going to be easy in this regard either. I bought my ticket for New York, and then a fog rolled in to the Cedar Rapids airport, and it looked as though I might miss the funeral. Nothing was arriving or leaving the airport, and driving was not an option. Even if I drove sixteen hours straight, I'd never make the funeral. So I canceled my first ticket and bought a second ticket, leaving from Chicago, a red-eye that would get me into LaGuardia at 8:00 a.m. I rented a car and drove four hours through the fog. I felt guilty enough that I had not been by her side when she died. I couldn't imagine what missing her funeral would do to me. On the way, I talked to her. In life she held grudges. I imagined in death she might well do the same. "C'mon, Mom," I told her. "Don't make it so hard for me."

My brother must have met me at the airport, but I don't remember this. I remember little until I arrived at the cemetery. Here, I sat on a bench among the graves and composed a few words to say at my mother's service. When I finally emerged from whatever hole the universe had tucked me in, my brother told me he had been calling my name, searching for me for ten minutes, though I sat not more than thirty feet away from him in full view. Neither of us had seen or heard the other.

Now that I had returned, the rabbi could start the service. He approached me, grabbed me by my shirt, and ripped it. My nicest shirt. I considered ripping his shirt. But then he did it to my brother too. I had forgotten about that part of ceremony. Ripping shirts at funerals. Breaking a glass at a wedding. Cutting off the foreskin at birth. There's a certain amount of breakage involved in being a Jew.

↶

As with my other do-overs, the evenings leading up to my South Bend house do-over bring nightmares. Variations on a guilty theme: my mother is either upset with me, though she never speaks, or Margie and I search for her, only to be told that we've arrived too late. She's not here anymore — though "here" is never a clearly defined place in the dream. I awake from one of these dreams reciting my mother's old phone number from South Bend, disconnected and discarded from memory for thirteen years.

You wouldn't think that living in a house you lived in when you were sixteen would cause as much stress as preparing for an ACT. But it surely does. When Mary, the woman who owns my old house, first moved in, a friend from her choir, Dea Andrews, said she had been in the house back when an English professor from IUSB lived there. As it turns out, Dea is the sister of Doug Kinsey, a retired art professor from Notre Dame. Doug and Marjorie Kinsey were two of my mother's closest friends in South Bend and have known me since I was fourteen. In a sweet and completely unexpected gesture, Mary decides to have a dinner party at her house in my honor and invites the Kinseys, Dea, and another one of my mother's close friends from Notre Dame, novelist Sonia Gernes. The Kinseys and Sonia — along with my mother's artist friend from Holland, Henny; a former student, Julie White; and her friend Gabrielle from Germany — were the saving graces of South Bend for her, a group of younger cosmopolitan artistic types whose company made her not yearn quite so much for New York.

I suppose that this coincidence is just another example of six degrees of separation. Still, considering that the metro area of South Bend, which includes its sister city of Mishawaka, is home to about three hundred and twenty thousand souls, it's at least mildly remarkable that the soul who occupies my old house has a connection to my mother's closest friends. The fact that they *were* my mother's closest friends only adds to my worry. I have no idea what they think of me anymore. I haven't seen any of them for at least a dozen years. Do they view me as a bad son who neglected his mother? Several years back, Marjorie tweaked me by e-mail when she saw a photo that made me look like some rugged explorer. "Who are you fooling?" she asked via e-mail. Certainly not her and not Doug and not Sonia. These are three insightful people who speak their minds. The thought of a dinner party with them takes on in *my* mind the aspect of a trial.

Getting to South Bend seems almost as difficult as attending my mother's funeral. First, my car wreck alters my plans. I have to appear in traffic court to plead guilty to being an ACT-addled idiot or something to that effect, and it's on the day I was originally supposed to strike out for South Bend. Fortunately, Mary is understanding and flexible in her plans, though she's warned me that she won't be able to spend much time with me because she's playing with the Notre Dame symphony the day after my arrival (she plays the bassoon), and she's got to go to a dress rehearsal the evening I arrive. But that's fine with me. I'll appreciate the time alone in the house.

In the same way that it was a trial simply getting to my mom's funeral, thunderstorms dog me the entire way to South Bend on the late April day I leave from Iowa City, and the road is littered with horrendous car wrecks. Early in the morning, a car crashed with a tractor trailer on the Indiana toll road, killing eight people. The hulk of a burned-out semi, not the same as the one that killed all those people, sits to one side of the road in Iowa, and in Illinois, another semi, still loaded with new cars, lies on its side at the bottom of a culvert ten feet below the road. I was planning to arrive in South Bend in the early afternoon, but because of various wrecks and traffic, I don't arrive until after five.

The house stands at the top of a hill, where I left it, if not *as* I left it, thirty-three years ago. When I lived in it, the house was white, but now it's a light shade of gray. A picket fence that wasn't there when I lived in it now surrounds a lovely perennial garden, new enough to be absent from my memory but old enough to look a little rangy and disheveled. There's still plenty of lawn to mow, but in the early seventies, it was all grass. Most remarkably, the empty lot where I tried with a friend to create an organic garden with the owner's permission is now occupied by a historic home from the early twentieth century, by the looks of it.

At the door of my childhood home, I'm greeted by a youthful, freckled woman with auburn hair cut in a pageboy style, and she invites me inside. I know the layout of this house with my eyes closed, though some features I have no memory of: the fireplace in the living room, for instance. I suppose we never used it, nor does Mary. She says that someone installed the flue upside down so that it dumps creosote. She has it taped up now. The floors are hardwood, something I don't remember, but that's because when she moved in she took up some "awful seventies shag carpet." *That* I remember. And her dining room furniture, a sideboard and table, are placed exactly as we had them. She leads me through the dining room and kitchen to the basement where I once set up a "rec room" with black-light posters in anticipation of my many friends who would listen to music with me down there. Never happened, of course, but those old posters remain in my memory: KEEP ON TRUCKIN', FUCK HOUSEWORK, FRODO LIVES!

Leading me to a utility room, she ferrets among some shelves, finally pulling out a swatch of dusty old orange shag, which she hands to me as though it's some powerful magic potion rarely needed. "I come from a family that keeps everything, thinking it might come in handy someday," she tells me. I don't even want to touch it.

When Poet Laureate Ted Kooser dropped in at his childhood home in Ames, Iowa, the owners presented him with some toy soldiers that had been dug up in the backyard. They had always wondered to whom they belonged. The soldiers belonged to him. As a child, when he and his friends had battles, they would give their "dead" soldiers burials. When Kooser saw the soldiers again, he burst into tears, as I know I probably would have too. But instead of toy soldiers, I get orange shag. I might sneeze, but I'm not going to cry.

Then, the thought of this hideous orange carpet starts to charm me. Why not? After all, it *is* a part of my life, and I've chosen to embrace all aspects of my past, even at its shaggiest. The carpet is the equivalent of a housewarming gift, but in this case freezing the past instead of warming the present.

Upstairs, Mary's cats, Max and Demelza, come out to greet me. Demelza, says Mary, is normally shy of new visitors, but she's rubbing up against my leg in no time. "You should feel honored," Mary says. I had two cats when I lived here too: a blue Persian with a smashy face named Anacris, and an affectionate white stray named Persephone. This is a two-cat house, and although I've come to love dogs, I didn't grow up with them. At heart, I'm a cat person, and cats, like dogs, know on whose team you're playing when you meet them.

Mary shows me to the guest room, which in my day was pretty much where I lived. It was my de facto bedroom if not my actual one. I had a little TV in this room, and I took all my meals here and slept here most of the time on a green foldout couch. I kept my comic book collection here and my stamp collection. And I had a poster here of an Indian goddess in an Eden-like setting that Nola, at her most ill, ripped to shreds one evening. And it's where I had a desk that I used to sit at and try to understand Plato and the history of Mesopotamia and the algebra I was taught at Magdalene, Bruce Fingerhut's little school in the church basement. This is also the room where my roommate at St. Andrew's and future host brother, Hiroshi, and I would sit and watch the Cubs when he spent Thanksgiving and spring break and part of summer with my family.

I didn't ask for this room. I didn't tell Mary which room had been mine, but, of course, this *would* be the bedroom she'd choose as her guest room, though the adjacent empty bedroom (the one I think might have officially been mine though I have absolutely no memories of it) is slightly larger. Another marvelous do-over coincidence. If the universe keeps dishing them, I'll gladly accept, though I'm hoping the bill won't be a shock.

When I put down my bag in my old room, a wave of nostalgia *doesn't* wash over me. I feel nothing really but relief that I survived the trip. The room is smaller than I remember because Mary claimed half of it to expand the upstairs bathroom. Now it holds a bed and a dresser, and that's about it. What do you do in your old house when you return for a visit and your old connections to it have faded like the dye in that old shag? If you're me, you make some calls to your new connections, my daughters in Wisconsin. I'd call Margie and Shoshie too, but they flew off to the Philippines to visit Margie's family a few days ago. Izzy picks up and starts telling me about her many activities. I've lost count of the number of activities she's involved in. Her latest is track, and tomorrow she doesn't get home until seven and then she's off to a statewide sleepover for student councils in Wisconsin. When I speak to her, I sometimes feel as though my life has been reduced to that old Harry Chapin song "Cat's in the Cradle," in which a type A dad never has time for his son, and when he finally *does* have time for the son, the son no longer has time for him. That damn song starts playing in my head half the time when I'm talking to the girls these days.

"How was traffic court?" Izzy asks, interrupting Harry mid-chorus.

"It was nothing," I say. "But there were a lot of people."

"All to see you?" she asks. "Was there a jury?"

I laugh, but, really, I almost built up traffic court that much in my own mind. I imagined a packed courtroom, a hanging judge. Actually, it was more like being sent to the principal's office. Not even that. Although the judge was dressed in a black robe and we stood for him, all my stereotypes of judges broke down after that. He didn't act like a judge. Not even a TV judge. He didn't even act like a principal. More like a jaded guidance counselor (is there any other kind?). There must have been seventy-five people in the room, and he split us into two lines: those who wanted to plead guilty and those who wanted a trial. I knew who my brothers and sisters were! I jumped into the guilty line, though I seemed the only person in the line who felt existentially guilty.

As outcomes go, traffic court was a breeze. Other outcomes weigh more heavily. At least I don't have to worry about Izzy's reaction to the new baby. A few days ago, Margie had an ultrasound and Isabel called up that night.

"Well? What is it?" she asked impatiently.

Unfortunately, the baby kept its legs clamped together, so the technician couldn't tell the sex, but she was leaning toward a girl. She was about the only one who leaned that way. The baby moved as though training for the Olympic gymnastics team, and so . . . Let the Baby Guessing Games Begin! Must be a boy, several people commented. Boys are more active, ya know. The shape of Margie's tummy supposedly foretells the baby's sex too. If the belly is round, it's a girl. Oblong, it's a boy. Margie thinks her tummy is oblong. I refuse to participate in this — maybe you can tell if a melon is ripe by knocking on it or sniffing it, but you can't tell the sex of a baby by the shape of its mother's tummy. What would I do with a boy? I don't know or understand boys at all, even though I've been one and have surrounded myself with them for the past nine months since my do-over at Camp Echo.

Tonight, Izzy tells me she thinks it's a girl. "Well, I want it to be a boy, but I think it's going to be a girl."

"What makes you think so?" I ask.

"I don't know. I just think it is," she says in that irrefutable way with which kids make statements about the world. I'm just glad she cares, though, of course, she follows up her statement with the "I don't care, just as long as it's healthy" clause. When talking about a pregnancy, you can't leave out the "I don't care, just as long as it's healthy" clause, or you're asking for trouble.

⌒

As do-overs go, staying again in my old house seems somehow subtler, less obvious than the others. I'm still unsure what exactly I'm doing over here. This is something that the woman in Athens, Ohio, wanted to know and that I couldn't satisfactorily answer, and something Mary asked me too. I still can't answer anything specific. It's not like getting initiated into a fraternity or taking the woman you had a crush on when you were sixteen to the prom or reprising a role in a school play, though I suppose it's most like reprising a role. Mary suggests that since I lived here as a teenager, perhaps I'd like to mow her lawn.

Yes, that's something I did a lot when I lived here, but . . . Oh, man. Do I have to? Can't it wait? It's not *that* long.

I spend most of the next day napping like an adolescent in my old bedroom and procrastinating about mowing Mary's lawn. It's still kind of wet, I reason. Maybe I should wait another day for it to dry out.

That night, I take a break from my productive napping to attend Mary's concert at Notre Dame. My mother would have loved going to this concert with me. The orchestra is playing selections from Mikhail Glinka and Alan Shulman, followed by Gustav Holst's *The Planets*. As luck would have it, there's an empty seat beside me in the packed symphony hall, and so I indulge my sentimental side and imagine my mother seated beside me wearing one of her trademark berets. Not the version of my mother I knew in the last eight years of her life, but the wisecracking independent woman I knew most of my life. During the final two years of her dementia, she often greeted me by saying, "They told me you had died." It's an unnerving greeting. "Tell them they're wrong," I'd tell her, and I'd give her a hug. One terrible day she didn't recognize me at all, and I felt that I truly had died for her. But the next time, she greeted me again as though I had returned from the dead. One of the stories she often told me when I was a child was that of Persephone (goddess of innocence and my cat's namesake), who ate six pomegranate seeds that she had been offered by Hades and so had to spend six months of the year as queen of the underworld away from her mother, Demeter. My mother hugged me as though I too had returned from the underworld. It was such a strong, clinging hug for someone so frail and old. When she let go, she looked up at me. "I told them I didn't want to live in a world without you in it," she said. But now, I lived in a world without her, and it was a strange world, in the way that the world becomes strange for anyone, no matter how old, recently orphaned. I imagine the tables turned now, my mother suddenly seated beside me as we listen to "Neptune, the Mystic," the last movement of the symphony. I imagine her squeezing my hand, leaning over, and whispering loudly in my ear, "I'm not really here. Don't be trite, Robin."

The following day, Mary and I visit the farmers' market, where I purchase the ingredients for the salad and some other goodies, my contribution to the dinner party. I also stop procrastinating and mow Mary's lawn. The lawn has changed more than the house and for the better. There's less to mow now, but it still takes me a good hour to complete the task. While mowing the lawn doesn't transport me back to my childhood, memories start seeping out of every stair and nook of the house. In front of the closet in the dining room, I see my sister Nola examining herself in the mirror, criticizing herself for looking too fat, though she wasn't fat at all. I see my mother pulling out a bottle of good vodka for her guests and just about dropping to the floor when she sees it has turned green. I turned it green. Actually, I turned the entire bottle of expensive vodka into a giant bottle of awful crème de menthe. From the time I was fifteen, I started brewing beer with my best friend in South Bend, Drew Lippert. We both hated the taste of beer, but our mothers liked it and so we made it for them. One day, I saw a packet of instant crème de menthe powder in the Wine-Art store in Mishawaka where I bought my beer-making supplies, and I thought that this was just the sort of thing my mother would appreciate too. I was wrong.

In the living room, I see Nobel laureate in literature Isaac Bashevis Singer, seated on a couch, chatting with my mother. She and my father had been his translators and editors for many years, and she invited him to be part of the Notre Dame Literary Festival in the 1970s. I see all of these things and more in the house. They're more than memories. They're more palpable, more present than memories. They play in front of my eyes whenever I enter the house, and I watch them unfold, spellbound.

Sonia Gernes is the first to arrive for the dinner party that evening. I always liked Sonia because she seems unpretentious and friendly. Although she's refined, even elegant with her light hair perfectly coiffed, there's still more than a trace of the Minnesota dairy farm girl she once was in her open smile. Unlike my mother, having grown up in the Midwest, I never felt conflicted about claiming it.

I bring Sonia some cheese and crackers and a drink, while in the kitchen Mary puts the finishing touches on her meal, a dish called Chicken with Forty Cloves of Garlic. This is the perfect dish to serve tonight. It reminds me of my mother in its extravagance and unabashed, unapologetic sense of pleasure and fullness. In a John Cheever story, one of his WASP antiheroes condemns a neighbor for being a "garlic eater." But that was Westchester County he was writing about, not Manhattan, where garlic eaters by the millions, immigrants once or twice removed, ate things and did things that suburbanites found strange, at least in my mother's generation. Dishes like Chicken with Forty Cloves of Garlic were my mother's métier, even a validation of sorts. A Manhattan kind of dish.

Sonia has never been in this house, from which my mother moved in 1976 before she and Sonia became friends. She and I reminisce before the others arrive, about the unhappy days much later in my mother's life, two decades after she lived here. Sonia tells me about the packing party she and seven other friends of my mother had before my mother headed to Bellingham to live near me. I wasn't able to get away to help, but I more than made up for it on the other end when I moved her first into her apartment, then into assisted living two months later, and put her enormous amount of belongings into storage. She refused to throw anything away, not even old issues of *TV Guide*. The entire contents of her house, unsorted, made the journey from South Bend, Indiana, to Bellingham, Washington.

Sonia tells me now that she and the others were shocked when they arrived at my mother's apartment, the last of several places she inhabited in South Bend, and saw what a mess it was. "I remember going up to the bathroom and noticing how dirty it was," she tells me. "And that wasn't like your mother. We kind of took over. Your mother kept thrusting things at us. We wanted to help her in any way we could." But they couldn't help because what she wanted was her entire life, as it was, transported lock, stock, and *TV Guide* to the West Coast where she imagined me, I'm sure, filling the role that her South Bend friends had so admirably filled. But I wasn't up to it. I had two young daughters and a job, and I managed to see her once or twice a week, sometimes not that when I was traveling. This house was the last place in which she had my undivided attention.

There's a knock on the front door, and Doug, Marjorie, and Dea step inside.

"Hellooo," Marjorie says, warmly hugging me.

"I can smell the garlic all the way out there," says Dea, the person I know least at this party besides Mary. For many years, Dea traveled, living in England for a decade, Kenya for five years, India for two. Now she manages an apartment complex for the South Bend Heritage Foundation and writes grants for an art gallery in South Bend, the best gallery in town, according to Doug. I don't remember her at all, though she remembers me, and I imagine my mother would have liked her for living the artistic bohemian life, if nothing else, and for being Doug's sister.

Doug, in his younger days, had almost Hollywood good looks: sandy brown hair, a chiseled chin, and a warm but ironic smile. Marjorie exuded a kind of exotic mystery with her long dark hair and large brown eyes. On their travels, she often passed for Italian or Jewish, even Indian, and Japanese once or twice during a two-year stay in Japan. In South Bend, she's frequently taken for an English woman simply because her diction is so good — as though the English all speak with perfect diction. She and Doug are both midwesterners, though if passing as east coasters or Europeans is the better part of refinement and sophistication in the eyes of other midwesterners (and in my mother's eyes), then they pass the test. She graduated from Wellesley, then went on for a theological degree from Yale, and received a PhD from Chapel Hill in art history. Doug, born in Oberlin, Ohio, to academic parents, went first to Oberlin and then received his MFA from Minnesota.

It's difficult for me to imagine Doug and Marjorie in any way but as I knew them when I was fourteen. Doug's hair is largely gray, and Marjorie's hair is not only gray but cut short, though still fashionable. She's in ethnic drag now (Doug's term, Marjorie, not mine!): a pair of dangly Indian earrings and a colorful dress with a Japanese pattern. Doug, virtually unchanged in his clothing style over these many years, wears a corduroy jacket and black jeans, but, of course, he's aged. As soon as they leave, Doug and Marjorie will snap back in my mind to the way they looked in 1974 — Doug's hair will turn brown again, and his skin will smooth. Marjorie's hair will turn a rich dark color and grow like the magic hair of Shoshie's Princess Jasmine doll.

I'm surprised how good it is to see them. Although I'm happy to see Sonia too, meeting up with Marjorie and Doug feels oddly like a relief, like one of those nightmares in which I've been searching for my mother — except in this case, I'm not told it's too late. They're not my parents, but they knew me when I was a boy, and that apparently counts for something in my subconscious.

"I *do* remember this house," Doug says, stepping into the living room. Both he and Marjorie look around in mild wonder.

"There was a bookcase," says Marjorie, pausing by the coffee table.

"You're remembering the bookcase over here," I say, pointing to the stairs, and the three of us take a virtual tour of the living room, circa 1973. I point out where the couch was. Marjorie mentions an antique drop-leaf table that my mother used as a dining table.

While Mary has taken care of the main dish, I've gone to town with side dishes and appetizers and bread and wines and the salad, all purchased (except for the wine) this morning at the farmers' market. I've probably gone overboard, as usual, just as my mother would have gone overboard. I offer the guests everything, from wine to goat cheese and Port Salut. I like offering goat cheese and Port Salut. Maybe these words highlight a certain brand of midwestern pretension and anxiety about worldliness. Even so, I've already had a couple of glasses of Shiraz (that's another good word — *Shiraz!*), so I have a hard time containing myself.

"Some goat cheese?" I offer Marjorie. "Port Salut? Some more Shiraz?"

"You went to Japan as an exchange student when you lived in this house," Marjorie says, uncertainly.

"Yes, as a matter of fact, I'm going back to my old high school in Osaka next week. It's all part of my project."

"You're going to know a lot about your life when you finish this," she says.

"Believe me," I say.

"I inherited from my parents after they died," says Doug, "a box that contained all the letters I had written to them. I had no idea they were saving them. This was over a period of thirty-five years. I haven't had the guts to even open up the box. Well, I did once, but then I found out I didn't really like that teenager I was reading about."

"I don't like the teenager I *was*," I tell him. "There's something terrifying about that."

"Charming but manipulative," Marjorie says, laughing again, cutting to the chase as usual. The charming part is okay, but that word *manipulative* stings a bit.

"It takes great courage to do this," Doug says.

"Very charming," Marjorie says, still laughing, almost choking.

"Well, coming back to this house, I was telling Mary, 'Doug and Marjorie know all my faults.'"

They laugh. "No," Doug says. Marjorie tilts her head and smiles but doesn't contradict me.

"When we first met you, you were still very short." They must have been in their late twenties or early thirties when we first met.

Very short? I was never *very* short.

"Just twelve or fourteen. You didn't spurt for a while, and then suddenly you were . . ."

"A beanpole," Doug says.

"A beanpole," Marjorie agrees. "And then the most dreamily aesthetic child who could just worm his way into anything."

"Very bright and very charming," Doug says at the same time.

Marjorie seems to have trouble using I-Care language of the kind I learned in Mrs. Statler's kindergarten class. *Charming, dreamily aesthetic* — those are all nice words. I'm not so sure about *manipulative* and *worm*. If she doesn't stop soon, I might have to tell her I-Care rule number four: We care about each other's feelings.

If that doesn't work, I might even have to resort to the I-Care amendments:

1. Ignore.
2. Tell to stop.
3. Walk away.
4. Get help.
5. Withhold goat cheese and Shiraz.

But it's not so bad really. I love Marjorie for her frankness. And her tone isn't condemning. She's simply amused, and perhaps what makes this all the more amusing is that I'm still all those things: all except for "dreamily aesthetic," alas. The positive side of being a manipulative worm is that I've been able to worm myself back into a life left behind. I've been able to manipulate the past and my relationship to it. Sometimes it's okay to simply meet your younger self, nod like passing acquaintances, and move on. There are things to leave back in 1973, and there are things to take away, like a box of old letters, opened and reread.

Perhaps this evening is my mother's wake, in a sense. At wakes, you eat and reminisce, and though you're sad, you also fill your stomach with the comfort of continued life. Without knowing my mother, Mary has prepared a dish that my mother would have approved of, that she would have made herself, that she would have cooked with pride for these very same friends. Mary calls us to dinner. *"Mangez vite!"* my mother would have added in a bad French accent, pretending to admonish us to eat quickly before it all grew cold.

At dinner, we tell stories of the houses in which we now live. Mary has records from a title search from the 1950s that came with the house. I don't remember ever seeing this history of the property going all the way back to the treaty in which the Potowatamies ceded the land to the United States. The house, as it turns out, was built on the old post road between Lake Michigan and Indianapolis but only dates to 1924. Still, Mary half expects, she says, to turn up artifacts in her garden, but the most she's discovered to date is an old bottle that shattered when her shovel hit it and some Legos. Still, looking at the old maps of the territory, circa 1830, fills us with an appreciation and wonder at the trail of people who passed through this one spot, including us, our younger selves.

The Kinseys have moved since I last saw them. Their old house, on Notre Dame Avenue, was torn down and a McMansion built in its place. They've moved to a historic property built in 1881 in the center of South Bend that they've renovated. While tearing off old wallpaper, Doug came across a piece of writing underneath, dated 1896: "Today is the Sabbath. I shouldn't be working today." We collectively marvel at this little tidbit of guilt, written into the walls of the home. If only all homes spoke so plainly. But there's more. In the course of tearing out an old staircase, they came across a metal box, written on its lid the words, "To Who [sic] It May Concern." They discovered in the box a letter from the family that had originally lived in the house, a letter written during renovations completed in 1904. The family wrote about their children attending college, and the house they were building next door for another family member, and the extent of the renovations they were doing. Doug and Marjorie read the letter, copied it, and added their own letter. Then they placed both back in the metal box and put it in the wall at a spot they figured would see the next renovations should a future family want to create even more space.

Under the circumstances, I could not have better dinner companions. Not only were they my mother's dear friends, but they understand something about the need to renovate and reassess, to look at old maps and old plans and letters and trace the sometimes indistinct line from the past to the present.

After dinner when the guests have all left, Mary and I clean up and do the dishes together. I wash. She dries.

"I always felt that the history of this house wasn't necessarily happy," she says. She always wondered if something had happened to a teenager in the house. She'd found cigarettes hidden in the basement ceiling, which hinted at teenagers. A drilled-out bedroom lock upstairs suggested trouble. She tells me also that before her, a couple who lived here divorced — the woman received the house in the settlement.

"My sister always said this house was built on a Potowatomie burial ground," I say. Where she got this information, I have no idea. Most likely it was simply a delusion of hers.

"I wondered when you told me about her if she had died here," she says. "But the thought didn't bother me. A lot of good and bad will have happened in a house of a certain age. That's just life."

"You know, the house seems fine to me," I tell her. "It just seems like a house. I think you've made it your own." She nods, and I hand her the largest pan, the one that held the main dish. My eyes aren't always the best, but I scrubbed it hard — it's dripping wet and sparkling, and not the slightest trace of our pungent meal remains.

CHAPTER TEN

OLD BOY

Exchange Program Do-Over

ORIGINAL AGE: 17	
DO-OVER AGE: 48	
ORIGINAL LOCATION: MOMOYAMA GAKUIN, OSAKA, JAPAN	
DO-OVER LOCATION: MOMOYAMA GAKUIN, OSAKA, JAPAN	

The last I heard from Hiroshi Oshiro was in a letter when we were nineteen, two years after I'd returned early from my exchange program. He wrote to me that he was forgetting his English but, even so, we would always be friends. That thought stayed with me for many years — we had been the best of friends. We'd roomed together at St. Andrew's when we were sixteen, and the next year he was my host brother in Osaka. For years, my mother told me she thought I should get back in touch with Hiroshi, and I had tried.

Nearly ten years before I started my do-over project, I had written to his parents' old address but had never received a reply. I had also asked various Japanese friends to help me locate him but with no success. I knew that his last name, Oshiro, had something to do with a castle. Either in front of the castle or behind the castle. But I didn't know the exact ideograms, and I couldn't simply plug the name "Hiroshi Oshiro" into a search engine and expect results. It's not that easy in Japan.

While arranging my other do-overs, I finally had the bright idea to contact my old high school in Osaka, Momoyama Gakuin, and see if they had any information on Hiroshi. My Japanese friend Yasuko, who lives in Iowa City, agreed to call up Momoyama for me. To start, I wanted to see if the school could locate Hiroshi. Perhaps, as Hiroshi had fretted in the last letter he wrote to me, he had lost all his English as I had lost all my Japanese. How could a friendship be rekindled when we had both tumbled long ago from the Tower of Babel?

But whatever happened with my search for Hiroshi, I wanted to return to Momoyama, though I wasn't sure the Japanese would "get" my do-over project, either its humorous or serious side. The whole idea might seem far-fetched and odd, and I doubted anyone would remember me. The head of my old exchange program, Mr. Nishikawa, a chain smoker, was certainly dead, as were, I felt sure, my other old teachers.

In Japanese, *Momoyama* means "peach mountain," but there was nothing either fragrant, fruitful, or hilly about the place. Located in the midst of a nondescript urban neighborhood in Osaka, Momoyama in my memory resembled a prison block more than a school, a dusty courtyard on which nothing grew, surrounded by several stories of featureless concrete. My time at Momoyama had been nothing short of a failure, and one that I had long wished I could erase. It had started out with such promise too. One day at St. Andrew's, the word *exchange* stuck in my mind. Hiroshi and I were such good friends, and I wondered if I might go to Japan as he had come to America. Father Martin seemed in favor, as did my mother, and that was all there was to it. There was no formal exchange, not even any preparation. The head of the Japanese exchange, Andrew

Nishikawa, had initiated the program when he had toured Episcopal high schools in the United States, and the first exchange student from the Episcopal schools in America had gone to Osaka shortly after Mr. Nishikawa's tour. I would be among the second wave, along with my friend Paul from St. Andrew's, a lanky runner whose meets I regularly photographed for the St. Andrew's yearbook as an excuse to get off campus. Paul and I would be joined by three other students from a couple of other Episcopal high schools in the States.

That August, in 1975, I flew to Tokyo with the other exchange students. We met on the plane from San Francisco and flew unaccompanied by any adults — this was before unaccompanied minor regulations. Besides my friend Paul, there was Stephen, with shoulder-length blond hair, parted in the middle; Jay, who wore big glasses and a protomullet; and Evan, with curly red hair of almost Afro length. I was the shortest and skinniest and had the biggest mouth, bouncing around the plane, unable to stay in my seat, trying to get to know them as though I had only a few hours to do so instead of a year. I was even out of my seat as the plane was landing, and the flight attendant urged me to sit down in one of the empty seats beside Evan, who was much quieter and regarded me with something between disdain and alarm.

We were met at Haneda Airport in Tokyo by Mr. Nishikawa and two other teachers, Mr. Toguchi and Mr. Hatsusegawa. Mr. Nishikawa had an urbane quality to him, though he spoke out of the side of his mouth like a gangster, perhaps as a result of the cigarette that was always dangling from his lips. He wore a blue suit and a red tie with the Episcopal shield on it. He kept his cigarette in his mouth and shook our hands vigorously, smiling and squinting from the smoke. "Welcome, boys!" he said in a husky voice, taking my hand in both of his. None of us knew more than a few words of Japanese. This was 1975, and exchange programs were the exception, not viewed as a necessary part of middle-class education as they are today. White Americans were largely ignorant of other cultures and cuisines. I had tasted sushi before, thanks to Hiroshi, but none of my friends had. My Japanese was limited to what I had learned from Hiroshi and from vintage World War II John Wayne movies, viewed on rainy days at Granite Lake Camp under duress. So I *could* hold a conversation in Japanese as long as it was limited to *Sayonara, Tojo!* and *Banzai!!!!!*

"*Oki ohayo momo, Kintama San!*" I said in greeting to Mr. Nishikawa, a phrase Hiroshi had taught me. And I bowed, almost prostrating myself, as though I were meeting the emperor. Hiroshi had taught me that too. I'd thought I was saying, "I'm glad to meet you, Teacher," but I'd actually said, "A big good morning peach, Mr. Golden Testicles!"

"Same to you!" Mr. Nishikawa said affably, as though he heard this greeting every day. "But Robin, who taught you those words?"

"Hiroshi did," I said, immediately giving him up. W. H. Auden writes that loyalty is the only developed value in adolescents. That was certainly true of Hiroshi, as when he refused to rat out the boy who had suggested he call our teacher a bitch on the first day of English class at St. Andrew's, but it wasn't true of me. I was much more adept and comfortable with betrayal than loyalty, as betrayal felt safer and more satisfying in the short term, and I made a catlike adolescent, satisfied to sun myself and lick my paws on the ledge of the present moment. Now it's hard to find a children's book that doesn't reinforce the sensible notion that loyalty is preferable to betrayal. Shoshie knows more about loyalty and other values at four than I knew at sixteen.

But in this case, there were no serious consequences. Mr. Nishikawa simply shook his head, smiled, and inhaled some smoke as if capturing in his lungs the memory of his own boyhood impishness.

He squired us first to the Takanawa Prince Hotel, and then we dashed off for a tour of Tokyo: Ginza, the Tokyo Tower, and the Imperial Palace, followed by dinner at a fancy Japanese restaurant where our lessons in Japanese began, though we were sagging with jet lag. Mr. Nishikawa possessed enough enthusiasm to light Tokyo, and his philosophy was You can rest when you're dead. When he saw my lids drooping at the table, he nudged me and said, "*Gambatte kudasai!* That means, 'Do your best,' Robin." I think he already sensed that I was not going to do my best if it meant having to suffer in the slightest. If I wanted to sleep, I'd sleep, or else I'd whine so much that he'd wish he could knock me out.

I sighed deeply and took the list of transliterated "handy Japanese phrases" Mr. Nishikawa passed out.

When the waitress approached me with the umpteenth platter of food, I quickly scanned the list for the words to say "I'm full." Sure enough, Mr. Nishikawa had provided this helpful phrase: "*Onaka ga ipai desu.*" I pointed to my stomach and loudly pronounced, "*Inaka ga opai desu!*" which means, "The countryside is a breast!" Actually, more like boob or tit. "The countryside is a tit!" I had no idea why my lack of appetite should bring tears of laughter to the eyes of Mr. Nishikawa and half the restaurant.

The next day we took the Shinkansen, the famous bullet train, from Tokyo to Osaka where we were met by our host families. When I was introduced to Mr. and Mrs. Oshiro, they seemed to me as though they had been designed to fit together, like matching salt and pepper shakers, the same compact height and build. Neither of them spoke a word of English, and I was hesitant to use the Japanese provided to me by their son or by Mr. Nishikawa's phrase sheet. We nodded and smiled a lot at each other, though I detected a hint of disappointment on Mr. Oshiro's face when back at the apartment I presented him with a gift of a fifth of Jack Daniel's whiskey. I thought it would be an appropriate gift, as Hiroshi and I had attended school in Tennessee, but Mr. Oshiro seemed baffled by it. He nodded and thanked me with a look that approached concern. "He doesn't know it," Hiroshi explained to me. "Johnnie Walker is what people usually give." My handmade (not by me) pot holders were met with equal befuddlement from Mrs. Oshiro as I soon gathered there were not many pots to hold, and looking back, I can't imagine pot holders making anyone rabid with joy.

Compared to the dwellings of my fellow exchange students, my quarters at the Oshiros' were luxurious. Mr. Oshiro was the vice president of a Taiwanese trading company, and the apartment was the penthouse (though not quite as luxuriously appointed as the term would suggest) of a building the company owned. I had my own apartment — actually, where the president, an elderly Taiwanese man, stayed when he was in town, an infrequent occurrence. I even had my own kitchen, though this was completely wasted on me. Hiroshi's room was a cramped closet with little space for anything other than a bed and was decorated with almost nothing but an American flag tacked to the wall.

Hiroshi and I quickly resumed our friendship. In the early days of the school year, we explored Osaka together, going to festivals and shrines, wandering the streets where even the smallest back alleys yielded fragrant tea shops and restaurants with ceramic white cats in the windows and cloth banners in the entryways. We spent much of our time in the entertainment district known as Shinsaibashi, a mile-long arcade in the middle of Osaka, full of the bustle of the city, lined with department stores in front of which stood young women urging shoppers inside, cafés where I listened to jazz and smoked Seven Stars brand cigarettes, pachinko parlors full of bells and lights and the clatter of thousands of pachinko balls as they shot in quick succession through the machines. Although illegal for us to play at our age, Hiroshi and I paid no attention and no one paid attention to us as we watched "pachinko professors" at their stations, their thumbs flicking balls with unerring precision into the little maws of the plastic flowers and creatures within the pachinko machines' glass cases. In response, the flowers and creatures birthed hundreds of balls into the silver ditch at the bottom of the machine. The professors had buckets of these balls, which they traded in for — what . . . prizes? Money? I can't remember anymore, and I didn't care then. Pachinko was pure sensation. Playing it was its own reward. I sat for hours, mesmerized by it, with or without Hiroshi.

As an American teen, I had almost star status. Kids tagged along behind me yelling, "*Gaijin, gaijin!*" literally "outsider." Strangers would approach me in the street or on the bus and ask if they could practice English with me, and sometimes they invited me home for dinner. I started to feel a bit like an exotic animal. One of the strangest encounters was when Hiroshi brought me to a friend's house and the three of us sat in a tatami mat room while the friend's mother brought us whiskey (Johnnie Walker, of course) and rice crackers — she never stepping foot in the room, but kneeling and setting the tray in front of us and bowing.

Hiroshi's friend asked if I wanted to see a movie. I was pretty sure it was going to be porn. I had never seen actual porn before,

though I had a vague notion of vaginas and their uses. I had seen a total of one vagina in my life, Erica Marks's when we were five and she took me down to her basement and said she'd show me hers if I showed her mine. "Gladly," I said, or the five-year-old equivalent. She went first. I nodded. Very interesting. As far as I could tell, she had nothing down there at all. Nothing worth showing at least. I felt I'd been cheated. So I refused to take off my pants. Since then, no one else had offered. Word got around, I guess.

But I had my big chance to see a few vaginas again when I found a stack of well-worn *Playboys* at a bazaar Momoyama held one weekend. The original owner of the *Playboys* had tried to erase the black marker on the heavily censored photos in the magazines but had succeeded only in smearing the marker so that the pubic area approximated a kind of swirling miasma as if a cartoon bomb had exploded there. Wile E. Coyote might emerge singed and disoriented from such a cave.

It wasn't porn we watched that day, but World War II footage, real footage. A film documentary of the battle of Iwo Jima. From the American perspective. I don't think anything could have shocked me more. The most graphic sexual scenario, though confusing, would not have confused me nearly as much as watching American soldiers shooting flamethrowers at Japanese holdouts. At first, I thought Hiroshi and his friend must be gauging my reaction, taunting me in some way. But they seemed completely into it, cheering wildly as their countrymen were decimated by carpet bombing, off-shore cannonades from battleships, and pitched close-quarters battle, corpses of snipers dropping from their hidden perches and slithering lifeless down embankments. The war had ended only thirty years earlier, closer to me in 1975 (though thirteen years before my birth) than Vietnam and 1975 are to me now. Some of my teachers in Japan, including my math teacher, Mr. Toguchi, had been in the war. An old man on a train had laughed bitterly when he saw me and Hiroshi seated together and had remarked to Hiroshi, "If all Americans were as small and skinny as your friend, we would have won the war."

But this . . . film. What was it about? I mean, what was it *about*? I had no idea. To this day, the scene baffles me. One thing I know is that for me it marked the beginning of culture shock. No one had told me about culture shock. I didn't even know the term, but after that night I started to feel differently about Japan. I didn't understand it. I didn't think I'd ever understand it. And so, I started to hate it.

All of the exchange students suffered from culture shock a bit, but I think I suffered from it the most. I own an artifact from 1975 that shows our culture shock in action, a slim volume that Momoyama published that fall, titled *The Exchange: 1975–1976*, on its cover a group photo of the five of us. I'm in the center, glasses barely visible under a giant helmet of hair, my arms crossed, my pants barely reaching the tops of my shoes (I guess my growth spurt had begun — about time!). I've got an idiot grin on my face. In fact, I'm the only one with a full-on smile. Paul stands to my right in a jacket and colorful seventies shirt (it has a kind of splotchy colorful look, though the photo is black-and-white), a kind of rock-star pose, ready to rumble. Over his shoulder curly-headed Evan pokes, and behind Evan, Jay, a slight smirk on his face, hands in pockets. Stephen, standing beside me, wears a more pronounced smirk than Jay and also has his hand in his pocket. I think Stephen by this time hated Japan as much as I did because right before the picture was snapped, he suggested that we all surreptitiously give our hosts the finger. That's what he and Jay are doing in the photo. In Jay's case, it's hard to tell because he's so far from the camera, but if you know what to look for, you can clearly see the middle finger in Stephen's pocket.

Inside the booklet are photos of the exchange students and text written in both English and Japanese. There's a photo of Jay on the stage playing guitar, a photo of the exchange students and Mr. Nishikawa in front of a WELCOME banner, another group shot of the five of us pretending to gawk and take photos of the person taking our photo (our response to feeling on display), and a photo of us onstage waiting awkwardly to give speeches to the school. About that speech. Jay was clearly the darling of the group. He played the guitar, was on the school basketball team, and gave an opening speech about as rousing as Lou Gehrig's farewell to the Yankees: "We are probably the luckiest high school students in Japan!" As for me, I figured something would come to me when I got up there. It didn't occur to me to actually write something down, as it had to my fellow exchange students. I mumbled a few words and shuffled offstage while they gave beautiful, lovely, gracious, smart, endearing, enchanting speeches and received thunderous applause compared to my feeble claps and coughs. The interior of the booklet was about the same. Jay's speech was reprinted as well as a bonus feature: Jay critiquing secretary of state Henry Kissinger's handling of the Mideast peace talks. Paul concocted a similarly mature and grateful entry, and Stephen wrote a neutral piece about our arrival in Japan, though the title hinted at his discomfort: "Look, It's a *Gaijin!*"

Evan wrote a piece titled "The Importance of Difference" that started out soberly enough, but quickly employed that most cherished of adolescent secret weapons: sarcasm. If everyone owned a Porsche, smoked "Lebanese lightning hash" and "Columbian gold dope," he explained, we'd soon be bored. Fair enough. At our home schools in the United States, the administration would never have allowed such an essay, but our Japanese teachers not only allowed it, they added an English-Japanese glossary to help define some of Evan's more idiomatic phrases:

Go buzzin' around
Get stoned
A wimp
A stud
Be screwed around

My entry was last in the book, a transparently bitter and terse critique of Japanese schools:

> One of the biggest differences I have found between America and Japan is their different approaches to teaching, the Japanese classroom presents a strict approach.
>
> The teachers do not seem very relaxed in their classrooms, and students do not call any of their teachers by their first names. This is the opposite from many American schools. Many teachers consider their students as equals, and some even want to be called by their first names.

That was it. The shortest essay I have ever written. Mr. Nishikawa and the others had displayed enough grace to allow me my peevishness and to allow Evan his sarcasm, though I can't help thinking that keeping the grammatical error in that first paragraph (a comma splice!) was a subtle dig at me for an incident that had occurred just a week earlier.

All of the subjects at school, except for English and Japanese class, were taught in Japanese. Mr. Nishikawa, who spoke perfect English, taught us Japanese, but I had no inkling what most of my other teachers or classmates said in most of my other classes. Calculus and matrix theory were taught to us by Mr. Toguchi, a skinny man with a long face who entertained us by smoking cigarettes without touching them with his fingers. As the ash accumulated, Mr. Toguchi slowly tilted his head toward the ceiling until he was looking straight up. He could smoke a cigarette to the filter in this manner, without flicking the ash away once. We didn't learn much about math, but it was a fine display of eccentricity, and he impressed us. Of course, calculus and matrix theory would have been lost on me in English as well, so at least the language barrier provided a convenient excuse for my poor performance in this instance.

I also had to take English. All of the exchange students took it, though we were scattered in different classes. My class had about forty boys, seated in neat rows, eyes fixed on the English teacher whose name I have forgotten. He would write a sentence on the board and then make the class repeat it in slurred monotones.

The quick brown fox jumps over the gate.

I sat in the back doodling, sighing, and sometimes reading science fiction. Then one day, I heard something that made me startle. My teacher had made a mistake. He said, "On *my* farm, the tractor is used for many things, includes hay rides."

I looked up from my book and saw him writing the sentence on the board, exactly as I had heard him say it. The class repeated it as though part of a posthypnotic suggestion: "includes hay rides."

I shot my hand up. "Sensei, sensei!" I shouted, almost gleeful. "You're wrong. That's wrong. That sentence is not proper English."

Did I mention that none of the exchange students had received any cultural sensitivity training?

The sensei bowed his head slightly and extended his hand with the chalk. "Would you like to show us the correct way?" he asked, his voice soft.

"Sure." I thought I was doing him a favor. I mean, he didn't want the students to learn incorrect English, did he? I stood up and made my way to the front. It seemed, however, like a long walk, much longer than the seven or eight steps it must have taken for me to go from the back of the class to the front. The class sat still, and I couldn't hear a voice, a scooted table or chair, a rustled piece of paper. Only the sound of Momoyama's hapless football team filtered through the windows. "*Ichi, ni, san, shi!*" ("One, two, three, four!") they shouted as they trotted in full gear around the school's dusty courtyard. The football team never did anything but practice because there wasn't another football team in Osaka, and, anyway, the team had only six players. "*Ichi, ni, san, shi!*" they chanted as I took that endless walk to the sensei's outstretched hand. *Shi* means "four" in Japanese, but it also means "death." It's the Japanese version of the number thirteen. That moment was a small death, for me, and certainly for the sensei. Only after I had committed to correcting him did I realize that I was humiliating him in front of his students. Still, I took the chalk, and I crossed out the word *includes* and wrote *including*. The coup de grâce. I may as well have been holding a sword instead of chalk.

My teacher thanked me, and I sat down. And that was the last day I ever took English in Japan. The next day, my schedule had changed, and I'd been placed in art class where I spent the rest of the semester making a decoupage dove of peace.

Although things were bumpy, and I proved the bane of Mr. Nishikawa's existence, I might have yet made it through the year. By December, I was starting to learn the language well enough that my dreams regularly included Japanese phrases of the approximate difficulty of: *On my farm, the tractor is used for many things, includes hay rides.*

But then, tragedy struck. My mother decided to visit me for two weeks over her winter break. Of course, I didn't view this visit as tragic at the time, nor did my mother have anything but my best interests in mind, I'm sure. Were I able to advise her now, I'd suggest planning her visit for the end of my stay, not the middle. But I was not savvy enough, and my hosts were too polite, and when my mother visited, they feted her like a visiting dignitary. Mr. Nishikawa hosted an elaborate seventeen-course banquet in her honor, and Mrs. Oshiro presented her with a lovely Japanese doll that now sits in my study.

My mother's return home erased any gains I had made in adapting to a foreign environment. She simply missed me as I missed her. My sister had died only two years earlier, and I was the last of her babies to leave the nest, my brother Jonathan long gone to college by then. After she left, I determined to go home too, and I'm sure I made Mr. Nishikawa's life miserable enough that it didn't take long for him to acquiesce. The other exchange students held a little going away party for me at Shakey's Pizza Parlor in Shinsaibashi the night before I left and saw me off at the airport the next day. As I shook hands with Mr. Nishikawa, he smiled with what seemed to me, even then in my most self-absorbed stage, great compassion. "I predict you will return, Robin," he told me. "But next time, you will come with your wife."

Two days later, I was back in South Bend, enrolled at Indiana University South Bend. I was two weeks late for classes, severely jet-lagged, hadn't taken the SAT, and for the next month kept using the Japanese word *hai* instead of yes when anyone talked to me. Still, I attacked my studies and managed to come away with a 3.75 GPA that semester, even getting an A in math. The next semester, I transferred to the main campus of Indiana University, and once again I arrived two weeks late for the start of the semester because my mother had not realized that classes at the two campuses began on different dates. My first inkling that something was terribly wrong was when I saw students, fully loaded with books, scurrying between classes when we rolled onto campus. Somehow, the thought of housing had not occurred to my mother either, and so I spent my first two weeks at IU sleeping in a student lounge.

While I earned a 4.0 that semester and the next, my failure to stick out my exchange program haunted me. And so, I invented a new story for myself. I told people I had been an exchange student in Japan for a year, not six months, nor did I tell them under what circumstances I had returned. Out of a sense of . . . what . . . failure . . . masochism . . . or a protoattempt at a do-over, I decided to major in Japanese. That first year, I devoted myself to Japanese as I had devoted myself to nothing else. I had a likable professor, Mr. Uehara, who enjoyed telling us about his acts of bravery during the war on Formosa/Taiwan ("And then I saw that he had not dug his own foxhole, so I threw him into mine and stood outside, laughing at the American bombers as the bombs dropped all around me!") Actually, Mr. Uehara was not illustrating his bravery so much as how beautiful life is when it hangs in the balance, a Japanese concept that even at eighteen appealed greatly to me. He went on to talk about cherry blossom viewing ("The best time to view the blossoms is when they are about to be blown by the wind from the trees; that is what you aim for").

This time, I applied myself. I spent up to eight hours a day in the library with flash cards learning my kanji, the ideograms of which you need nearly two thousand to read fluently. By the end of the year, I knew almost a thousand.

But something happened the next year. A sophomore slump. I fell in love with a young woman I'd met in a literature class. I started slacking off, and my new Japanese teacher, a white American named Mr. Ellison who viewed Mr. Uehara with contempt and thought I didn't have the dedication I needed to learn Japanese, told me the only reason I had done so well in first-year Japanese was because of my "year" in Japan. And so, I started skipping classes and skipping tests and before I knew it, I had an F in Japanese.

The rest of my college career I received almost all As, and I assumed that five credits of F would not hold me back in the eyes of anyone else. I was right, though this episode marked me. I began to think of myself as someone who could start things but not finish them, and in some ways I spent the rest of my adulthood fighting against this notion, trying to prove to myself, if to no one else, that I wasn't a quitter. Still, the fact remained . . .

↶

That September, while making arrangements for my other do-overs, I initially made contact, through my friend Yasuko, with a Mr. Okada at Momoyama, who requested an e-mail from me detailing (1) who I was, (2) the person in question and my relation to him, and (3) the purpose of my contact. Then they'd get in touch with him, and if he was willing they'd give me his address.

I sent the e-mail right away. A month went by and there was no response, so I asked Yasuko to call Momoyama once again. This time, she reached a completely different person, a teacher named Mr. Nukui in the school's International Center.

Once again, I was requested to send an e-mail, this time to Mr. Nukui, and then he'd set about trying to locate Hiroshi. As for my request to attend Momoyama again, I'd need to send *that* request to the new head of the exchange program, a young teacher named Mr. Toshiyuki Hamai. I did both and promptly received a warm reply from Mr. Nukui, in which he remembered me as an "impressive student both in the good and bad sense."

He remembered me? Obviously, he did — the part about the "bad sense" was proof enough. But I was astounded to find someone who still remembered me from thirty years earlier. I had no memory of him.

Within a day, Mr. Nukui had found Hiroshi's address. What's more, Mr. Nukui *loved* the idea of my project and stood ready to assist me in any way possible. Grateful, I lost no time in writing to Hiroshi. I sent Hiroshi as well as Mr. Hamai copies of one of my books that had been translated into Japanese. This book was the closest I'd come to redeeming my miserable experience with Japan and the Japanese language, even though I couldn't read a word of it. A month passed before I heard from Mr. Hamai, who was slightly more reserved than Mr. Nukui, though not discouraging. He told me he thought the project *might* be possible, though no final decision had been made. However, he didn't think it likely that he'd be able to find a host family willing to take in a forty-eight-year-old exchange student.

As luck would have it, that part of the equation proved unnecessary. Another Japanese friend of mine, a world-renowned linguist named Ritsuko Kikusawa, whom I had met because her husband, also a linguist, had helped me with a previous book, not only lived in Osaka but was going to be gone the entire year as a visiting researcher at Leiden University in the Netherlands. Her apartment was vacant, and she told me I could stay there as long as I wanted.

Over the next six months, Mr. Hamai and I entered into a spotty correspondence about my trip. Up until April, I wasn't confident that the trip would actually happen. There was a long spring break to contend with as well as Golden Week, a week-long family celebration during which Japan stops work and plays. I couldn't blame him, but Mr. Hamai didn't seem to know quite what to do with me either. His subtext always seemed to be a hearty "Uh, okay." As I'm married to someone from Asia and have spent a fair amount of time there, I'm used to the fact that few people say no in Asia. Anywhere. People might mean no, but they don't say no. That's not to say that no is nonexistent. It's simply often disguised as yes, and you have to understand when yes actually means no, as in, "Yes, it is possible for you to attend our school," which might actually mean "No, please stay in your own country, Mr. Golden Testicles." Mr. Hamai, however, *did* tell me that Mr. Nishikawa was still alive. He had retired five years earlier, but that's all Mr. Hamai knew, as he didn't know Mr. Nishikawa. Finally, after a drawn out e-mail discussion, Mr. Hamai sent me an e-mail saying that the dates in May I suggested were fine with him.

I was relieved to learn that Mr. Nishikawa was still alive, but that didn't mean I wanted to see him again. I'd feel too humiliated. I'd made his life miserable when I was under his supervision. He'd shown me nothing but generosity, even bringing me a giant plate of sushi one day in the midst of our constant feuding. I refused to touch it until he left the Oshiros' apartment, after which I devoured it. I couldn't imagine he'd want to see *me* again. But he had been correct about one thing: the next time I visited Japan was with my wife and family. I had returned to Japan two years earlier when Ritsuko invited me to give a lecture in Tokyo. Not only did I bring Margie, but also Olivia and Isabel and Shoshie. We'd visited Nara, Kyoto, and Tokyo, and the trip had kindled in Isabel and Olivia a love of Japan. At the time, I'd thought often of Hiroshi and Momoyama but had virtually given up on ever seeing Hiroshi again.

Two weeks before my trip back to Momoyama Gakuin, I read a bedtime story to Shoshie about losing and finding things. Franklin the Turtle finds a camera that doesn't belong to him and makes great efforts to find the true owner, though only after taking a bunch of his own photos with it. After I'd finished the book, I saw that Shoshie was still pondering what it had to do with her own life, as she does with most of the bedtime stories I read to her. In this case, she saw a direct link to her "blankie" and a toy she left that afternoon at her friend Peter's house. Peter is Yasuko's son. Shoshie plans to marry him someday.

"Sometimes I'm sad when I lose things," she told me.

"Everyone loses things," I said. "Even Mommy."

"Like when she lost her sunglasses, and you were mad at her?"

"I wasn't mad. I was just annoyed."

"Dad, tomorrow can we hang out together? Because it makes me happy when we're cuddling and hanging out."

"Me too," I said.

"Okay, and I'll tell you when, okay?"

"Okay," I said.

Shoshie is a planner, like me. She too has a hard time living in the present. For her, the future seems bright but also fraught with possible loss. Of course, things never turn out quite as you plan. Dad isn't always available to cuddle with. Sometimes he's got to go to eighth grade or to Atlanta to be the Heavenly Messenger or to Japan to be an exchange student again. Dad is a little odd, it's true, but he's got good intentions like Franklin.

After putting Shoshie to bed, I grabbed my phone and headed for the patio. I'd written to Hiroshi in September, but by mid-April had still not heard a peep. I *had* his phone number, but I hadn't been able to bring myself to call. I sat under the patio umbrella. Though a breeze had kicked up, and a downpour might begin at any moment, this was one of the first truly warm days of spring, and I was determined to enjoy it. I felt a pang of regret that I was soon going to leave Iowa City for the entire summer. Shouldn't I simply be content to sit on this patio in a town I knew, in a time that itself would soon enough vanish forever, rather than chasing all these ghosts from my past?

Taking a few deep breaths, I tentatively dialed the international number. A girl (his daughter?) or possibly a young woman (his wife?) answered: "*Moshi, moshi!*"

My Japanese wasn't good enough to hold a conversation, so I carefully asked, "May I speak with Hiroshi?" in English.

"Yes, please may I ask who's calling?" she asked after a moment.

The theme music from *The Sting* followed.

"Hello, Robin." His voice was a middle register, reserved though not unfriendly. "Where are you calling from?"

"From Iowa."

"From Iowa?" he said and laughed as though Iowa means something funny in Japanese.

"I'm going to be traveling to Japan soon, and I want to see you when I'm there," I said.

"Yes, why not," he said. I was a little taken aback by this response, though I tried to keep in mind that he might not have intended this as coolly as it sounded. English, after all, wasn't his everyday language, and "Yes, why not" might have been meant in a casual friendly way rather than a casual apathetic way. Margie often makes fun of me for my overpowering American enthusiasm. "That's fantastic!" she says, or "That's great!" in imitation of what she calls my "plastic" Americanness. She refuses to participate, but, on the other hand, when we travel in Europe or elsewhere, she misses the "friendliness" of Americans.

Obviously, I'd built this up a bit too much. Probably nothing short of incoherent shouts of joy lasting many minutes would have satisfied me.

Even though I hadn't spoken to him in thirty years, Yasuko had. She'd called him on my behalf months earlier and had liked the sound of his voice. She told me he had remembered me warmly, referring to me by the endearment "Robin *kun,*" a fact that had cheered me, though not enough to call him until the trip was almost upon me. And it's one thing to speak affectionately about an old friend to a third party, but when you actually make contact again, there's bound to be some awkwardness.

In clear if halting English, Hiroshi apologized for not contacting me and asked me where I was staying in Osaka. After we went over the logistics of my visit, I asked him what he did for a living. "We have a lot of catching up to do."

"I work for a trading company."

"Like your father." I wanted to ask him if his parents were still alive, but I imagined not, and this felt like an awkward question as well.

"Yes, but a different company. We trade steel."

"Who was that who answered the phone?" I asked.

"That was my daughter. She is thirteen."

"Oh, I have a thirteen-year-old daughter too," I said, eager to establish as much common ground again as quickly as possible. "How many children do you have?"

"I have two. The elder is sixteen. Robin, when you come to Japan, is there anything you would like to do?"

Absurdly, I said I'd like to eat *okonomiyaki*. Of all the things I could have chosen! It was like someone wasting a genie's wish, asking for a hundred dollars rather than a million. Why had I said I wanted to eat *okonomiyaki*, a simple pancake, a kind of Japanese fast food? I suppose I said *okonomiyaki* because I had a vivid memory of Hiroshi and me, age seventeen, stopping in a little restaurant somewhere near Shinsaibashi.

"Robin, have you tried *okonomiyaki* yet?" he had asked me then. "You will like it! It's made best here in Osaka." And we stepped into the crowded restaurant, greeted by a shout of welcome from a woman at the cash register, *"Irashaimase!"* and the sizzle of *okonomiyaki* cooking on individual griddles in the center of each table. Hiroshi and I smoked a cigarette, and he ordered quickly for me, proud, as he always seemed, to be showing me his city. He was right too. I loved the dish. I loved that afternoon. When I said I wanted *okonomiyaki,* I suppose it was code. I was saying, I want that afternoon. I want that friendship again. I want it all back.

⌒

I arrive in Osaka at the end of Golden Week, on Children's Day, which seems somehow appropriate for my project. This time, I've come prepared: I'm carrying *two* bottles of Johnnie Walker Blue, one for Hiroshi and one for the head of the exchange program, Mr. Hamai. I've arrived on a dreary day, and Osaka doesn't readily display its charms even on the best of days. After all, it was bombed to near oblivion in World War II. But on a rainy day, on an endless ride from the airport to the center of the city, past countless drab edifices and virtually no green space, only isolated trees and roof gardens here and there, the city feels nothing short of forbidding. And it doesn't take long, not even the entire eighty-five-minute bus ride to the train station from which I'll make my way to Ritsuko's apartment, for me to feel akin to one of those isolated trees, for me to feel crowded by old feelings of failure and regret. *You can't change the past,* I repeat in my head. This all happened so long ago. *You can only change how you feel about the past.*

Ritsuko and her husband, Laurie, live in a development known as Cosmos Forest, pronounced in Japanese: Kosumo Foresta. Perhaps the Japanese, like Americans, are equally fond of naming their apartment complexes and subdivisions after the very thing that the subdivision has displaced and destroyed. I take an admittedly cynical pleasure in seeing block after block of poorly built ranch houses in America located in such developments as Prairie View, Eagle Crest, Moose Hollow, Buffalo Grove, and Indian Heights. But in the case of Kosumo Foresta, at least, there is an actual forest on a series of actual hills that the massive apartment complex abuts. The forest is a national park on the outskirts of Osaka in the district of Mino-o, and walking the trails you are in danger of being pickpocketed by one of the aggressive monkeys that live in Mino-o and go after anything loose in your pockets.

The place is a city unto itself, a cosmos of people, a forest of apartments, two enormous buildings linked by a long crosswalk. Ritsuko sent me the keys to the apartment, located on the seventeenth floor, and from their back balcony I stare out into what I imagine as old Japan and listen for monkey calls and watch birds wheel over the hills. From their living room window, I gaze out into the gray of what I imagine as new Japan, the megalopolis of modern Osaka stretching as far as the eye can see, Ridley Scott's inspiration for *Blade Runner*.

My sense of isolation only increases that first night. I can't get Ritsuko's Internet connection to work, which seems somehow appropriate. In 1975, we had no Internet. I wonder how my experience might have been different if I'd had such a lifeline. There was no communication stateside at all with our parents except for prohibitively expensive long-distance calls, reserved for emergencies and special occasions. The phone service is off as well in the apartment, and I can't even purchase a cheap cell phone because Japanese law makes it virtually impossible to own a cell phone if you don't have a permanent address in Japan. Seventeen floors below me is my only link to my family, a phone booth by the curb outside the building. Of course, we're not talking about an episode of *Survivor* here. I'm in a comfortable apartment. But I'm a social animal. I can't last long without company. I can watch the news on TV, but it is as incessantly repetitive and depressing as news in America. It might be Children's Day, but no one gets special treatment, not even children. A teen girl was thrown from a roller coaster today at an amusement park in Osaka and killed. So I settle in for the evening on Ritsuko and Laurie's couch in the living room, munching on the Japanese rice crackers I loved so much when I was an exchange student, watching grief and loss replay themselves in time-honored fashion.

The next morning, I wake early and catch a bus to Senri-chuo station. Ritsuko, who is both brilliant *and* thoughtful, a rare combination, has left me detailed instructions on every possible need I might have: where to catch the bus, where to catch the train — she even sent me a train ticket with the apartment key. Senri-chuo station is the end of the line — waiting for my train, I'm both charmed and creeped out by the Japanese penchant for personifying everything, even trains. As the train pulls into Senri-chuo, a sickly sweet female voice coos, *"Tadaima!"* (I'm back!), followed by strains of music that I recognize immediately as "There's No Place Like Home." I'm starved for company, ready to converse with a homesick train if necessary, but the train is out of language, and the people *in* the train, my fellow commuters, seem as studiously uninterested in my presence as they were fascinated by me thirty years ago. On the hour-long ride to Momoyama, no one asks to practice English with me. Back when I was a student, the constant *gaijin* attention wore me down. Now I wouldn't mind some. Bring it on! Let's practice English together! No such luck. Maybe it's the fact that I'm no longer a cute and skinny seventeen-year-old. Maybe everyone knows English. Maybe no one wants to learn it anymore and they're sick of *gaijin.* Maybe iPods are more fun; half the people on the train seem cocooned in music, the other half focused on their laps.

I arrive at my stop, Showacho station, an hour early, a perennial problem of mine. I am the original Eager Beaver. I'm supposed to meet Mr. Hamai in front of the school at 10:00 a.m. this Monday, and that's all I know. I figure he's lined up some classes for me to take — we've corresponded a little about this. He's suggested I sit in on some classes in their International Studies program, conducted in English, and that seems fine to me. Beyond that, I don't know what to expect.

As I walk up the steps of Showacho station onto the street I visited almost every day for six months when I was a boy, I try to remember what the place looked like in the midseventies — but there's no memory, really. Small businesses and low-rise buildings line a wide street. Bike riders navigate around pedestrians on the sidewalks, a few businessmen stroll along, some women with small children — and I remember *being here* at the top of these subway steps with Hiroshi, but that's all. Nothing distinct remains in my memory. I'm not even sure which direction to walk in to get to Momoyama. My intuition or memory's faint residue tells me to walk in the same direction I'm pointed in as I emerge from underground, but I ignore memory's advice and start off in the other direction for a few blocks, until I reach a little bakery where I approach one of the clerks.

"*Sumimasen.*" Excuse me. "Momoyama Gakuin . . ." Here, I stumble. Should I add the word *wa* or *ga* or neither? "*Doko desuka?*" Where is it?

She understands me at any rate and points me in the opposite direction from the one in which I was headed. Ten minutes later, I see an imposing institutional building looming in the distance, a Circle K convenience store across the street. That's got to be it — where better to put a convenience store than across from a high school? Then I spot the name etched into the wall: ST. ANDREW'S SCHOOL above the Japanese kanji characters for Momoyama Gakuin. St. Andrew's is its English name, the same as my old school in Tennessee, though no one ever refers to it as such.

The building is getting a facelift. Helmeted construction workers mill about, and one of those delightful signs shows the building as it will look in the future, less like a prison complex and more like the kind of hallowed hall one might find on the campus of St. Andrew's in Tennessee or some tonier boarding school up north, complete with decorative Episcopal crests adorning the building.

But I'm still much too early, so I walk around the neighborhood, eat a doughnut at a nearby coffee shop, and soak in the atmosphere of the neighborhood, smelling curry from the doorway of a restaurant, which reminds me of the curry shrimp I ate almost every day at Momoyama. I follow a group of uniformed Momoyama students as they walk past me, lost in conversation, tracing their familiar path until I'm back at the locked gate of the school, where I gaze at the traffic and bicyclists rushing past as though looking at a sunset over the ocean. I never imagined I'd be back here.

When Mr. Hamai has *still* not shown up at 10:02 a.m., I worry that I've got the time wrong or the place wrong, the country wrong, the life wrong. I don't even know what he looks like, though I figure he won't have much trouble spotting me.

Finally, after waiting an excruciating amount of time (it must be 10:06 by now!), I decide to walk around the side of the building to see if there's an entrance there. Sure enough, on the other side of a bicycle rack where dozens of bikes are parked, there's a doorway wide enough to drive a truck through, and in the same instant I see the entrance, I remember it, the entrance we always used, not the unfamiliar front gate. Here, a receptionist calls up Mr. Hamai, who comes down to meet me. I don't know how old I expected Mr. Hamai to be, but I didn't expect him to look as though he's about to go out for an evening of clubbing. I understand he's new to the job, but he seems new to the world, a mere baby. He's dressed casually in a white, body-hugging shirt and gray slacks, and wears a fashionably stubbly beard and mustache. He has a kind of harried energy about him, neither friendly nor unfriendly as he whisks me into the school proper where the vast courtyard in the middle of the complex looks exactly as it did in 1976. Something like an enormous taupe Quonset hut with a green peaked roof is most familiar to me: it housed both the gym and the lunchroom in 1976. But memory lane will have to wait. It's all I can do to keep up with Mr. Hamai — we skirt the courtyard and enter a building where Mr. Hamai directs me to take off my shoes and put on a pair of guest slippers. Even in Japanese schools, one doesn't wear street shoes.

One thing that's changed dramatically since my day is the influx of foreign English teachers to Japan. Now native English speakers are so commonplace that they form a kind of barely respectable underclass, the lowest of the professional *gaijin* in status-conscious Japan. When I was here, there were no native speaker English teachers at Momoyama, but now there are three among those whose desks crowd the exchange/English office, a cramped room on the fourth floor of the main building. The native speakers aren't all present when Mr. Hamai first shepherds me into the office, but here I meet David, a Brit in his thirties hailing from Newcastle, a new father married to a Japanese woman. He's here for the long haul. Even the nonnative English speakers seem somewhat better trained than in the old days; Mr. Tanaka, for instance, who tells me he studied at the University of Northern Iowa in Cedar Falls in the 1990s. "A lot of cornfields," he tells me. "It allowed me to concentrate on my studies."

Mr. Hamai sits me down in a corner of the room behind a screen — a little anteroom with a couple of red leatherette benches, and here I make the presentation of the Sacred Johnnie Walker Blue to Mr. Hamai. I'm not sure what I expected, but he looks at it the way my host father, Mr. Oshiro, looked at my gift of Jack Daniel's thirty years ago, caught off guard, like, what am I supposed to do with this, as if I've given him a bottle of fingernail polish.

Are you kidding? I'm thinking. *This is Johnnie Walker Blue, man! Top of the line.*

He sets it on the table beside a kind of stuffed cartoon Japanese head thing, as though it too is a stuffed Japanese cartoon head thing and not something much more valuable and, in moderation, more pleasurable than a stuffed head thing.

As if this weren't depressing enough, Mr. Hamai tells me his age. He's old enough to drink Johnnie Walker Blue, but just. He's eighteen years younger than me and was born *a year after* I returned from here as an exchange student. This is crushing news. I should probably just slink off and forget this whole thing. Mr. Hamai seems uncomfortable with me, and it's hard to blame him. I'm turning forty-nine at the end of the month. He's young enough to be my son. Who isn't? And what's the protocol? I'm sure there's no precedent for this in the *How to Be Japanese* handbook. I don't even know how I should address him.

While I'm sitting behind the screen, waiting to be told where to go, what to do, like some postmodern version of a game show contestant in the soundproof booth, David from Newcastle comes over with a big bound book, titled *The Exchange*. He opens it up, and there I am on the cover of the first pamphlet, many pounds lighter, my hair long, Stephen smirking up at the viewer, giving us, our future selves, the finger.

"That's me," I say, embarrassed.

"You don't say?" he says, noncommittally.

At lunch with David, Mr. Hamai, and Mr. Tanaka, I ask Mr. Hamai what I should call him. "You can call me Hamai-*san* or Hamai-sensei or . . . Toshi." Well, that clarifies a lot.

"Just don't call me late for dinner," I mumble.

David tells me of Mr. Minobe, who also taught here when I was a student. He teaches English. The enthusiastic Mr. Nukui, whose day off it is today, is an English teacher as well, as it turns out; Mr. Nukui, who remembers the bad about me as well as the good. The urge to flee suddenly comes upon me. I'm not sure I want to meet either of them. Could one of them have been the English teacher I humiliated in front of his entire class?

"You don't soon forget Minobe if you meet him," David tells me.

But can the same be said for me? Mr. Hamai/*San*/Sensei/Toshi spots someone in the lunchroom who was a teacher when I was a student here and approaches the man. Mr. Hamai points to me, and I smile and give a little wave. Maybe I was this man's favorite student, for all I know. But when Mr. Hamai returns, he shakes his head, "Yes, he was here when you were an exchange student. He doesn't remember you at all, but he *does* remember Jay Whitehouse."

After lunch, I meet my present counterparts in the exchange office, two young students from North America: Brian from Toronto, and Mark from Austin, Texas. They both seem cheerful and smart, both nearly as skinny as I was when I was their age, but Mark at least adds height to his lankiness. He's got an open, friendly face and dresses casually in an NYC T-shirt, while the equally friendly Brian is actually wearing a sweater and a tie like the teachers. There's something endearing about that, taking his role here so seriously. I remember being told constantly that in Japan I was an ambassador of the United States (though without the embassy staff), so I should make sure my actions reflected well on my country. They didn't. But Brian seems to take this admonition to heart.

I should be expert by now at explaining my project, but I find myself as uncomfortable as ever. Apparently, Mr. Hamai has told no one about my visit. Or, if he did, they seem to have forgotten it. Not that I expected a marching band (a few flutes playing "Yankee Doodle" would have been nice), but it's as though I've just parachuted in from the past. "Hey kids! Mind if an old *gaijin* pretends to be a young *gaijin*?" Thankfully, Brian and Mark humor me. They're kind. They say, sure, follow us around, though they don't know what classes would be most beneficial to me, what I'd even understand. Mark tells me he's taking Japanese lit.

"Oh, who are you studying?" I ask.

He thinks about it but can't come up with a name. "I don't know what's going on in that class," he says. "But neither does anyone else. So I don't feel so bad." That, at least, is like the old days, that feeling of being utterly and completely lost. If I had stayed on, I would be him or some version. He's been here eight months now, is practically fluent, and knows six hundred *kanji* already. He has the easy confidence and knowledge of someone who's stuck it out, not someone who's lost at all.

At 12:30, I flee Momoyama, suggesting to Mr. Hamai that maybe it would be preferable for me to leave for now and return tomorrow. He greets this idea with what seems an unmistakable look of relief.

On my return trip to Mino-o, no one wants to sit next to me on the train. The train is crowded, and there's an empty seat beside me, but no one dares approach until a man gets on reeking of alcohol and sits down. He starts bobbing his head as he holds it in his hands and moans. Having forgotten the words for "Please don't puke on me, Mr. Very Drunk Man," I get up and pretend to study the subway map, but really, why bother? I'm not going to offend him. The only reason he sat beside me was because he has no idea where he is or who he is. We make a lovely pair.

At lunch, I think Mr. Hamai poured a packet of Instant Culture Shock in my miso soup because that's the only explanation for the almost instantaneous sense of profound isolation and despair that has come over me today. The first time it took a few months, but I'm suffering a relapse, as with an ancient case of malaria.

Like the trains, the elevators in Japan are regular chatterboxes. They welcome you when you enter. They wish you farewell when you leave. They probably say nice things about you to other elevator users and dream of you at night. The elevator at Kosumo Foresta seems happy enough to see me today. But when I enter I notice that my fly is wide open and probably has been wide open the whole day. What a good representative of my country I make. I zip up my fly and grimace and curse before remembering that the elevator, like me, is a bit of an exhibitionist. A constant video feed shows whatever is going on in the elevator to other Foresta dwellers for their entertainment and edification. I retreat to my corner like a weary boxer, stick my hands in my pockets, and give whoever is watching the finger through my pocket as my old friend Stephen Becker once did.

The next morning I arrive bright and early at Showacho and follow the packs of school kids toward Momoyama. On my way, I see Brian at a corner waiting for the light. He's cheerful as yesterday and once again wearing a tie. Only the students in the international program at Momoyama wear school uniforms, so it's completely unnecessary, but I admire his resolve to make a good impression. "*Gambatte kudasai!*" I'd like to tell him.

"You're here early!" he tells me.

"I want to start classes with everyone else," I say. "What's your first class?"

"International relations," he says and asks me if I want to come.

"Of course," I say, eagerly. "That's why I'm here."

He gives me a slightly puzzled look that sets off a little alarm in me. "So what's your level of education in Canada?" I ask.

"Um, you mean, what have I completed? Well, I got my bachelor's just last year."

The penny drops. He's a teacher, not a student. That explains the tie.

"So who are the exchange students?" I ask.

"Mark and Brian."

"And you're Brian."

"Another Brian."

I guess that should be obvious that he's "another Brian." But I'm a bit flummoxed, and when I'm flummoxed, I immediately turn into the village idiot, with a skull as thick as Osaka Castle. It dawns on me that now I'm stuck going to the international relations class that he *teaches*. Brian, *Teacher* Brian, has been in Japan for seven months and teaches fifteen classes a week. At the exchange office, an announcement comes over the loudspeaker, and I ask Brian if they're making morning announcements. "I don't really know," he says. "I don't pay attention to them. My Japanese isn't so good."

I'm grateful that Brian is so accommodating, but I can't think of anything I'd less like to do than visit his international relations class. And I can't think of any polite way to get out of this. *Actually, I'm not so interested in you. I thought I was following around an exchange student, not an English teacher.* I hate to use the K-word, karma, but it strikes me as I'm sitting in the back row of Brian's class over the next hour listening to thirty-five students repeat in droning fashion such scintillating sentences as "May I see your passport and your I-ninety-four please?" that a Mack truck of karma has just plowed into me. *On my farm, the tractor is used for many things, includes hay rides.* I might

282

as well be back in the class that causes me the most shame, though at least Brian is in no danger of making any mistakes. Still, the moment is not lost on me. Score one for Destiny.

I seem to be on my own, more or less. Mr. Hamai isn't coming in until noon today — and my bottle of Johnnie Walker Blue has been set in a pile of papers and books beside his desk — so I decide to take my destiny into my own hands. When I run into Mark in the exchange office after international relations, he suggests I go with him to *onraku,* music class.

I imagine this will be a good class. The Japanese, after all, are famous for the Suzuki method. While I rebelled against what I considered the rigid discipline of Momoyama as a student, I've come to feel differently about discipline, especially when it comes to practicing an art. This class has about forty students seated in chairs with empty music stands in front of them. They rise as one at the beginning of the class, and Mark exchanges a few words with the teacher in Japanese. The sensei, a man in his thirties, looks my way and smiles, then introduces me to the class as a *ryugakusei,* an exchange student. The class claps for me.

Seated at the piano, he knocks out a few measures of Beethoven and talks to the class about what he's just played. Then he releases them, and they stampede to the back of the room, where they grab their instruments. So much for Japanese discipline. The students play a cacophony on instruments ranging from the trombone to some kind of big bicycle horn (played by Mark) and the clarinet, played by a pale, studious-looking boy I take to be the Real Brian. The experience is akin to the Drum Lady from Camp Echo, but with horns. It's worse than kindergarten, worse than hordes of sixth graders on the recorder. After fifteen minutes of little clownlike grunts of "Ode to Joy," the class falls eerily silent, as in some Japanese horror film. I sense impending doom. The sensei starts to isolate the sections. A group of four girls in uniform who make up the trombone section barely get out a trombone fart between them, and one girl drops her mouthpiece, which bounces on the floor and hides in shame underneath another student's chair. She kneels down to retrieve it and giggles.

Withstanding this musical banzai charge for nearly an hour, I sit stunned at the aural carnage as they come toward me en masse to put away their instruments. Mark tells me the bicycle horn he's playing is called a euphonium.

"Kind of a random instrument," he admits. "No one ever thinks of it." He chose it almost by default. The school has a limited number of instruments, and the students don't take them home. Obviously. When I was a student, I remember reading in the English-language edition of *Mainichi Shimbun* almost weekly accounts of neighbor killing neighbor over piano noise. The thought that anyone would kill over the sound of an instrument amused and amazed me back then. But now I see why the right to bear instruments is not universal in Japan.

Next, I follow Brian and Mark to religion class, held in a chapel built in 1964 that I'm sure I never set foot in when I was a student. The curriculum is completely different from my days here, but I wouldn't have minded this class, a haven after the mayhem of the previous two classes. Mark and Brian are the only two students in religion, which is nonetheless taught in Japanese by a middle-aged woman who speaks no English. She welcomes me and calls me an *obi*. An *obi?* Sure. Mark and Brian seem as perplexed as I am by this word, and Mark takes out his pocket translator to see what she's talking about. I shake my head. I can barely hide my envy. What I would have given in 1975 for an electronic translator.

"What is the kanji for that?" Mark asks.

It's not written in kanji, but in katakana, one of the two phonetic alphabets, this one reserved mostly for words, such as *Coca-Cola*, adapted from foreign languages. *Obi,* as it turns out, is OB, and it stands for "Old Boy," alumnus. I'm an old boy.

At lunch, I finally get my chance to bond with the exchange students, though it's Mark with whom I feel the most connection. He seems a lot like me when I was his age. We both have big feet — I wear a twelve and he wears a fourteen. He loves photography as I did when I was seventeen. Maybe that doesn't sound like much: big feet and a love of photography. Maybe that's not *a lot* like me. But I'll take what I can get.

"You're lucky to have e-mail and blogs," I tell them.

"The flip side," says Brian, "is that some people abuse e-mail. Not every change is for the better."

One thing that hasn't changed: even now, it's a battle getting Japanese kids to speak to the exchange students in Japanese. They all want to practice English. But unlike me at their age, Mark and Brian know how to draw boundaries.

"I'll only speak to them in Japanese," says Mark. "My Japanese is better than their English anyway, so it's easier in Japanese. Eventually, they give up. I tell them when they come to the States, we'll practice English."

"Mark is a lot stricter than I am," says Brian.

I'm *still* not very good at boundaries. When Mr. Hamai invites me to visit his English class, I find myself once again trapped. I can't say no. I don't want to say yes. I don't know how to say yes and mean no. Thirty years ago, I failed miserably as an ambassador of my country. This time, I'll try my very best to make any necessary sacrifice, even basic English.

Mr. Hamai's class meets in the morning, so the next day, I rise with the salarymen of Osaka and take the train back to Momoyama only to discover that Mr. Hamai is not in the exchange office and no one seems to know where he is or where his class meets. Brian the Teacher and David from Newcastle offer to help search for him, and we find him eventually on the second floor, where we nod at each other. "I was supposed to go to your English class?" I say.

"Yes," he says, and nods again.

Perhaps I misunderstood. Perhaps, in the same way that yes can mean no, the words "Please come to my class tomorrow morning" actually mean "Stay the hell away from my English class."

Mr. Hamai's class is full of boys who gaze at me with the open, uncomprehending stare of newborns. Mr. Hamai asks me to introduce myself to the boys and then gives me a grim little intro in Japanese, his face completely emotionless, as though I'm a case study for a criminal law class and not a returning *ryugakusei*. Mr. Hamai must be the reincarnation of the English teacher I humiliated, who obviously committed hara-kiri after I was in his class. The evidence is mounting, and after all, there's precedent: I have a detrimental effect on teachers. My kindergarten teacher, Mrs. Collins, was committed to a mental hospital and died after I was in her class. And I recently saw a Japanese horror film called *Reincarnation* in which a crazy professor kills eleven people at a hotel in the early 1970s and then commits suicide. Thirty-five years later, he and his victims have all been reincarnated, and the victims proceed to reenact their gruesome deaths while exacting their revenge on the male professor, who has been reincarnated as a cute Japanese actress. Other than the cute Japanese actress part and, well, killing eleven people, the situations are similar. Crazy professor. Me. Mr. Hamai. Born a year after I returned from Japan. Now I'm back in his class. And he obviously seeks my blood.

"Robin, we are studying line five on the right side," he calls to me from the front of the room. Why? I must have looked bored. I try to perk myself up. The students in this class are deathly quiet as they follow Mr. Hamai's scribblings on the board. One boy in front of me jumps in his sleep, startled awake by something.

"*According to this book,*" Mr. Hamai writes on the board.

"*Mr. Weerkin was very angry at losing so much money at Coe,*" he says, and the students murmur the sentence as though reciting morning prayers.

"*They thought Mr. Duff carry Mr. Weerkin . . .*"

"*He didn't look very clever either.*"

"*Notto very,*" says Mr. Hamai, and I repeat with the other fifty boys, "*Notto very.*"

By the end of the hour, I'm convinced this is all part of an elaborate plan to drive me crazy. Imagine how long the English teachers have awaited the chance to exact revenge on me. I've undoubtedly occupied all their waking hours and haunted their dreams. It's a good horror film concept at any rate: *Revenge of the Nonnative English Teachers of Momoyama Gakuin: He thought he return for second chance . . . Never has practice English look like this!!!*

When I return to the exchange office, I'm introduced to a balding, chubby-cheeked man wearing a vest and tie. It's the legendary Mr. Minobe, the English teacher who, like Mr. Nukui, was here when I was a student.

"Do you remember me?" he asks bluntly, smirking at me.

"Well, yes, vaguely," I say, which means, "Well, no, not at all."

"Vaguely," he repeats, considering the word. "Well, you've changed," he says. "You were a skinny kid."

"Yes, I'm afraid that's changed," I say.

"Have you spoken to Mr. Nishikawa?" he asks. "Mr. Nishikawa had lung cancer a few years ago and something else. He still smokes. He says the smoking didn't cause his cancer."

"I don't know how to get in touch with him," I say. Actually, I had fully expected him to be dead. A part of me wanted him dead, long dead, so I wouldn't have to face him again.

"Oh, I'll call him now," he says, and before I can stop him, he sits down at his desk and makes the call. Mr. Nishikawa answers, and the two chat for a minute before Mr. Minobe hands me the phone, smiling.

"I didn't tell him who was on the line," he says.

I'm completely unprepared for this. What am I supposed to say?

"Mr. Nishikawa? This is Robin Hemley."

"Robin Hemley!" he says in that throaty smoker's voice I haven't heard for thirty years.

"I'm here in Japan." Of course, this should be obvious to Mr. Nishikowa, but I'm flustered.

"You know the word, *natsukashi*, Robin?"

"No."

"This is how I'm feeling. *Natuskashi*."

Nauseated? I wonder. We agree to meet either Saturday or Sunday, and he asks that I bring along Hiroshi. I'll try, I tell him. After we hang up, Mr. Minobe becomes a whirlwind of *natsukashi*, not nausea but nostalgia, barreling through the massive complex of Momoyama Gakuin, looking for anyone who might remember me. He brings me first to the ground floor where the exchange-program room was located in my day. Now it's used as an office by the physical education department. Three somewhat elderly men sit inside, and Mr. Minobe points to me and speaks quickly in Japanese. They shake their heads and stare at me blankly while they converse in Japanese. I can't make out their words except for "Jay Whitehouse."

Despite the shock to my system, I'm grateful for Mr. Minobe's take-charge personality. For the past few days, I've felt unmoored in this old school, but now he brings me to the headmaster's office, where he introduces me as Robin Williams (at least it's not Jay Whitehouse), and then he takes me to a second-floor office where I finally meet the elusive Mr. Nukui, who, to my amazement, looks about twelve. He, like Mr. Minobe, wears a sweater vest and a shirt with a collar, but no tie, and wire-rim glasses. Boyish in the extreme, Mr. Nukui is skinny and has a wide smile and wavy black hair and not a wrinkle on his face. This guy started teaching a year before I arrived at Momoyama, but he looks ten years younger than me at least. While we take the requisite photos of me posing beside them, I ask the question I've been dying to know, "Were either of you my English teacher while I was here?"

"No, not me," says Mr. Minobe.

"Not me, too," says Mr. Nukui. "Maybe it was Mr. Hatsusegawa. He left a year or two after you were here." "And died in an asylum," I wait for him to add. I try to detect if either of them is lying to me. It's a possibility. Who would want to admit I was their student?

Mr. Minobe hands me off to Mr. Nukui, who takes me to lunch at a little restaurant in a nearby alley. Here, we discuss my project. From the beginning, Mr. Nukui was enthusiastic about it, and at lunch I see why. Our tea has been laced not with *natsukashi*, but with *koukai*, "regret." He tells me readily of the things he wishes he could do over. Like me, he's lost his mother within the past few years and wishes he had been a better son. He wishes he had been a better parent.

"I wish I'd stuck with my piano lessons," he says, and we laugh at that. The world over, people wish they'd stuck with their piano lessons. Although perhaps quitting piano saved his life, some neighbor on the verge of strangling him.

Mr. Nukui keeps smiling throughout lunch, but he has a sly look in his eyes, almost conspiratorial as he leans across the table, a mug of tea in his hands. He appears as though he's about to pour it over my head. "Tell me, Robin," he says. "Were you sent home for misbehavior?"

"I did misbehave," I say. "But I left voluntarily. That's not why I went home."

But he seems unconvinced. "Did you get drunk at a bar when you were here? Were you found at a bar?"

I shake my head. "No?" he says. "I think that was Evan then. But one time you went to Kyoto alone and were lost there. I remember your host mother called me up and was very worried. You didn't come home until very late." Another fabrication. I have no memory of this either. Still, I can see how I might be tagged with this misdeed the way well-known robbers in the Wild West were blamed for any unsolved bank robbery, simply because of their notoriety. At Momoyama, I am the opposite of the Jay Whitehouse Legend. He took them to the All-Japan basketball championship in 1976. I got drunk at bars. I went off alone to cities far from my home. I was sent home for misbehavior.

"The other students broke the rules," Mr. Nukui tells me. "But they knew how to get away with it. One is a bank president now. Another is a stock trader."

I, on the other hand, am a writer, the profession of miscreants who, far from getting away with things, go back for more punishment, for seconds and thirds. Still, if I'm allowed for a moment to indulge in the sin of pride, this is how I feel at lunch with Mr. Nukui. I've finally found my way back here. My regrets have not overwhelmed me.

Last night, alone in the apartment in Mino-o, I hated Japan all over again, but my attitude has completely turned around now that I'm finally making some headway. After lunch, I give Hiroshi a call at work from the exchange office. He likes the idea of meeting Mr. Nishikawa in Nara on Sunday but says he'd like to bring me home to have dinner with his family on Saturday. Happily, I learn that both his parents are still alive. Good. Then I have a chance to redeem myself on this score too, to give Mr. Oshiro the coveted bottle of Johnnie Walker Blue instead of giving it to Hiroshi. I wish I had bought an extra bottle, but he and Hiroshi will have to share.

"Robin, my father wants to know if you like sushi."

"I love sushi," I say.

"Because long, long time ago, you were pretty peculiar."

"Picky," I say. "Not peculiar. I'm not picky anymore."

"I'm going to a drinking party the night before for a new member of our company. So I might be hung over when we meet the next morning. You must promise not to laugh when you see me."

"You're more likely to laugh when you see me," I tell him. We agree that he'll pick me up on Saturday in front of the Mino-o train station, and from there we'll do a little sightseeing.

"How will I recognize you?" he asks.

"I'll probably be the only *gaijin* hanging around the Mino-o train station."

"What would you like to see in Nara?" he asks.

"It's up to you," I tell him.

"Robin," he says. "I'm Japanese. I can see Nara whenever I like."

I decide to skip the rest of my school day in celebration of the many reconnections I've made today. What better way to celebrate than to take the train to Shinsaibashi, where I inevitably headed whenever I skipped school the first time around. As some people have Daily Affirmations, I have Daily Rationalizations. The Rationalization of the Day: if I stick around Momoyama, I'll undoubtedly wind up in another English class anyway.

Shinsaibashi. The very name sends a charge through me. Outwardly, I suppose it doesn't look like much, but this was the place where I explored the world on my own terms for the first time. It's gaudy and superficial, full of stores with names like Big Joy and Lotteria and Nova, crowded with shoppers and neon and casino-like sounds drifting from the pachinko parlors. Through the large glass doors, the pachinko professors are clearly visible, seated in front of the machines in the same attitudes of wired concentration that I left them in thirty years ago. I pause outside one of these parlors, Osaka Hall, and read the sign written in typically nonsensical English:

Challenge The Neon Genesis
an Impressive Amusement Space
Let's Enjoy Pachinko

Impressive as it may be, I'm not tempted to walk inside. It's enough that I'm here and that I recognize that in some ways this noisy place is one of many that shaped who I am, for better or for worse. I love the noise of the world. I love to be one among many, anonymous and wandering the crowded streets of London, Paris, Rome, Amsterdam, New York, Manila, Buenos Aires, to be carried along by conversations and the laughter of strangers, to stop on a whim at a store or coffee shop, to pretend for a moment that this is where I live. Like all of us, I *do* live here and here and here, and yet I'm only visiting, and it's in the Shinsaibashis of the world that I feel most keenly the precarious joy of living alone among multitudes.

By Thursday, I seem to have hit my stride at Momoyama. That morning, Mr. Tanaka, the teacher who studied in Iowa, welcomed me with a hearty *Otsukaresama!*

I ask Brian the Student what it means, and he tells me it means something like "Good job, great, tired person!"

Great, tired person, is it?

But now that everyone seems to know who I am and why I'm here (Mark and Brian tell me the first they heard of my visit was when we were introduced!), they all seem on board with my project, and I've started making friends across the generations. I get on especially well with the two Brians, Confident Brian the Student and Brian the Self-Effacing Young Teacher from Toronto whom I mistook originally for an exchange student. Born in Taiwan, he moved to Toronto when he was seven and studied to be a violinist but changed his major to Asian Studies after a teacher told him it would be too difficult to make a living as a musician. Now he's biding his time teaching at Momoyama while trying to figure out what to do with his life. He spends his weekends going to places such as Kyoto and watching Kabuki (though he fell asleep during a couple of performances). When I mention graduate school, he says, "I'm not so good at studying." I point out that maybe he *is* good at studying, just at his own pace. What can I say? He brings out the paternal in me. If he were my son, I'd tell him to forget that teacher and pick up the violin again. But no one listens to parents. We'd all be virtuosos if we did. When Olivia took up the French horn, the word *scholarship* blinked liked the BIG JOY sign at Shinsaibashi somewhere in my cerebral cortex until she gave it up in favor of choir, and *scholarship* was replaced by *debt* and *student loan*.

Today, Brian the Student wants me to accompany him to his English class. Not another English class! Don't I get a pass? I *am* an English professor. Please, why won't anyone believe me?! But he tells me that this is one of his favorite classes, and, actually, it's more like social studies. It's taught in a computer lab by an American, Matt Walsh, who's lived in Japan for more than twenty years. He's a baby-faced, affable man, clearly smart, if not brilliant, in a disarming way as he lectures his students on current events — in Japanese, of course. While the fifty or so Japanese students in the class must write their papers for him in English, Brian has to write his in Japanese.

"You probably didn't have a computer lab, did you?" Brian asks me.

"We didn't even have computers," I tell him. "I didn't get my first computer until nineteen eighty-four."

"Did you have typewriter labs?" he asks. A typewriter lab. I imagine some secretarial pool out of a thirties film.

"No, not even that," I say. He gives me a look of disbelief, if not abject horror.

Distracted by my presence, Brian would rather use his computer to show me his Web site than pay attention to Mr. Walsh. There are hundreds if not thousands of photos on the site, and he proudly shows me his favorites, among them a photo of a rose beside a chain.

"It has deep meaning," he informs me. "The background is black at the top and light at the bottom. To get from the black to the white is painful."

I have my camera with me, so I return the favor and show him my photos, though they have no deep meaning. When I show him my photo of the pachinko parlor, Osaka Hall, I tell him I used to hang out there when I was a student at Momoyama.

"You played pachinko?" he asks. "Whoa. That's totally illegal."

He turns to a group of Japanese boys his own age and tells them this news about me in Japanese. *"Wah!"* they exclaim with a forceful expulsion of breath and look at me as though I'm still seventeen and might get them all in trouble for my bad decisions.

At lunch, I successfully negotiate the lunchroom ticket machine for the first time all week. This is a test for all *gaijin,* and even Brian and Mark admitted to me they had difficulty with it at first. The names of various dishes are written in Japanese on a machine that gives you a ticket once you deposit the requisite coins for the dish. You're in trouble if you don't read Japanese, and the kids crowding around you aren't much help, milling about like commuters in front of a subway turnstile. But today, I recognize the Japanese for *tonkatsu,* a breaded pork loin, or I think I do, and I bring my ticket to the women at the kitchen counter, one of whom takes my ticket, says something in Japanese to me, and hands me a tray of *tonkatsu.* What do you know? Not even a week here, and I've overcome culture shock, the language barrier, and the ticket machine. Ambassador Hemley: our most adaptable man in the field, according to the Home Office.

The English teachers invite me to dine with them again: today it's Matt Walsh, David from Newcastle, and Brian. I tell them about Mr. Tanaka calling me a great, tired person: *Otsukaresama!* But Matt says that Mark was translating the words literally. "It means, you're doing a good job. He was speaking to you from above as though you're a student. He appreciates your effort."

What I appreciate is the fact that he was addressing me from above, as though I were a student. The demotion in status doesn't bother me a bit. I left here as a student, and I have returned as a student, though not so much a student of Japanese as a student of my younger self, trying to decipher who he was, where he went wrong. Matt, as it turns out, is the perfect teacher for me today. He's a version of me, what I might have become had I kept up with my Japanese. He also worked for Mr. Nishikawa during Mr. Nishikawa's last year at Momoyama.

"You know, back when Mr. Nishikawa started the program, there was nothing like that," he says. "He just went over to the U.S. and set it up, said he represented Momoyama and it would happen. When he came back to Japan, he told the headmaster, and the headmaster had to go along because Mr. Nishikawa had promised.

"I used to be Mr. Exchange Program. I was a counselor for the kids for a while, but they switch people around now every couple of years."

"I could have used a counselor," I tell him.

"Well, Mark and Brian have fit in well, but every year we have one or two who are rebellious. Still, they find their individuality here. So that's a good thing."

He goes on to tell me about one exchange student from Australia who was caught in bed with his host sister by his host mother and how Mr. Nishikawa never wanted the exchange students to have girlfriends.

That sounds like the Mr. Nishikawa I knew. A bit of a God figure. A micromanager. But on the plus side, he did things up big, throwing lavish parties and bringing us on elaborately organized excursions. That was his style.

"Mr. Hamai is new at the job," Matt tells me. "He's capable, but this isn't his passion, as it was Mr. Nishikawa's." Even so, I regret giving Mr. Hamai the precious Johnnie Walker Blue. I should steal it back, I think, and give it to Mr. Nishikawa when I see him.

While Matt has been filling me in on the history of the exchange program, the lunchroom has been thinning out, and David and Brian have been comparing schedules, confused about whether they need to be somewhere or not. But now David tells me something I hadn't even considered. "You know, there were a number of bad Japanese exchange students to Canada and the U.S. A few of them were sent packing back to Japan."

"They were?" I say. "When was this?"

"Maybe in the nineties," he says. I have never heard of such a thing, Japanese kids acting out the way American kids do. But I guess everything changes in thirty years, even Japan. I feel like shaking his hand, hugging him, kissing him. I wasn't the worst exchange student ever!

"They were quite legendary," he tells me. "After all, sixteen- and seventeen-year-olds will be sixteen- and seventeen-year-olds."

And forty-eight-year-olds will sometimes be seventeen-year-olds too. I have had my sentence commuted. I have been given permission by Destiny to act bad. My Daily Rationalization. The next day, I sleep in. I skip school. I call my daughters and my wife. I tell them how much I miss them. I take the train around Osaka and get off at random stops and wander aimlessly. But I studiously avoid those dens of iniquity, the pachinko parlors of Osaka.

On Saturday, full of the energy of my youth, not a great tired person, I awake early and hike down the long hill, at the top of which perches Kosumo Foresta, and await my old host brother, Hiroshi, whom I haven't seen since 1976. I peer at every approaching car with anxiety, trying to glimpse the driver. A young woman wearing a black skirt and white go-go boots bounds from one, gives the driver a kiss, and walks toward me. I'm sure Hiroshi has changed but not into a young woman with go-go boots. More cars turn into the roundabout in front of the station, then a bus blocks my view, and I stare at it with irritation, as though it's purposefully done this to keep Hiroshi and me apart. An insidious bus. It strikes me that I probably take too many things too personally.

Then a blue Toyota sedan pulls up, and I see him. Like me he was a thin kid, but athletic. Now, he looks fuller, but not like an old man, his eyes still shining with intelligence, something still youthful in them. We shake hands, and he gives me a wry smile that I recognize across the years. His car smells of smoke — we both started smoking when we were sixteen at St. Andrew's, but I quit more than a dozen years ago. As we drive from the station, we spend the first few minutes asking the usual questions: We talk about our children, our wives, our jobs. He asks if I'm still in touch with anyone at St. Andrew's and I mention Lizzie Clark. I ask if he remembers Claire Reishman.

"Reishman," he says, like a convict remembering the cop who put him away. "Always MNS on papers . . . Makes no sense."

We drive into the mountainous countryside, about twenty miles north of Osaka, and stop at a quaint crossroads called Inagawa, where he parks the car beside a trailhead. On the edge of a grid of rice paddies sits a steep-roofed traditional house the size of a small mansion, with a white wall around it. Green but stunted woods spread out in the distance.

"That's my house," he says.

"Really?"

"Just kidding," he says.

This is what made us friends. Both of us tricksters.

Our destination isn't the traditional house, but a rustic little restaurant on the other side of the crossroads, with faded paint and a sign that reads OPEN in English. By the looks of it, hikers and bikers stop here for a quick meal. An old-fashioned bike with one giant wheel in front and one small in back graces the front of the restaurant — one of the main decorations inside is a bicycle hanging from the ceiling and a jersey draped by the window. A warm wood bar and a sign that lists daily specials (in Japanese, of course, though the board they're written on reads HOME COOKING) gives the place the cozy atmosphere you might find on the outskirts of Yellowstone or Yosemite. The reason Hiroshi brought me here is evident, I think. The better part of our friendship was in a small town in the mountains of rural Tennessee. This is like one of our old haunts, the sandwich place called Shenanigans where we used to hang out. We're not our old selves. We're not in our old contexts. But the greatest portion of anyone's day is spent daydreaming alone, and with old friends we daydream together.

That afternoon, Hiroshi plays the host, driving and driving and driving through more countryside than I thought modern-day Japan possessed. We stop at an old mine turned into a museum ("No earthquakes, please," Hiroshi says, the microversion of a prayer as we enter the shaft), but mostly we stay in the car and talk. Slowly, as the day progresses, we open up. I tell him about my daughters, my divorce, my new marriage. He tells me about his job. Oddly, his company, which, in typical Japanese fashion, he's been with since he was a young man, sells two commodities not often associated: fish and steel. He's in the steel end of the business. His company has four plants in China, but he spends most of his time selling steel to customers throughout the Japanese countryside. He used to be in the seafood end of things, and this, it's easy to see, he loved and misses, though he doesn't tell me so explicitly. The company sent him around the world to twenty countries to assess the quality of the seafood they were purchasing. He spent several years in the early nineties in New Jersey, where his daughter was born. There, his American co-workers knew him as Jack because they could not pronounce his Japanese name. They called him Jack because it's a typical Irish name, they said, and that Oshiro could almost be Irish: O'Shiro. I could never call him Jack, and it's hard for me to imagine that Hiroshi is such a difficult name to master, but then I remember that it took me all day to master his name when we first met at St. Andrew's. I kept calling him Hiroshima, to which he, unfazed, responded by calling me Pearl Harbor.

A month after he was married, his company sent him for a week to inspect crab on a huge container ship in the Bering Sea, but the week turned into a month. "We couldn't step outside. The weather

Old Boy

295

was so fierce, worse than a typhoon. The ship was a huge floating plant, a city." Like me, Hiroshi has his adventurous side. He's not meant to peddle steel to a group of steady customers. As delicately as possible, I ask him why the company transferred him.

"I don't know," he says simply, and I drop it, though it's typical of Japanese companies, even schools like Momoyama, to shift employees around without any apparent reason. At the very least, it shows who is the boss, even if it kills morale.

In midafternoon, we cross a mountain pass with a pristine lake, where several fishers stand on the banks, and I know that Hiroshi is playing the good host by showing me these sights, but one sight is as good as another to me, even the back of a truck transporting rice plants we're stuck behind.

"Robin, how do you spell *foreign?*" he asks me out of the blue. "Once, you asked me that when we were studying, and I was amazed that one of the geniuses of St. Andrew's couldn't spell the word *foreign.*"

Because it's me and because it's Hiroshi and because we have history, even if it's ancient history, we start to talk politics the way we did when we were at St. Andrew's. Back then, the subject was whaling. Now the subject is the militarization of Japan. "Should America defend us forever?" he asks.

"China won't let you have a military again," I say, "and why would you want it? The rest of the world should follow Japan's example rather than Japan following the rest of world by building up its army again."

I always enjoyed this kind of sparring with Hiroshi, but we're not seventeen anymore. After a prolonged silence, I ask him if he's tired.

"Tired of thinking in English," he says and laughs.

Finally, as the afternoon is waning, the small towns start to blend into subdivisions and office buildings, and we're once again on the outskirts of the twenty-first century. Hiroshi and his family live in a modest house on a pleasant and quiet street of mostly elderly people. The house is big enough for him and his wife and two children and his parents, but just. As we step into the small foyer and remove our shoes, Hiroshi yells, "*Tadaima!*" and I echo him. "*Tadaima!*" I'm back.

Mr. and Mrs. Oshiro walk into the room, white-haired of course, but virtually unchanged in their appearance other than that. They beam at me and bow and take my hand, laughing at how big I am, how much *I've* changed. I'm whisked into the dining room where I meet Hiroshi's wife, Etsuko, and his teenage son and daughter, Akira and Naoko Grace. Etsuko, who's several years younger than Hiroshi, though she looks many years younger, speaks fluent English — she teaches English to kids — and both Akira and Naoko understand English, but they're a little shy to use it. In Japan, badminton is a serious sport, and both of Hiroshi's kids are serious badminton players. Hiroshi thinks they're a little too devoted to badminton and not enough to their studies. Akira is skinny and about to overtake his father in height. Naoko is Isabel's age, and when I meet her I wish Isabel were with me because I can see them striking up a friendship.

Before dinner, I make the Presentation of the Sacred Johnnie Walker Blue to Mr. Oshiro.

"Thirty years ago, I brought Jack Daniel's when I should have brought Johnnie Walker," I say.

"Thirty years ago, scotch was very hard to come by," Hiroshi says, sitting down and opening the box. "And very expensive. The only brand Japanese knew was Johnnie Walker. But until now, I didn't even know there was such a thing as Blue Label. Now my father has developed a taste for bourbon."

Bourbon? Bourbon! You mean I should have brought a bottle of *Jack Daniel's?* I give up. We sample the thirty-year-old Blue. Hiroshi pours four fingers of the damnable stuff. I take a sip and so do Hiroshi and his father. It doesn't even burn. This is what Blue tastes like. This is the feeling of thirty years gone by.

"Smooth," says Mr. Oshiro, perhaps one of the only English words he knows.

"Smooth," Hiroshi echoes.

At dinner, I apologize to Mr. and Mrs. Oshiro for having been a brat, and Hiroshi translates for me. They wave off my apology and laugh. But still, she remembers Mr. Nishikawa coming over one day, and there I was, smoking in front of him. We were strictly forbidden by Mr. Nishikawa to smoke and drink. I'm sure I saw him as a hypocrite and, in my self-righteous adolescent fervor, decided to blow smoke in his face, so to speak. A tad embarrassing for her, I imagine — especially since she's remembered it for thirty years. A tad embarrassing for me to hear it now. Mrs. Oshiro and I also feuded a lot over how "peculiar" an eater I was.

"Have I eaten enough?" I ask her now. We've feasted on tuna, mackerel, salmon eggs, octopus, scallops, and squid, and there's hardly a morsel left. Except for rice. Always rice. Mrs. Oshiro thought I was sick unless I had two bowls at every meal.

"No," she says, her eyes searching for the few pieces of sashimi left on plates on the table. "You should have more."

↶

The next day, Hiroshi picks me up at Kosumo Foresta and we drive the highway between Osaka and Nara, where we're going to meet Mr. Nishikawa in front of the train station. I've been to Nara a number of times, most recently with my family. Last time, we fed the tame deer of Nara and saw the great wooden Buddha in Todai-ji Temple, the largest wooden building in the world. Isabel, who was nine at the time, was the only one of us small enough to crawl through a hole in a pillar there, assuring her good luck according to legend, or at least tourist brochures. I dutifully aimed my digital video camera (which supposedly doubled as a still camera) at her, but Margie, Izzy, and Olivia made fun of me mercilessly because the photos had so few pixels that Izzy's face looked like a cartoon face. She was reduced to a little thumblike person with barely discernible nostrils and a linelike mouth bent in a crooked smile. I have dozens of photos like this from Nara.

I had *thought* of Mr. Nishikawa when I visited the last time. I knew this was his city. He had taken a special interest in me because I was such a troubled child, I assume, and had invited me to stay with him and his family in Nara. He even let me ride his motorcycle around his neighborhood — at snail-like speeds, something that struck me even then as generous if slightly foolhardy. But I never considered looking him up when I returned. I simply assumed he was dead and that if he *were* alive he wouldn't want to see me.

But he's alive. He's had one lung removed and part of the other, and Hiroshi surmises that he wants to meet us at the station so that he won't have far to walk. We can have lunch there. Hiroshi parks the car off of Nara's wide main street. I'm lost in thought as we walk toward the station, so Hiroshi takes me by surprise when he suddenly asks, "Robin, how do you say *hospital?*"

I'm not sure what he's asking, and so I turn the word into its Japanized equivalent: "Hospitaru?" I say absurdly. You can make any word Japanese simply by adding the right vowels. In Japanese, McDonald's becomes *Makurodonutsu*. That's one of my favorite words. "Let's go to Makurodonutsu!"

Still, this is not what he meant. "*Byoin,*" he says. "How do you say *barbershop?*"

This time I stay quiet. I'm not going to say it. *Baba shapu.*

"*Byoin,*" he says. "I remember you had a hard time pronouncing them."

I still do. I can tell absolutely no difference in his pronunciation, though apparently there *is* a difference in the tone. Although Japanese is by no means as tonal a language as Chinese, there *are* some words, like *byoin* (which can mean either "hospital" or "barbershop") or *hashi* (which can mean either "chopsticks" or "bridge") in which tone matters. And I can tell that Hiroshi, who has stopped to light a cigarette, is feeling pretty smug right now. This is always the way we showed affection, by knocking one another down a peg, the verbal equivalent of punching your friend in the arm. I'm about to tell him to pronounce the word *railroad,* the hands-down most difficult word for Japanese to pronounce, *r* and *l* being as tortuous for them as the Japanese combination *r/l* sound is for native English speakers. When I hit upon *railroad,* I derived endless pleasure at St. Andrew's asking him to say the word. But before I can regress to my seventeen-year-old self, Hiroshi points across the street. "There he is," he says.

At first, I can't make him out through the pedestrians crossing both ways, but then I discern a solitary figure in a gray suit but no tie, natty as ever, his back straight, one arm on his hip as he smokes a cigarette. Then he sees us and waves. I expected a gaunt, slumped figure, but you couldn't tell how gravely ill he's been by looking at him. His hair is thin and dark, and his face has a couple of age spots, and he wears gold wire-rim glasses I don't remember, but other than that . . .

"He looks better than me," I tell Hiroshi as we cross the street.

"You're looking very good," I tell him as we shake hands.

"I almost died last year," he says. He points to his right side. "I had lung cancer here, and then last year the other side. I cannot walk too far, so why don't we go to a restaurant in the station?"

Located on the second floor of the station, the restaurant is decorated with the kind of photos of Japan one might see in a Japanese restaurant in the States. Scenes of Nara no less. All very nice, but they seem like overkill here. Is there any danger that a patron of this restaurant might think he's eating at a Zaxby's Chicken restaurant in a strip mall in suburban Atlanta? As soon as we sit, he and Hiroshi proceed to chat with each other in Japanese as koto music plays softly in the background.

Yoo-hoo. *Gaijin* alert. Can't understand you. Give me the chicken fingers, slaw, and Texas toast, please.

After a while, they remember me, and we settle down to eating and some heavy reminiscing. The funny part, or maybe not so funny, is that the things I remember Mr. Nishikawa has forgotten and the things he remembers I've forgotten. I remember, for instance, going on a field trip to a small seaside village with the school. The five of us exchange students, wanting to get in some trouble, worried that Mr. Nishikawa would send spies to report on our whereabouts in the town when we went off on our own. We wanted to buy some beer and figured we needed some kind of disguise. It's hard to disguise five *gaijin* in a small Japanese village, so someone had the bright idea to pretend we were French as we tried to buy beer in a convenience store. Stephen and I went inside the store and, in the worst French accents imaginable, asked the old woman at the counter, "*Où est la bière?*" She had no idea what we were saying, so finally Stephen said, "*Kirin! Asahi.* You know, beer!"

"*Hai, biru!*" she said and led us three steps to our left. We were standing right in front of the beer, of course. We had seen the beer. We knew where it was. But we were hell-bent on being French, not Americans.

We bought the beer, joined our friends outside, and popped the tops. Not five minutes had passed as we sauntered down a seaside road swigging our beers when we saw a car speeding toward us from a tunnel. "It's Nishikawa," someone yelled. "Pitch your beer!"

I needed no convincing it was Mr. Nishikawa, though we couldn't make out the driver from the distance and darkness. All we saw were the headlights. How Mr. Nishikawa might have known our whereabouts or our nefarious activities, in an era before cell phones, I'll never know. But I believed it was him, so I threw my beer can as far onto the beach as I could, and so did the others, all except for Evan, who tried to hide his can by his leg. "What are you doing?" Jay asked Evan. "Get rid of it."

"What if it's not him?" Evan said.

The car pulled up beside us, and Mr. Nishikawa peered out. With a kind of superhuman eyesight, it seemed to me, he immediately spied the beer can Evan was hiding.

"What's that?" he asked.

"A beer," Evan said, as though he wanted to be helpful and practice English with Mr. Nishikawa.

"Get in," said Mr. Nishikawa. He brought us in silence to the hotel where we filed into his hotel room and sat on the floor while Mr. Nishikawa railed about what bad boys we were and how he might just send us back to America. Feeling defiant and sensing that Mr. Nishikawa was bluffing, I refused to show any repentance. "Go ahead," I dared him. "Send me home."

"You're *very* bad," he told me. But he didn't send me home. I did that to myself a couple of months later.

Mr. Nishikawa doesn't remember the incident at all, which disappoints me. I had wondered all these years how he had known. Spies? The old woman in the convenience store? A lucky hunch?

What he *does* remember surprises me. "I remember a time when you were lost in Kyoto, and you were out very late. Your host mother called me. She was quite worried."

This is the same incident that Mr. Nukui reported. How could I have forgotten such a thing? "I have no memory of this," I tell him.

"Mr. Nishikawa has a good memory," Hiroshi says.

"I probably blocked it out. I guess I took the train to Kyoto alone." This wasn't simply a matter of going to another neighborhood but to a different city entirely. How I accomplished this and, more important, why I would do such a thing is beyond me. Certainly, I was a thoughtless kid and can imagine that I would not have considered what my host mother would be going through. But what was I looking for in Kyoto? Maybe I simply *wanted* everyone to worry about me. That seems like the kind of self-pitying adolescent motivation I might have had.

A horrifying thought crosses my mind. What if, as Mr. Nukui wondered, I *was* sent home for bad behavior? Much of my project has been about reevaluating the past, and for the most part that's been a positive process. But what if, in this case, I really was *worse* than I've always believed?

"I'm sorry for putting you through so much trouble," I tell him now.

"That was a long time ago," he says and smiles.

The waitress comes to the table, and Mr. Nishikawa orders a beer, and so do Hiroshi and I. I look over at him and say, "I won't get in trouble, will I?" and Hiroshi laughs.

Mr. Nishikawa lights up another cigarette. "Mr. Nishikawa. Don't smoke," says Hiroshi, lighting a cigarette too. "It's not good for you." Hiroshi and I started smoking on the same day, the same hour, the same minute. This is not something I want to do over. I'm not one of those self-righteous ex-smokers, though perhaps in this instance I can lay claim to a little plot of the moral high ground. But not much. I admit enjoying the occasional cigar, one of which in any case packs the nicotine of seventy-two cigarettes. I don't do anything, even self-destruction, halfheartedly.

"Over the years, did any other students go home early?" I ask Mr. Nishikawa. Notice how gingerly I ask the question. I leave open the possibility of correction, the possibility that Mr. Nishikawa might say, "Do you mean, were any others *sent* home early?"

But he doesn't correct me. He sits back and thinks about it. "Not so many," he says. "Maybe two from Mississippi."

"After my mother visited, I became homesick," I say. "Not that I'm blaming her, but I left because I was homesick."

"It was natural for you to be homesick," Mr. Nishikawa tells me. "Stephen Becker was homesick too. He bought a ticket and was going to go home."

"When was this?"

"Shortly after you left. But his father was headmaster of St.

Stephen's in Texas, and he wouldn't allow him to return. He told him he had to stay."

"Good for him," I say.

"He was even more homesick than you."

Of course, Mr. Nishikawa picks up the tab for lunch. I suppose I should make more of an effort to protest, as Hiroshi does (perhaps I should have my ambassador's license revoked for not insisting), but I know it would do no good. In fact, I know it does Mr. Nishikawa good to pick up the tab, that this is as close to a banquet for a visitor as he gets these days. We spend the rest of the afternoon driving around Nara in Hiroshi's car, chatting about the past until it's time to bring Mr. Nishikawa back to the train station. After our good-byes, Hiroshi turns to me and says, "I'm sure Mr. Nishikawa was very happy to see you. Do you want to bet how long Mr. Nishikawa will be alive? One year or two?" I'm silent. Hiroshi seems slightly hardened to me, not the ebullient Hiroshi I remember. But maybe he's just realistic and I'm not, living as I do in Fantasyland. "And how long will we be alive?" he adds. "Ten years?"

"I hope more than ten years," I say. We're stopped at a light, and I see a building with green kanji on its roof. "What does that say?"

"*Byoin*," he says.

"So it's a hospital?" I ask.

"Yes," he says, and we laugh.

We spend that evening wandering around Shinsaibashi as we used to. As we walk, Hiroshi points out places I liked to visit. "You took me to a coffee shop here once," he says, and we spend the next ten minutes searching for it. He finds the spot, but of course there's no trace of it. There's simply a corrugated shutter, and several buzzers with the names of small businesses or tenants. "It's not here," he says, as though he expected otherwise. And we stand at the spot for a minute, as if we might push one of the intercom buttons, and the past would buzz us up.

⌒

The next evening, my last in Japan, Mr. Nukui has invited me for dinner and drinks. He and his wife, empty nesters, have recently moved to the hopping Umeda district of Osaka, and he wants to take me out on the town. I've never been averse to that, and after another sushi dinner, we wind up at his favorite bar, literally a hole in the wall. It's simply a bar, not even as wide as a railway car and half as long. There are ten seats at a counter where he and I sit and chat, and another take-out counter where passersby can order drinks on the fly. I order a *shochu* (a kind of Japanese vodka) on the rocks and Mr. Nukui orders a scotch, neat.

"Robin," he asks. "If you could be reincarnated as a person from any country in the world, what country would you choose?"

"I'm not sure," I admit. "I'd have to give it some thought. What about you, Nukui-sensei?" I've taken to calling him sensei because even if he wasn't my English teacher, he was a teacher of mine in the general sense and is owed my respect.

"I'd come back as Japanese," he says. "Because it would take me many lifetimes to get to the bottom of what it means to be Japanese."

Our bartender, an attractive college student with whom Mr. Nukui, a regular, likes to chat, nods and smiles.

I raise my glass in a toast. "To who we are," I say, and Mr. Nukui raises his glass too.

"*Kampai!*" he says, the Japanese toast.

Although I've never said it in my life, it enters my mind to say the same thing in Italian, perhaps because I'll be in Italy for a month with my family this summer.

"*Chin chin,*" I say.

The bartender looks at me and then at Mr. Nukui and says, "I feel some embarrassment," and she laughs.

Mr. Nukui leans toward me and says, "Robin, *chin chin* means 'dick' in Japanese."

Oh well. Touché.

To who we are.

TEACHING MOMENTS

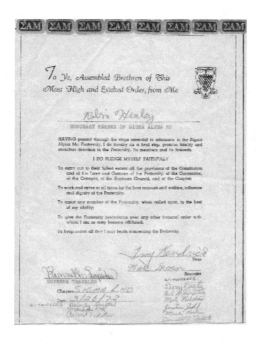

That summer, shortly after my trip to Japan, I turned forty-nine, two years shy of my father's age when he suffered his fatal heart attack. My daughter, Olivia, turned sixteen, and my wife, Margie, was due in August with a baby whose sex we had been unable to determine after two ultrasounds, and our insurance wouldn't allow us any more. So the baby was going to be a surprise whether we liked it or not. The idea of a boy terrified me, but I thought if God is vengeful he'll definitely give me a boy to pay me back. A merciful God would give me another daughter. I was used to daughters, and there would be a certain symmetry in having another. Two from my first marriage. Two from my second. A boy would throw my universe off balance. How could I raise a boy when I had spent the last year re-raising myself?

The decision was out of my hands as so many things are. I decided instead to focus on the things I could control, such as our travel plans. I had not traveled to Italy since I was fifteen, the summer after my sister Nola died, and I thought it was about time, as a reward for all my grueling doing over, to return. So I went on the Internet and rented an apartment in Florence, sight unseen, for the month of June. The apartment had a couple of drawbacks. Its closest neighbors were a sex shop, a gay sauna, and an adjacent apartment full of men who smoked so passionately and continuously that our common hall had a shroud of smog hovering in it twenty-four hours a day. Not that I'm a puritanical American, but Shoshie was fascinated by the edible undies in the sex shop window, and by the word *sex,* which she spelled out and said loudly every time we passed the shop, not to mention her high-volume complaints that "It *stinks* here!" every time we ventured into the apartment hall. Other than that, we had few problems with our accommodations, and we spent the month rather blissfully. Of course, this was June, and Margie was expecting in late August, so we were cutting it a bit close, and there were a number of times as the month went by that Margie preferred to stay in the air-conditioned apartment rather than venture out with the rest of us. As we were in Italy, I took Olivia to a couple of classic opera performances: *Tosca* and *La Traviata* — Izzy preferred the equivalent cost of the tickets in clothing. I kept Shoshie in the dark and promised her nothing.

She reveled in any case in her older sisters' attention, and I reveled in having all my daughters at my side as we strolled around Florence or took the train to Siena or Lucca or Pisa or to the beach at Viareggio, sometimes in Margie's company, sometimes not as the weather grew hotter and she grew bigger. Shoshie became so familiar with Michelangelo's *David* that any time she saw a replica she'd shout, "Hey, guys, there's David," as though he were a personal family friend. On the Ponte Vecchio, Margie pointed out a jewel-encrusted Star of David in a shop window. "And there's the heart of David," Shoshie said, pointing to a heart pendant beside it.

Shoshie was always good for comic relief in Italy, my protégée. She had no notion of being foolish. Everything and anything was worth taking a stab at. And, of course, everything was new to her, contradictions unimportant. The day the four of us walked through the Boboli Gardens of the Pitti Palace, an intensely hot day nearing a hundred degrees, we paused by a small waterless fountain, where there was a little shade. Shoshie danced around the fountain as her sisters and I rested on a bench. Suddenly, Shoshie screamed. "A bee! A bee!" She dashed toward us, her eyes alarmed. And then, after a moment, with perfect timing, she said softly, "Maybe."

The laughter energized us, and we shook off the heat and trudged up the hill toward the palace where before us, Florence, in all its terra-cotta splendor, baked. For me, Shoshie had just perfectly encapsulated my feelings about this past year, about my life: "A bee! A bee! . . . Maybe." If written in Latin, it could be my personal motto.

I wasn't sure what was chasing me, but I felt safer with my family. While doing over some troubled patches couldn't solve all the problems of my life or the problem of life itself, I had become a connoisseur of childhood, with Shoshie's help, with the help of my older daughters and Margie, and the teachers and students I had encountered along the way. I knew more about my life and the things that had shaped me, and I knew more about the lives of children today, and maybe that would make me a better parent. I had grown up without a father since the age of seven, and I hoped that Olivia and Isabel weren't growing up similarly. I couldn't be a part of their everyday lives, but still I hoped they would not think of me as absent. None of my children had been with me during my do-overs, but in a sense they were with me every step of the way, as perhaps were my own parents.

When we returned from Italy at the beginning of July, we concentrated as a family on the future rather than the past. Ready or not, another person was entering the world and our family, and we all meditated on this fact in our own ways. Margie grew tomatoes. Olivia read in her room. Isabel taught Shoshie cheerleader routines and dance steps. And I prepared for one last do-over trip. I had received word while in Italy that my bid to become a Sammy had finally been approved, and the Sammies were going to induct me in a secret initiation at their annual conference on August 9 in Phoenix, Arizona. Despite my delight that I was going to become an actual Sammy and not an honorary member, the date was close enough to Margie's due date of August 23 to make both of us nervous. Luckily,

Margie's mother, also a nurse, was coming from the Philippines in late July to spend a few months with us, but I wouldn't forgive myself if I missed my child's birth and neither would Margie. I *had* missed Shoshie's birth when she arrived three weeks early. I had been on sabbatical with Margie in the Philippines, finishing a book project, but had to return to the States briefly for a teaching commitment. On my last day in the States before returning to the Philippines, I received a call from one of Margie's sisters that Shoshie had come early. I was in Vermont. Margie was in Manila. It took me two days to get to her side and meet Shoshie, and this was something I did not want to repeat.

This time, Margie's subconscious spoke out. One night, she had a dream that she had gone into labor. After driving her to the hospital, I told her I needed to leave so that I could fly to Phoenix to join my fraternity. "Go then," she told me, and bopped me over the head.

So . . . yeah . . . that wasn't the ideal scenario. *Maybe I should just skip the whole thing,* I thought. I didn't want Margie resenting me on either the conscious or subconscious level, and I didn't want to risk the possibility that I'd miss the baby's birth. If this happened, in any event, it might well turn into my last do-over: a repeat of my first divorce.

I decided to postpone until the last minute, if possible, a decision on whether I could risk the trip and to put my fate in the hands of Destiny. I can always count on her to turn my life into what we in the education field call "a teaching moment." I had weathered plenty of these during the past year — every do-over had been Destiny's Teaching Moment in one respect or another.

For this reason, when Friday, July 13, rolled around, I decided to stay off the roads and get nowhere near standardized tests, David Hasselhoff, or anything else that might pose a possible threat to existence. Instead, I went into the garage and randomly picked up an old metal file box of papers that I hadn't opened in twenty-five years. I took the box onto our sunporch and started flipping through the contents with the intent of seeing what I might put in the recycling bin. Oddly, this box seemed to contain various stations of my do-overs: on top, I found a program from *Antigone* with a sketch of a seventeen-year-old Lizzie Clark on the front. Below that lay several issues of our school newspaper, *The Daily Planet,* the front page devoted to opposing editorials on whether we should have locks on our doors. And below that was something I couldn't believe — my honorary membership to Sigma Alpha Mu. The certificate was just as I remembered it: Black-and-gold stickers with the Greek letters for Sigma Alpha Mu adorned the top edges of a sheet of heavy bond paper that proclaimed to all who cared to know that from this time forward I was an honorary member of the fraternity. It was signed by a dozen or so witnesses, including Mr. Bounce-for-Beats himself, Terry Dietz, and someone designated as the "Supreme Traveler," Kenneth Lapides. No doubt about it, this was the original. I was positive that I had given the certificate to the head of the chapter at Indiana University and that it had never been returned. For years, I had believed this story, but I had been carrying around the thing this whole time, rediscovering it only when I no longer needed it.

I ran inside the house with the kind of excitement that I usually only witness in Shoshie, and I announced my find to my family, all of whom were in our family room watching TV. "Can you believe it?!" I nearly shouted.

Apparently, they could. *America's Next Top Model* was on, and I was interrupting the suspense of it all.

"Are you going to show it to them?" Olivia asked.

"I don't know," I said. The Sammies had made such a big deal about there being no such thing, I felt irrationally as though they might confiscate it this time and never give it back. Or destroy it!

"This Friday the thirteenth turned out better than the last," said Izzy, and then they turned back to learn the fates of the models, no longer interested in mine.

I immediately climbed up to my study and e-mailed Roger King, the executive director of the Sammies, telling him of my find. He was eager to see it, he replied the next day, and suggested I bring it with me to Phoenix.

That settled it. I went ahead and purchased my ticket. The ticket I had booked would bring me in to Phoenix in the afternoon of the ninth, and I'd leave early in the morning on the tenth. While delays are always possible, I'd be gone less than twenty-four hours, and if there was any uncertainty at all, I'd simply cancel the flight. This plan seemed to satisfy Margie, both in her dreams and her waking hours, and staved off my guilt. The last thing I wanted was any more guilt associated with childhood, my own or my daughters' or (potential) son's.

In advance of my initiation, I corresponded mostly with David Goldfarb, the treasurer of SAM who had allowed me to go along on the Argentina trip that got this whole thing rolling. David reminded me that the ceremony was a secret and that, once initiated, I couldn't reveal any aspect of the ceremony, not even the handshake or the Sammy Booty Grind. He also told me I needed to bring a pair of new black socks. I didn't ask why, of course, assuming it was an important part of the ceremony. Maybe I'd burn them. Or drink a potion made from sock water. Maybe that's why it was important for them to be clean. You wouldn't want to drink dirty sock water.

Of course, there are always complications. On the day of the trip, my flight was delayed, and so I had to dash from one end of the Minneapolis airport to another to make my connection. I barely made it. My luggage didn't. Inside my suitcase was a good pair of shoes, my tie, and my new black socks.

In Phoenix, I picked up my car rental and drove to the Arizona Biltmore where the convention was taking place this year — I had just enough time before dinner to drive to a local mall and purchase another pair of shoes, my black socks, and a tie. Then I checked in with Margie for the third time that day to make sure she wasn't going into labor as I just *knew* she would. But she hadn't. I hate to be one to convene and dash, but under the circumstances, my soon-to-be Sammy brethren understood that I couldn't hang around with them and reminisce about our old fraternity days, which didn't exist for me in any case. This was a commando do-over: I would be initiated right this time, but quickly. Before dinner, I ran into Roger, dressed in a striped seersucker suit, who introduced me to the fraternity muckety-mucks, including the supreme prior, Larry Leib, who would preside over my initiation ceremony.

"I brought the black socks," I told Roger, eager to show him that I would follow the Sammy dictates to the letter.

Roger raised his eyebrows. "Black socks?"

"David told me to bring new black socks to the ceremony."

Roger laughed. "I don't think that's part of the ceremony. David was having a little fun."

I suppose it could have been worse. He could have sent me on a snipe hunt, in the grueling desert heat of Phoenix in August to try to flush a snipe out of its cool burrow.

Terminally early as always, I hovered around the entrance to the banquet hall where dinner was scheduled, like a nervous maître d' worried about seating an important party. A huddle of young fraternity members, who had shown up early too, impatient for food, eyed me with curiosity. My name tag pegged me as an initiate. I felt like the forty-year-old virgin. Shouldn't I have taken care of this when I was their age? Thankfully, David and Phil, my tough-talking Republican friend from Chicago, wandered by and rescued me from the stares of the others. They greeted me warmly and shook hands (though not secretly) and invited me to sit with them during the banquet. I was so happy to see them I didn't even mention the black socks to David. We sat at the front of the room, which held a hundred and fifty or so Sammies from around the country, mostly undergrads, regional representatives, officers from various chapters, and regular members. A woman from the Alzheimer's Foundation, which had replaced the American Heart Association as Sigma Alpha Mu's official charity, addressed the group — they had raised $26,000 last year for the foundation, and she spoke movingly of what that could buy, challenging them to raise more this year. This type of call would have roused me when I was in college, slightly less so now. The next morning, the group was going to eat breakfast at 7:00 and take a bus at 7:15 to a food bank where they would work as part of their community service obligation, something I was relieved *not* to do, though I surely would have if I didn't have that convincing baby excuse, as well as the equally convincing Old Fart excuse.

At 10:00 p.m., I was initiated in a ritual that lasted an hour. I can't say anything about it except this: It didn't involve paddling. The ceremony had integrity and emphasized things that I could have benefited from when I was an undergrad, that I can benefit from now. After the ritual, a roomful of undergrads burst into applause. I was taught the secret handshake and shook many hands that night.

Afterward, I bought drinks for David, Roger, Drew, and the rabbi presiding over the invocation at dinner. I showed them my original "illegal" (Phil's word) honorary certificate. I told Phil I'd show it to him only if he promised not to tear it up. David and Roger recognized a couple of the names, Terry Dietz and Ken Lapides, Supreme Traveler, who had once been on the national staff. "Could I take this back with me to headquarters to make a copy?" Roger asked.

"I'd rather not," I said. Look what had happened the first time! Well, actually it hadn't happened. I had made it up. But it could have happened. It might yet happen.

"Okay, you can make a copy and send it to me. I'd like to put it in your membership file."

I had a membership file now. I relished that.

The next morning, I awoke early and at checkout asked an alert young woman if I could enter my Hilton Honors number, which I had forgotten to do on check-in. I didn't have my card, so she looked up my number and found it.

"You're a gold member," she said, beaming.

"Oh, what does that mean?" I asked.

"It means you're not silver," she said. "It means you're not platinum."

Her co-worker, a man, stopped what he was doing a moment to add to the general merriment at my expense. "It means you get to wear a gold crown."

Okay, already. I got it. I understood loud and clear. Membership does not necessarily have its rewards. There are memberships that matter and memberships that don't. The fragile little club that I belonged to had members in Iowa and Wisconsin and in the womb. I was one of the presiding officers: the Supreme Traveler. We had no secret handshake, but we were about to initiate a new member. And I needed to get home to help preside over the ceremony.

When I returned from my trip to Buenos Aires with the Sammies in January, I had found that a small tree we had planted in our front yard had been destroyed, and a ring of beer cans adorned the shattered plant. I assumed (unfairly, Margie thought) that fraternity boys had caused the destruction. Unfair or not, when I returned this time from my initiation, I found the *other* tree we had planted that same day destroyed in a similar way. The circumstances were bizarre. A couple of drunk students had crashed a party at our neighbor's house the night before and had eventually been booted from the premises because of their rowdiness. In retaliation, they went in search of some missile they might hurl at their rude hosts, walked around the corner and found my poor little crab apple tree. They broke it off a few inches from the roots and then hurled it at my neighbor's house, where it landed ineffectually on the front porch. Upon my arrival home, I immediately saw my tree, its leaves already drying, propped against a larger tree in my neighbors' yard. This time, I didn't jump to the conclusion that frat boys had murdered my plant, merely a couple of stupid students who could have been anyone and probably had no memory of their actions the next day. Still, I mourned my plant and sought revenge, even going to the police, who thankfully don't have enough to do in Iowa City, at least in the summer. A young officer showed up within ten minutes of my complaint and interviewed my neighbors with the seriousness of a true murder investigation. The young man gave me his card and told me to call him if I wanted to know the progress of the investigation. *That tree deserved some justice,* I thought.

We all had our little dramas going on. For Izzy, at thirteen, it was boys. She'd had a series of secret "boyfriends" whose names she would never tell me, as though I might know them. We didn't even live in the same town. Olivia and Margie knew the names of the boys, but, for some reason, it was a big deal that I should be kept in the dark.

One evening, Isabel accompanied me on a walk to our local co-op where I needed to pick up a few ingredients for dinner. On the way, I asked about her mysterious boyfriend.

"He's not my boyfriend anymore," she told me.

"Did he break up with you?" I could tell from her tone of voice.

"Yeah, but I'm over it. He was annoyed that I was gone for four weeks in Italy, like I had any choice about that. Plus, he liked one of my friends, and he's dating her now, but no one will tell me who it is. He even had a friend tell me."

"That he was breaking up?"

"Yeah, that was real manly. No one else in the family knows this, Dad," she said. "Not even Olivia."

"Why not?"

"She'll make a big deal over it."

When we reached the store, shopping interrupted the conversation, but it resumed right where it left off on the walk home.

"It's so stupid that they won't tell me who the mystery woman is," she said. "They're acting like . . ."

"Thirteen-year-olds?" I said.

"Yeah. I think it might be Amanda, but it could be Ali. They both have said they like him."

"You're well rid of him, I'm sure," I said. "What's his name?"

"Dwayne."

"Dwayne," I said. Yuck. I hate that name. "I never would have guessed the name Dwayne in a million years."

"I know."

In the scheme of things, the conversation was unimportant. She'd find a new boyfriend. Not that I wanted her to find a new boyfriend until she was thirty at least. But she would, and eventually they'd break up and life would go on. But this was the kind of conversation I yearned for with my older daughters. As part of the divorce process in Washington State, I had watched a film about a boy whose parents had joint custody but who lived in different states. He had talked about how painful it was to live for six months with one parent and six months with another, how traveling between states had made it harder for him even if it was easier for his parents. The film urged divorced couples not to make such arrangements, that if you truly loved your children, you wouldn't put them through such a thing. I truly loved my daughters. I didn't want to put them through such a thing. So I hadn't fought for joint custody. Perhaps if I had fought for joint custody, my wife wouldn't have been able to do what happened next. She moved out of state. My lawyer told me if I tried to fight this, I'd probably lose.

I suppose that could have been the end of the story, that I could have faded away from the lives of my daughters, and we would have become figments in one another's lives. But that didn't happen, and for this I was both grateful and proud. None of this had been easy, but I knew that they never doubted my affection for them, nor would they think I took them for granted. We were still important to one another, and I hoped this would never change.

⌢

On August 14, Margie went into labor, and twenty-two hours later she gave birth to her second daughter, my fourth: Naomi Pearl Hemley. Twenty-two hours. It's hard to imagine. But I was by Margie's side the whole time, and when all was over she turned to me as though I had done the hardest part and said, "You were pretty good in there."

Olivia, Isabel, and Shoshie were nearby, and they soon visited their new sister. I took a photo of them standing by Naomi's bassinet in the hospital room — such a spread of ages. It was odd and wonderful to have four daughters ranging in age from zero to sixteen. Even so, they had this much in common besides being sisters: their lives were still very much in flux, the outcomes uncertain. Only time will tell what any of them will become, what they'll do in their lives and with their lives. There's only so much I can do to help them along, and I have to accept the fact that they'll all make mistakes, have regrets, wish they had done this thing or that thing differently. Naomi doesn't even know who she is yet, who we are, and what this strange place is where she's landed. But I'm eager to watch her as she finds out. Olivia might become an opera singer, a psychologist, or neither. And Izzy will sing on Broadway, become a doctor, or neither. Shoshie, who changes almost daily, will become a golf course or a golfer or someone who lends people money or a mother or someone who takes care of lots of animals. Who's to say? Not me.

Of course, I still have regrets. Who doesn't? Doing over one's life doesn't change those. But I'm beginning to see them in perspective at least. And I can honestly say that there's nothing major I would change in my life, that the dissatisfactions are finally small and inconsequential.

Someone recently asked me if I wanted to do over anything that I had done well the first time. Unfortunately, I couldn't think of anything I'd done well the first time. What would be the point? If I'd

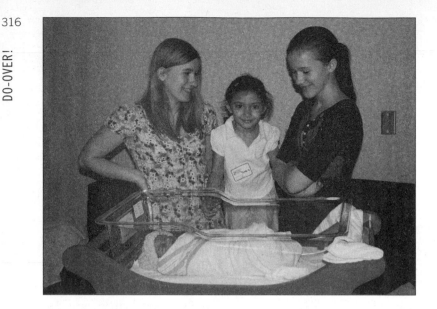

done it right the first time, what good would come from doing it over and maybe flubbing it? The simple categories of success and failure can't begin to measure my life or anyone's, I suspect.

In my case, the renovations on the structure of my life have long been overdue. I've kept the scaffolding up for a year now while the workers have pounded away. Now it's all done, the scaffold can come down. My wish is that someday my daughters might read this record of those renovations before tucking them back into the walls of their own personal histories and that it might help them, in some small way, carry on with the hard but necessary work of living.

Acknowledgments

To thank everyone involved in the making of this book would be a monumental task and might take as long as doing my taxes. It's not that I'm lazy or ungrateful. On the contrary, I'm indebted to all the many people who helped bring this project to fruition and who shared with me a certain mischievous joy in trying to set back the clock. To all who supported me in this endeavor, cheered me on, and encouraged me with their do-over fantasies, I give you my sincere thanks. In many cases, I've changed names in this book for the sake of privacy, and to single out people now might nullify that effort. All of the teachers I encountered were smart, dedicated, and had the kind of sense of humor necessary to teach public or private school and to allow a forty-eight-year-old man into their midst. I'm especially indebted to them. So please forgive me if I don't mention you by name. My intentions are good and my gratitude true.

But there *are* some people I must single out.

First, I'd like to thank my family: Margie, Olivia, Isabel, and Shoshie, as well as N, our latest little plot twist. Without them, there would be no reason for writing this book.

I'd also like to thank several of my students in the Nonfiction Writing Program at the University of Iowa, who were generous in their enthusiasm when I told them one evening at an Iowa City watering hole that I might like to go back to summer camp: Alex Sheshunoff, Katherine Jamieson, Colleen Kinder, and Ori Fienberg. Alex also has my deep thanks for taking some wonderful photos of me in my kindergarten and sixth-grade do-overs, including the photo of me on the cover of this book.

Faye Penn and Adam Moss at *New York* magazine said yes almost immediately and with great zeal to the initial idea of going back to summer camp. I appreciate the gamble on their part, as I also appreciate Marla Coleman and Camp Echo's staff and campers, for allowing me to be part of their fun. I'd return to Camp Echo every summer if I could.

My friends Tim Doody and Peter Barbur not only lent me their house in New Jersey to write my initial *New York* piece, but it was in their kitchen, while I babbled to them as they prepared dinner, that I first concocted *Do-Over!* as a book.

While neither Katharine Culverius or Elizabeth Nagle were able to see the project through to its conclusion, there's no doubt that the book would have faltered badly if not for their efforts and support. Katharine shepherded the idea as my agent, and Liz took on the project as my first editor at Little, Brown. I'm indebted to them both.

Reagan Arthur saw me enthusiastically through the middle territory of my project. Happily, Little, Brown is the type of publisher in which everyone is familiar with a project from its inception, and so I never felt in any way uncared for as *Do-Over!* and I navigated our way through the process.

Another happy match was made between me and my current editor, John Parsley, who has unerring instincts, an eagle eye, and who edited the book with great care and generosity. I keep hearing that real editors don't exist anymore, but I've not found that to be the case at all. John took on the project as though he'd been with it from the outset — I feel fortunate to have had this book pass before his discerning eyes.

I'd like to thank John's savvy assistant, Cara Eisenpress, who certainly has loads more aplomb than I did at her age. Also at Little, Brown, Marie Salter has been the most respectful and the most thorough copy editor I've ever dealt with.

Kate Lee at International Creative Management has been supportive, keen for the project, and open to my many flights of fancy. I hope that we'll work together for many years to come — the same goes for the ever-friendly and capable Larissa Silva.

Others who have supported me greatly in this endeavor by smoothing the way, making contacts, offering me a place to stay, supplying photographs, giving a thumbs-up when needed, and/or permitting me to reenter the world of childhood, include Bonnie Sunstein, Yasuko Akiyama, Ritsuko Kikusawa, Marc Perlstein, Aaron Girson, Annie Cook,

Shiro Nukui, Nyle Klinginsmith, Nell Jackson, Richard Sowienski, Rolajean Sowienski, Lizzie Clark Duncan, Rick Duncan, Elliot Duncan, Claire Reishman, Hiroshi Oshiro, Andrew Nishikawa, Jay Semel, Neda Barrett, Susan Core, John Kortlander, Virginia Adams Bloom, Elizabeth Fisher, Erica Marks, Theresa Morrison, Gary Keller (and all my other childhood chums from Putnam), Lia Purpura, Craig Warwick, Judith Kitchen, Stan Rubin, Brenda Miller, Amy Weingartner, Paulette Studley, Robert Hoagland, the Reverend William Wade, Toshiyuki Hamai, Scott Eggerding, Lawrence Reid, Russell Valentino, Adina Hemley, Gail Boldt, Kathy Whitmore, Karla Brendler, Jodi Rickels, Jay Vithalani, Josie Freedman, Wendell Brock, Kate Hrdina, Lindsay Hebrank, Susan Hebrank, Sarah Tyrlick, Susan Tyrlick, Diane Strotbeck, Cherie Rieskamp, Jeff Mermelstein, Paula Donoho, Jill Rosser, and a certain home owner in South Bend, Indiana, who shall remain anonymous, even if her cats Demelza and Max do not remain so.

The students, faculty, and staff of my three alma maters featured in this book have my undying gratitude; St. Andrew's-Sewanee, Momoyama Gakuin, and Jefferson Junior High.

The students, faculty, and staff of the two schools featured in this book located in my adopted hometown of Iowa City made me feel very welcome, and so I now consider these schools alma maters as well: Horace Mann Elementary and Longfellow Elementary.

I am very grateful to the cast of *The Littlest Angel* and the now (sadly) defunct Big Top Theatre in Marietta, Georgia. I'm keeping my angel wings at the ready if you ever want me back.

Thank you to the officers and members of Sigma Alpha Mu. I'm delighted to finally be one of you, though I'm sorry to say I've forgotten the handshake again.

I thank my wonderful colleagues and students in the Nonfiction Writing Program at the University of Iowa, as well as my colleagues in the English Department and in the College of Liberal Arts and Sciences.

Grateful acknowledgment is made to the John Simon Guggenheim Memorial Foundation for its generous support as well as the Obermann Center at the University of Iowa, where much of this book was written.

Last, Mrs. Collins, wherever you are, all is forgiven.

About the Author

ROBIN HEMLEY is the author of seven books of fiction and nonfiction. He has published his stories and essays widely in such places as the *New York Times, New York* magazine, the *Chicago Tribune,* the *Southern Review, Conjunctions, Boulevard, New Letters, Prairie Schooner, Creative Nonfiction, Fourth Genre, Ploughshares, Shenandoah,* and many other literary magazines and anthologies. He is the recipient of a number of awards, including a Guggenheim Fellowship, two Pushcart Prizes, and the Nelson Algren Award for Fiction. He is a graduate of the Iowa Writers' Workshop and directs the Nonfiction Writing Program at the University of Iowa.